THE MORAL STATE
WE'RE IN

THE MORAL STATE WE'RE IN

A MANIFESTO FOR A 21ST CENTURY SOCIETY

Julia Neuberger

HarperCollins*Publishers*

HarperCollins*Entertainment*
An Imprint of HarperColins*Publishers*
77–85 Fulham Palace Road,
Hammersmith, London W6 8JB

www.harpercollins.co.uk

Published by HarperCollins*Entertainment* 2005
1 3 5 7 9 8 6 4 2

A catalogue record for this book is
available from the British Library

ISBN 0 00 724012 0

CONTENTS

INTRODUCTION

In March 2004, a wonderful story appeared in *The Guardian* headed: 'Q. How many care workers does it take to change a light bulb? A. Ask a risk assessor.'*

The Department of Health had devised an advertising campaign to attract people into becoming care workers that showed a care worker reaching up to put a new bulb in for an old man – without any obvious assistance. The advertisement read: 'If you could do the small things that make a big difference, you could earn a living in social care.' But many care workers say they are not allowed to change light bulbs – not on their

---

* Article by David Brindle, *The Guardian* (27 March 2004).

INTRODUCTION

own, at least. One local authority said it might take four people to do it: one to hold the ladder, one to turn off the electricity at the mains, one to stay with the old person, and one to change the light bulb. This is to comply with both Health and Safety rules and electrical safety legislation, but it obviously leads to some considerable difficulties. It is this kind of risk aversion – extreme though this case is – that this book is about: rules and regulations, well founded, well meant, even theoretically sensible, that yet lead to an extraordinary situation in which a care worker cannot change a light bulb for fear of the consequences, and which makes the lives of vulnerable people more difficult than they need be.

This is an extreme example, but it is not unusual. For six years I was Chief Executive of the King's Fund, a charity devoted to the health and healthcare of Londoners, with a watching brief for the National Health Service as well. During that time – and indeed before – I have watched bemused as we have apparently become less and less caring for, or even aware of the suffering of, the most vulnerable in our society. This is not to say that there are not hundreds of thousands of people who, every day, carry out acts of kindness for a variety of people in trouble. Nor is it to say that we are bad people, or uncaring – though we may be – or insensitive to the needs of others, or incompetent, or somehow unaware in other ways. Nor is it to argue, as religious leaders have often done, that we have become selfish – though that, too, may be partially true. I believe that something else is going on: a complex pattern of interacting ideas, events, the Zeitgeist, and personal human attitudes that has somehow allowed us to reach this position. In this book I hope to tease out some of the contributing factors by examining what has happened to some of the most vulnerable groups in our society – the elderly, the mentally ill, children in care, offenders, and asylum seekers.

As I began the thinking for this book, I realized that I was not alone in my concerns. I was astounded by the number of people of all political persuasions, all backgrounds, classes, and creeds, who told me I needed to write it, that it was somehow important.

INTRODUCTION

They were not necessarily going to agree with me, but they believed we needed to ask ourselves some questions, and that the stories in our daily newspapers, the material with which we argued over politics – insofar as anyone did any more – or social issues or economics suggested some deep-seated problems in thinking about how we might sort our society out.

Concerns varied. There was a passionate concern about how we treat the elderly in our society, about the welfare of people with mental illness, and about what happens to children in care.

There was also a widely expressed view that our penal policy is a mess: we are putting more and more people into prison, but we have less and less idea about whether we are trying to punish, rehabilitate, contain, or simply forget about them.

Then there was a growing body of opinion that felt our policies towards asylum seekers were plain cruel, that if we could not sort out our immigration and appeals system then it was hardly fair to blame those who were trying to come to the UK, even if some were – to use the jargon – economic migrants rather than true refugees.

These are some of the issues that concern many of us – and may also touch us directly. The proper care of our elderly relatives is an issue that we all have to face at some time. Many of us know someone with mental health problems, and we may ourselves have had some period of depression or some other relatively minor mental illness and so will have seen first-hand something of what the system offers (or fails to offer) by way of help and support. Most of us will have read horrendous stories about children in care and what happens to them when they leave – we may even have experienced this ourselves. We may also have read about, or have first-hand experience of, ex-offenders, some of whom will have been in care and many of whom have mental health problems. And whilst most of us will not have direct experience of today's asylum seekers, many of us may know someone whose family came to this country as refugees.

What kind of society is it that locks up those with mental illness in prisons, rather than placing them where they can get help and care, that fills them up with drugs but shows them little kindness?

What kind of society is it that allows our young care leavers to gain access to the criminal fraternity so easily and denies them the support of mentors and befrienders in their late teenage years and early adulthood?

What kind of society is it that makes so little effort regarding ex-offenders that many of them feel so unsupported that they fall back into offending for want of anything else to do?

What kind of society is it that locks up children from asylum-seeking families, that fails in its duty of kindness towards the stranger, and that fails to recognize the rights of children, who are in no way to blame for their lot?

And what kind of society is it that fails so lamentably to protect older people from abuse whilst also failing to offer proper long-term care for those who need it?

We have made it more difficult to help such people. Part of this book will examine why it is so hard for ordinary people to help those less fortunate than themselves – the kid in care, the old lady next door whose life is getting tough. For, as a result of scandals surrounding some of our institutions – for example in children's homes, schools, and foster homes – we do not allow ordinary people to help. For instance, an obsession – not wholly misplaced – with sexual predators has made it necessary for anyone who works with children to undergo a police check. Until recently it also meant that a child in the care of foster parents could not spend a night with a friend unless the friend's parents agreed to undergo police checks too. The need for school teachers and helpers to be checked for their past record also means that those who might be willing to help on an occasional basis must also be checked by police.

Such vigilance in itself may be no bad thing. But the fact that we have become so stringent in our requirements for checks on those who work or have any relationship with children means two things: first, that children themselves are encouraged to be suspicious of adults in a way that may be quite unhealthy, both for themselves and for society as a whole; second, that those who are inclined to look after a child or young person who is distressed – who is, for instance, lost, or is being attacked by older children – will be very nervous of getting involved. Suspicion of motives has forced some people, particularly men, to restrain ordinary common decency and kindness. Yet many of our most troubled young people – though by no means all – have no regular, stable male role model in their households. Add to that an ever-growing worry over paedophilia and you have a picture of a society that wants to protect children from potential attack but which may end up by destroying valuable relationships between young people and their elders, purely because fear of sexual attack takes precedence over a belief in ordinary common humanity. When photographs of children at nursery school cannot be taken without parental consent, for fear of pornographic use, we have a problem. When we are so suspicious of adults' motives in wanting to help a child that one cannot help in a school – even one's own children's school – without a thorough and lengthy police check, we may have a

Introduction

legitimate point of concern, but we will deter all but the most determined helpers.

Our fears are not wholly unfounded. We have, in recent years, lived through the Soham murders and through a series of scandals surrounding children's homes and special schools. In the USA, one smart California nursery was thought to be the centre of a wave of bizarre sexual and other attacks on small children. The Roman Catholic Church is still reeling from revelations about the number of attacks on young children by priests and from stories of violence and abuse by priests and nuns in Catholic-run children's homes, about which senior church members knew and did nothing – or, worse, simply moved the offending priests or nuns on and did nothing to protect the children or heal their wounds. Yet, for all that, such a level of protection of children will lead to them being unable to trust anyone. Anyone accused of an attack on children is likely to go underground. The situation may well arise in which those who want to help children whose own families may be the worst abusers, or children whom circumstances have let down in a big way through parental death or family break-down, are deterred by the bureaucracy through which they have to go. It is as if we are trying to create a risk-free society, which we know in our heads and our hearts is impossible. The result is that we restrict and regulate, hoping to make terrible things impossible whilst knowing we cannot, and, in the process, deterring the willing and the kind.

Then there is the unwillingness of many nurses to do what they once did best – holding the hand of an elderly person and dispensing simple TLC – through fear of being accused of assault; or being unwilling to offer a dying person a drink in case they choke, thereby risking legal action against themselves or, more likely, the hospital. The bureaucracy involved in serious untoward incidents, as they are called, is now so enormous that many senior nurses spend huge amounts of their time in filling out forms, making a nonsense of their nursing and caring roles in an increasingly risk averse culture. Professionals have become polarized into those who do case management – including when things go wrong – and those, more junior, who do the actual caring. Because of the requirements of the Health and Safety Executive, nurses cannot even lift an elderly person who has fallen out of bed: they often have to be left until suitable hoists can be found.

None of these things is necessarily wrong in itself. But the cumulative effect of a risk-averse culture results in an erosion of simple human kindness. A nurse will put a line into an elderly person for drugs to be given intravenously, but she will not hold a hand or stroke an aching back. An ordinary decent man, in his thirties say, with energy and skills that could be put to good use working with young people, will give a charitable donation to Childline or to the National Society for the Prevention of Cruelty to Children, but is unlikely to sign up to a mentoring scheme that would give him regular contact with an individual disturbed and deprived 14-year-old boy: it is simply too much trouble to go through the checks. If the man is himself gay, then official doubt and suspicion will be all the greater. If he is heterosexual and wants to mentor a girl, yet again suspicions are aroused – and his computer will be checked for pornographic images.

Aversion to risk pushes out common sense, and the smallest of risks now takes precedence over what we used to call kindness and care. The result is that the kindness one sees in hospitals often comes from porters and care assistants rather than from senior staff. Similarly, kindness to people with severe mental health problems often comes more from the owners of the cafés in which they sit for much of the day, or from the staff in public libraries, than from the nurses and outreach workers who are in a position to really extend a hand. This is not because of ill will or lack of feeling but because the system is increasingly unwilling to allow nurses and carers to take on any risk. An arm around the shoulders might be thought to be common assault. An invitation to have a meal might be seen as some of kind of sexual lure. And so we reach a situation in which social care assistants are told that it will take four people to change a light bulb for one vulnerable old person, whilst one of the teachers' unions has called for an end to school trips for fear of accidents after three children have died in recent years.*

Risk aversion has made for part of the difficulty and has increased a natural human reluctance to get involved. That reluctance has been exacerbated by urban living. Many city dwellers lead isolated lives, in contrast to the sense of community still possible in rural or suburban areas, and have an unspoken, unofficial code of not interfering in each other's lives. This means that those in trouble can become totally alienated. Around Christmas and New Year, when many of the regular support services close for ten days at a time, the needy can find themselves totally unsupported. No friends, no family – and the reluctance of strangers to get involved. Kindness is in very short supply.

That reluctance will grow unless we look carefully at why we have deliberately allowed this culture of risk aversion to grow, why we are so suspicious of sexual motives, and why we no longer trust the stranger. And this requires examining our

---

* *Evening Standard* (19 March 2004).

own personal experiences. If we fall in the street, it is the stranger who picks us up and dusts us down. If we have a car crash, it is the stranger who calls the police and stays with us to give comfort. If we are mugged, it is the stranger who all too often gives us the wherewithal to get home. If we suddenly become distressed, or ill, or overcome with fatigue, it is often the stranger who carries our bags, asks if we are all right, and offers to take us to the Accident and Emergency Department of the local hospital. Of course there is always risk: the person who carries our bags home may proceed to burgle the house; the person who takes us to the emergency room after we have been raped may turn out to be the rapist. But these are exceptions. There are still people out there who give up their seats on the underground or the bus to older people. There are still people who pick you up and dust you down. And yet we are making it more difficult for such people to do good deeds. Why, as evidence grows that crime is down, are we ever more fearful, ever more timid?

To answer this, I think we have to look in detail at some of the major inquiries that have been carried out into abuses of the vulnerable. In each section of this book, I shall try to examine some of the reports, the newspaper stories, and the official responses to such inquiries looking for clues as to why we are increasingly reluctant to get involved and why that reluctance may have its root, at least in part, not only directly within ourselves, but also in the culture we have created for ourselves with the best of intentions: to protect the weak and to deter the aggressor.

Today, it seems we have a desire to do everything possible. We want to stretch the limits: cure the incurable, reach the unreachable, do the undoable, explore the inaccessible, travel to the most exotic and impossible places. Yet at the same time we have never been so internally reflective, so obsessed with ourselves and our feelings, so dedicated to understanding ourselves. Our gaze runs both to the furthest horizons and into the deepest recesses of ourselves. Yet by our desire to go to the extremes in medical treatments we often cause damage and bring suffering, as well as sometimes achieving miraculous cures. By our desire to go to the furthest reaches of the world we may cause environmental damage or destroy the lives of those we encounter. And, as we look deeper and deeper into ourselves, we lose the will to think beyond ourselves to others, lose the inclination to help others, to serve others, to work for others, to look into the middle or near distance. We fail to deal with what we find at our feet or in our communities.

This is, of course, a huge generalization. Yet our obsession with self – which may not necessarily be selfish but is perhaps self-indulgent – does lead to some strange behaviour. As the death of Princess Diana recedes into the middle distance, it is hard to remember the reaction many people had to it. Yet a walk through London's parks in those days immediately after her death was a curious experience. All over, there were groups of people – largely women – sitting in small groups, often round a lighted candle, contemplating, reminiscing, remembering, memorializing. But they were not, after the first few minutes, thinking of Princess Diana. Their grief, though real and genuine at the time, was not truly about the death of the fairy princess. This was something quite different. They were remembering themselves, grieving for those they had not grieved for before, remembering mothers, fathers, siblings, even children, remembering the grandparents whose funerals they had not been allowed to go to. This was a sentimental wash of grief, hitherto unexpressed and even unrecognized. But the mood was not one of enormous sadness over Princess Diana's death. The sadness was for them, and it played out as something truly self-indulgent. It also meant that those participating were looking inward, at themselves and their experiences, one of the curses of our age, rather than thinking about what outward action they might be taking to improve things for others worse off than themselves.

This, perhaps, has been the most dramatic recent example of group behaviour that caused a combined rush of sentimentality and genuine grief. Self-indulgence was combined with necessary grieving processes, sometimes much delayed. Yet the light was not shone externally. We were not looking to see who else might be suffering, or why.

INTRODUCTION

Instead, the light was directed inwardly, on ourselves. What *we* felt became what mattered. When the Queen did not come straight back to London from Scotland, we complained – irrespective of what her feelings might have been, or her desire to protect her two grandchildren. The Queen needed to be back at Buckingham Palace because *we* wanted her there. It was an astonishing example of the triumph of the group desire for personal gratification over common sense and understanding. Yet part of this desire to look inside ourselves is precisely what leads to that lack of a longer, more measured view. Though psychotherapy has brought great gains, it has encouraged an emphasis on personal priorities over those of the group; and whilst counselling has made a huge difference to many people with a variety of mental health problems, as a tool for everyday self-examination it can, at worst, lead to an inability to act.

What has happened might be argued to be an unfortunate confluence of events – or of intellectual and emotional pressures. At the same time that individualism became paramount, the then Prime Minister, Mrs (now Lady) Thatcher was alleged to have declared that there was no such thing as society and consumerism hit its heights, making the consumer king, rather than the citizen. Concurrently, the obsession with introspection grew in intensity, combined with a political and philosophical view that the individual should control what happened to him or her. The combination of all these factors led to a distaste for looking at the welfare of society as a whole. As a philosophy, utilitarianism – the doctrine that the correct course of action consists in the greatest good for the greatest number – was held in severe disrepute. Individual endeavour was what was needed. Utilitarianism might deter the huge efforts, for huge gains, of the talented entrepreneur. Society looked less at the welfare of the whole and more at the welfare of the individual, whilst the intervention of the state was seen to be less than desirable, and often less than benevolent to boot. In addition, it was perhaps inevitable that a utilitarian state found it difficult to deal with minorities of whatever kind since it was predicated on the idea of a one-size-fits-all approach to the world. There was little appreciation that minorities might choose not to fit, something that needs to be remembered when ideas about multiculturalism are becoming unfashionable and the opposing idea that we should all comply with something uniquely British is growing again.

This contrasts curiously with a strongly held belief in the values of the National Health Service, the only truly universal service in the UK, used by everyone. The NHS was predicated originally on the idea that the best possible care would be provided for the greatest number of people. It encapsulated utilitarianism at its height, in an immediately post-war world in which having a population fit enough to work well to rebuild Britain was a priority. The original view was that universal health care would lead to a country in which everyone would be healthy and less state care would be necessary. It did not work out like that; indeed, pressures on costs have continued throughout the history of the service. The NHS expressed a philosophy – these days a series of values which do not wholly fit together – about the obligation of society to look after the sick and the needy. We pool the risk, and we share the care and the responsibility. Despite worries about quality and standards, and worries as to whether the service will be there for us when we need it most, the NHS is still highly trusted and much loved, even though there are concerns about its ability to provide a service fit for the new millennium. The welfare state may have its difficulties, but the UK population still believes in it. The way it works may change: there needs to be greater choice, greater acknowledgement of diversity. But by providing health services relatively cheaply and efficiently to the whole population, the NHS is part of the glue that holds British society together.

For we are individuals now. We demand things. We go for the personal. We understand our own needs. The idea that we might not be able to have what we believe we want and need is anathema to us. We have become demanders, not citizens; we look to ourselves rather than to society as a whole. This tendency is not new, but it has acquired far greater weight. The words so often uttered, particularly by elderly people, until just a few years ago, that 'I have had my

INTRODUCTION

turn, it's someone else's go now' are becoming rare. We see no need to moderate our demands. We see no reason to say that we have had our share. It is no longer about our fair share, but instead about when *we* feel – as autonomous individuals – that we have had enough.

The idea of an obligation to society, beyond the demands we ourselves wish to make, has become unfashionable. Utilitarianism is out of the window, as is mutualism. We are into understanding ourselves, into self-improvement, into improving our homes, our looks, our minds. Our view of faith is also increasingly individualistic. We choose the elements of faith that suit us. Individual salvation is part of the appeal of the evangelical movement. Personal salvation is the carrot held out. But the requirements which our faiths put upon us to consider others may get less than their fair expression. Despite all the surveys demonstrating widespread belief in God, despite the huge readership of religious books and the increasing attendance at evangelical churches, the idea of social solidarity – about evening up the inequalities, about making a difference to groups or individuals who suffer – has taken a battering.

This book seeks to examine some of these issues. It does not attempt to be a philosophical work, nor a work of political theory. Rather, it is an attempt to show the ordinary reader where we have got to with our system of care for the less fortunate, and why, and to examine whether there are things we can do to improve it. Though the welfare state will be seen by some as being critiqued in the book, I am a profound believer in its values. But I also believe that, in the light of social change and huge increases in wealth and expectations, we will need to reassess what we can reasonably expect to provide for everyone. Throughout my adult life, we have tinkered with the welfare state at the edges, be it in changing the provision for the very elderly – the greatest consumers of the welfare state's provision – or in how we provide health care. The question that arises is whether such tinkering has gone on long enough and whether we might now need to rethink some aspects of the welfare state and its basic value system as we assess what we can and should do for the most unfortunate.

This is both a political and an ethical issue. In a society where voting figures are reducing and where trust in politicians is at an all-time low, reassessing what we provide for the most disadvantaged is difficult to do. What we have is a failure of trust combined with an aversion to risk: those who work in our health and welfare services do not trust the politicians not to blame them when things go wrong. And we have a society that thinks politicians lie when they promise various services for all of us, including the most disadvantaged. Improvement in education? Show me. More higher education? Where is it, and why have I got to pay for it? Yet trust is essential if we are to value our services, and risk aversion will make for bad services, where no one will do what seems natural and kind in case they get accused of behaving improperly or riskily. We look at ourselves and make our demands. But we fail to look out at others. Our sphere of endeavour is both vast – we see the world and beyond as never before – and tiny, as we sit glued to our television screens and fail to go out of our front doors.

I believe we have reached a stage where trust is under threat, where politicians – often unfairly – are regarded as being only out for their own ends. Yet we cannot just turn our backs. If we want a society where people feel that fairness is part of the ethos, we need to be seen to be involved with our politicians and thinking about our society. We cannot just let our concepts of fairness and mutuality go, and then complain. If we are too individualistic, then we will suffer, for our happiness, as Richard Layard argues so cogently,* will suffer, but so will our sense of belonging.

Ultimately, this is a book about who belongs to our society and how we regard them. It is about insiders and outsiders, the trusted and the distrusted. If we recognize mutual obligations, how far does that mutuality extend? Who is 'us', and to whom can we legitimately say we have no obligation? If we only look to ourselves, we narrow our field of vision and in the end become

---

* Richard Layard, *Happiness: Lessons from a New Science* (2005).

automata: selfish, self-obsessed, habitually shirking our responsibilities. If we only take the longest view, we somehow forgive ourselves for not noticing what is under our feet or in the next street. But both the longest and the nearest gaze negate the need for trust. It is in the middle distance – amongst our neighbours, our police, our fellow citizens, our politicians – that trust can be found and where debate about making the world a better place can effectively take place. Escaping inside will simply negate our experience of friends and colleagues. Escaping to the ends of the earth will bring excitement but no permanent gain. The issues we need to grapple with are in the here and now, in our cities, towns, and families. Unless we rethink our social obligations and reassess the issue of trust, we will become even more cynical, even more atomistic, even more individualistic – and there will then really be no such thing as society.

If I am not for myself, who will be for me?
And if I am only for myself, what am I?
And if not now, when?
(Mishnah, Ethics of the Fathers, 1: 14)

ONE

THE ELDERLY

Once upon a time there was an old donkey who had worked for the same owner for many years from being a very young and energetic donkey. One day he saw his master talking to the local butcher and that he was eyeing him up and down. He thought he knew what that meant – that they were going to make him into cat's meat. He wasn't having any of that. So that very night he kicked the stable door down and escaped.

Whilst recovering from his exertion in a field full of thistles, which he munched his way through, he thought what to do. He would become a musician in the famous city of Bremen, not too far away. That decided, next morning, with a belly full of the best thistles that ever grew in a cruel farmer's field, he set out down the Bremen road.

He had not gone very far when he met an old dog lying panting in the road. He asked him what was wrong, for the dog was distressed, with obviously sore paws. The dog replied that he was an elderly dog who had served his master well for eleven years, but, as he got older and more rheumatic, he could not chase and round up the deer as once he had. And so his master was going to have him put down. They both agreed that this was appalling, and then the donkey offered the dog the chance to join him and become a town musician in Bremen along with him.

So they went on together. Soon they tripped over an elderly cat lying in the road with sore paws, her claws split. She was panting. They asked her to tell them her story. She explained she had been a fine fit young cat, a great mouser, and very popular and much loved by her mistress. But now that she was old and tired, and liked to sit and dream by the fire, her mistress thought she was useless and not worth feeding. So she threatened to drown her. The cat heard this and ran away from the house where she had once been so happy. Then she had stopped, thinking that there was no easy way for her to survive. The donkey and the dog were very sympathetic. They said the same thing had happened to them. So they asked her if she would like to join them on the way to Bremen, since with her fine singing voice she could easily become a town musician.

And so they carried on together. As it was nearing nightfall, they saw a cock hopping towards them, making the most terrible noise. They asked the cock what was the matter. He replied that he was getting old and he had heard his master say that he was not much use any more for waking up the farmyard and that a younger cock was needed for the task, as well as for impregnating the hens to ensure they laid enough to make a living for the farmer's wife. But the worst thing had been hearing his master threaten to cook him up for the soup for Easter Sunday!

The donkey, the dog, and the cat were all very sympathetic. They invited the cock to join them in their journey to Bremen, and then to become a town musician with them. And so he cheered up, and went with them. And they journeyed on till nightfall, when they stopped in a forest and went to sleep, though it was cold and they were very hungry.

But then they saw a light a long way off. The cat cheered up. It must be a house and she could sit warm and snug by the hearth and think her old cat's thoughts. They decided to go towards the light. When they got there they found a pretty cottage, but it was full of robbers eating a huge meal around the table. They looked at each other. Then the dog jumped on the donkey's back, the cat on the dog and the cock on the cat, and they looked into the window and made the most terrible noise. The robbers were terrified and ran away into the forest. The animals sat down round the table, had a great meal, and then went to sleep in a cosy cottage that seemed just right for them.

But the robbers began to think they had been silly to run away. They thought it could only have been a group of animals who had found them. So they moved nearer. The chief robber told the younger ones to go into the cottage. All the animals were asleep, and he thought it was safe to attack the sleepers, kill them and take back the cottage – to which, of course, he felt entitled.

But the cat could hear in her sleep, old though she was, and she woke up, and as the robber passed she scratched him viciously with her claws. As he ran from what he thought was a knife, the dog bit into his leg and would not let him go. He wrenched himself away and, as he ran, the donkey lashed out at him with a hoof, and then, for good measure, as he began to get up some speed, the cock swooped down and pecked at his face and ears. He was terrified; the people in the cottage were all armed. The robbers would have to give up and go far far away.

And the animals lived there happily in retirement ever after.*

In the week before Christmas 2003, a case hit the headlines in all the papers entitled variously: 'Betrayed', or' Frozen to death', or, in *The Guardian*, 'Cold and Old'. An

---

* 'The Bremen Town Musicians' (with thanks to the Brothers Grimm).

elderly husband and wife, who had lived in the same house in London for 63 years, had died at the ages of 89 (of emphysema and hypothermia) and 86 (of a heart attack) respectively. No real surprises here, except their gas supply had been cut off for non-payment of bills. Yet they were not poor. There was £1,400 in cash in their home and a further £19,000 in a building society account.

They were finding it harder and harder to cope, a nightmare that overtakes many older people and is feared by even more. They may not have Alzheimer's disease, but at the end of their lives they often find it hard to organize things and get their paperwork sorted, to catch up with the bills and the personal administration, and to keep their affairs in order. Two of the commonest causes of winter deaths are, as we know all too well, heart and chest diseases. Yet the excuse used by British Gas for cutting off their gas supply but not alerting the local social services was the Data Protection Act – i.e. on privacy grounds. The Data Protection Act's Information Commissioner responded immediately by saying that this was a nonsensical excuse, and there is no doubt that some considerable incompetence was involved. Yet the seriousness of the case lies in the fact that two perfectly innocent, old and frail people – hitherto just about coping with the vagaries of life in their own home – died because no one noticed that they were a bit confused.

This chapter discusses how we view older people, whether we treasure them or simply want them to die. It looks at whether older people can control their own deaths, or whether they are liable to be abused and neglected in their last months and days, and at the question of euthanasia and how we ration healthcare.

It also examines the poverty of many older people, and the general neglect they often experience within the health and social care system and asks: is this how we want our parents to be treated? Is this how we want to be treated ourselves? Has our aversion to risk made us mechanistic and unkind? Has government made a mistake in refusing to allow more funding for the care of older people in care homes and nursing homes?

Finally, it looks at the question of how older people have been slow to use their political muscle and whether that might change.

Poverty

As well as the difficulty of coping with personal administration, nightmarish though that may be, many old and frail people also have to cope with extreme poverty. Whilst the focus of much public policy in recent years has been on child poverty, poverty is still a major issue for many older people. This is especially true of what is described by the Faculty of Public Health as 'fuel poverty', which is where any household has to spend more than 10 per cent of its income on keeping warm. For older people, this is not uncommon: they need their houses to be warmer than younger people do, and often live in poorer quality housing than younger people. Though there are government programmes to address this, the 'warm front' programme, aimed at preventing some of the worst excesses of winter deaths by providing better insulation and heating, is only worth £400 million. But the £1.9 billion spent on winter fuel allowances may be a less than efficient way of tackling the problem. For many older people are still seriously poor. Inequality amongst retired people is even greater than amongst the working population. The top 20 per cent of pensioner couples have a retirement income averaging around £45,000 per annum, whilst a quarter of all pensioners – over two million people – live below the poverty line (£5,800 for a single person.) *The Guardian*, on the day of the particular story cited above, called for the Government to add to its target for the abolition of child poverty by 2020 a similar target for the abolition of older people's poverty as well.

The Very Old and Frail

Terrible though the problem of poverty is for many older people, and disastrous though some parts of our pensions system have turned out to be, particularly for those whose company pensions have simply disappeared, the main focus of this chapter is not older people in general. For the majority of the relatively young 'older people' – the Third Agers, up to 75 or 80 – life tends to be quite pleasant, reasonably financially stable, and, until ill health sets in, fun. There is much to be written about this age group and its changing expectations, and our own, as working longer seems likely to be the norm in order to fund future pensions.

But for a particular group amongst the elderly, life is very different: the very old, the very frail, people who need continual care of one kind or another. Much of the media's attention has focused either on older people who make up the bulk of patients in any NHS ward – especially those amongst them who do not need to be there and who are termed, unflatteringly and unfairly, bed blockers – or on those who have Alzheimer's disease and other forms of dementia. But the majority of very frail older people are neither bed blockers nor people with dementia, yet they need our support and respect.

So who are they? There were some 737,000 people between the ages of 85 and 89 in the UK in mid 2002,* and a further

---

* *Population Trends* (summer 2004), no. 116.

387,000 aged 90 and over. That's over a million people over 85, and growing. The total population of England and Wales is only expected to grow by 8 per cent between 1991 and 2031, whilst of those aged 85+ it will have grown by 138 per cent. So the so-called dependency ratio will escalate. By 2031 there will be 79 dependants for every 100 of working age. This is expensive, and new. It is costly for both pension provision and healthcare, for the over-85s already cost the health and community services five times as much as those aged 5–64. Some 10 per cent of all hospital and community health resources are spent on people of age 85 and over.† The impact on families will be huge. The State is unlikely to be able to provide the full costs of care. The implications for families, and for the individuals themselves, are colossal.

It is a vast change, and we have not kept pace with the changes it demands of us, either ethically or politically. The 'time bomb' argument was very fashionable in the late 1980s and the 1990s, and still rears its ugly

---

† Department of Health, Departmental Report, 2004.

head, despite the fact that people are now more worried by growing suspicion that our increasing longevity has only resulted in pushing the period of frailty to a later age. Indeed, it may be that by increasing our calendar age we are imposing upon ourselves a longer period of frailty and dependence than hitherto. We are certainly seeing an increase in the numbers of people with Alzheimer's disease, and the Alzheimer's Society suggests that there will be around 840,000 people with Alzheimer's in the UK by 2010, rising to more than 1.5 million by 2050. This echoes US figures, where the Rush Institute for Healthy Aging claims that more than 13 million Americans will have Alzheimer's by the middle of the 21st century.*

Whilst demographic predictions have been wrong before, the increase is certainly taking place and the theory that longevity may not always give one a healthier old age is beginning to look worth examining. However, others argue that the high-dependency period, particularly in terms of NHS hospital

---

* N Salari, 'Are health and care services ready for a surge in Alzheimer's cases?' *Community Care* (2003).

use, has simply shifted to an older age and is still roughly parallel with previous experience, being the last three years of life at whatever age.† But it also has to be said that since 1969 admissions of people over 64 to NHS beds has quadrupled, whilst for the rest of the population they have barely doubled. It is not clear how much of this is to do with more recent technology – cataract surgery and hip replacements, for instance – and how much to do with the longer term disabling conditions for which there is no 'quick fix'.

There are also many who argue that concern about the ageing of our society carries heavy ideological baggage – precisely the people who believe we cannot afford welfare support for the frail and needy. If we have more elderly people, frailer and more dependent, then somehow we will have to provide welfare support for them if they cannot provide it for themselves; and that, for those who wish to draw back the provisions of the State, is a highly unsatisfactory situation.

---

† N. Pettinger, 'Age-old myths', *HSJ* (27 August 1998).

This is perhaps best expressed by the author Phil Mullan in his excellent book *The Imaginary Timebomb*. Mullan argues that the preoccupation with ageing has little or nothing to do with demography in itself but is much more to do with ideology – in this case, the curbing of the welfare state. He also argues – as does Frank Furedi in his excellent introduction – that the 'problematization' of older people coincides with 'the tendency to marginalize the elderly from the labour market and from society at large'. The real problem, according to this argument, is not that there are not enough younger people working to support a growing population of older people, but that older people still find it hard to find employment. In the late 1970s and early 1980s, the employment rate of older male workers declined sharply. These rates have improved slightly in recent years, but they are still below the employment rates seen in the 1960s.*

---

* *Simplicity, Security and Choice: Working and saving for retirement*, Department of Work and Pensions (December 2002).

The argument here is that it is the shortening of the period of working life that is likely to be the cause of difficulties, in financial terms, rather than demography per se. There is plenty of evidence to support this theory. The Chartered Institute of Personnel and Development (CIPD) surveyed its members, arguing that Europe's population would age faster than almost anywhere in the world, and found that two out of every five workers felt they had been discriminated against on the basis of age. Older people are seen as doddery and out of touch, whilst the young are seen as immature and unreliable. In looking at the data, Patrick Grattan, Chief Executive of the Third Age Employment Network, identified the media, fast-moving information technology, financial services, and manufacturing as industries that have yet to embrace an equal age policy.* Mike Saunders, the 66-year-old owner of an employment agency entitled Wrinklies Direct, argues that older people also sometimes lack the right attitude at interview, arguing that 'They have to sell their

---

* Ben Richardson, BBC News Online (16 June 2004).

experience; they have to stand up against the young and be counted.' There is cynicism amongst employers, too. Older workers in traditional sectors like banking tend to have built up expensive employment rights, such as increments and pension entitlements. By making people redundant early, firms save themselves a lot of money.† Nor are government schemes particularly effective: 'New Deal 50+', launched in 2000, is open only to those already on benefits, rather than to all those over 50 who are finding it hard to get new jobs.‡ Even more significantly, Mullan argues convincingly that the fear of the demographic time bomb, rather than its actuality, is what promotes insecurity and a lack of inter-generational trust. If older people cannot trust the next generation down to look after them when they are frail and dependent, an increasingly individuated way of caring for oneself will develop. Meanwhile, if the next generation down fears that the older generation will consume

---

† N. Gillies and N. MacErlean, 'Tell me the old, old story', *The Guardian* (23 July 2000).
‡ H. Mulholland. 'Fifty reasons to be cheerful', *The Guardian* (3 April 2000).

all the assets of the family or the state, then respect and care are likely also to be in short supply. This truly is a vicious circle, and Mullan is on to something when he points to the fear of the demographic time bomb as an example of the generalized lack of trust between individuals in our society, particularly between the generations.

So the responses to this apparent demographic threat are many and numerous. Some say that this supposed time bomb is not all it seems because the UK will be importing a huge amount of labour from overseas to carry out the caring jobs and to feed our economic growth. According to this argument, the panic is unreasonable, we should stop worrying and simply get on with providing better care for very frail older people. At the other extreme is the enormous change in attitude, both in younger and older people, towards the euthanasia argument.

Euthanasia/Assisted Dying

There is a view expressed by some that there is no need to have 'useless' old people around who can no longer make a contribution to society. Though no one is suggesting that they should be forced to die, there are some who think that it should be possible for them not to have to continue living if they do not wish to. These are people who might be said to be arguing for euthanasia on the grounds of age and uselessness.

At its most extreme, the 'uselessness' view is one that could be compared to that held by the Nazis about people with severe mental and physical disabilities. There was already a respectable view of 'mercy killing', as propounded by Ernst Haeckel (1834–1919), the scientist and philosopher. So when the Nazis came to power in Germany, they set up the General Foundation for Welfare and Institutional Care, or T-4 as it came to be known, made up of doctors and psychiatrists, and carried out 70,000 killings of men, women, and children in institutions before the programme was stopped as a result of protest, largely from clergymen.

Obviously, those who are in favour of euthanasia for older people have no desire to go that far. But in arguing that very frail older people are of no use to society they are going down that road, though they would naturally be appalled at the comparison. Their aim is to make it respectable for older people – particularly those who really are near the end of their lives, who are suffering, and whose continuing care is costing the health and social services considerable amounts of money and resources – to ask for euthanasia. In order for that to happen, it has to become morally acceptable to eliminate (with their consent) older people who cost the state too much to maintain.

Other countries have euthanasia, after all. In Holland some argue strongly in its favour, whilst others are far less happy about it. Bert Keizer, a physician in the Dutch state-run nursing home system who has written extensively about death and dying, argues that there is virtually no abuse of the system and that people themselves do genuinely ask to be put out of their misery.*

The Dutch Catholic Church tends to take a different view, claiming that children put pressure on their parents in order to inherit.

---

* Keizer, B. (1997).

It has to be emphasized, however, that, unlike in much of the UK (Scotland being the exception), nursing home care is free in Holland and there is little in the way of private-sector provision. So how strong is the pressure from children likely to be once elderly parents are ensconced in a free nursing home, when they have reached a stage where relatives can no longer manage to provide care at home?

In Britain, on the other hand, the bulk of nursing home care for older people is provided by the private sector and children may well see their parents' nest egg, which they often regard as theirs by right, swallowed up in nursing home fees. Parents certainly have a strong desire to pass on their wealth and savings – and often the house they live in – to their children. The result is considerable anxiety about the lack of free provision and about the need to draw down on savings. Anyone who has capital of their own above £20,000 will be assessed as being able to pay the standard rate. In the case of a care home providing nursing care, this would be the fees less the contributions the NHS might make towards the cost of nursing care. Those whose capital is between £12,250 and £20,000 will be expected to make some contribution from their capital on a sliding scale, until the capital goes down to £12,250. Pensions and provision for older people have become major political topics in Britain, as discussed below.*

Those in favour of euthanasia argue that it might be easier if older people, instead of costing the country so much, could simply ask to have themselves put quietly and painlessly to death before the money runs out. The argument is rarely spelled out that way. But remember the story of the dog, the cat, the donkey, and the cock at the beginning of this chapter. Their owners thought them useless and felt that it would be fine to finish them off. We are not the owners of our older people, but as a society we see them as a problem. Hence the political issue that has blown up over long-term care for older people, which the Labour government promised to sort out on coming to power in 1997. It soon realized that this was a truly

---

* Age Concern Fact Sheet 10, *Local Authority Charging Procedures for Care Homes*, issued April 2004, updated June 2004.

difficult task because of the conflicting and complex moral and financial arguments. Are older people entitled to free care by virtue of being old? Or should they pay for their care on the grounds that it is an unreasonable burden to place on the younger people who will end up paying the bill? Should they, in fact, regard it as a normal part of the costs of life?

In this climate of concern about ageing and its costs, the Patient (Assisted Dying) Bill was introduced in Parliament in February 2003 by the cross-bencher peer Lord Joffe. As it did not have government support it had virtually no chance of becoming law. Nevertheless, it was seen as an opportunity to air, once again, the complex and varied views held by all kinds of people and organizations on the subject. It had its second reading, unopposed, in accordance with tradition, in June 2003. After that, significant changes were made to it, to deal with some of the objections. These reduced its scope in a variety of ways, including limiting application of the Bill to terminally ill patients and stating that in assisting someone to die the attending physician might only provide the means to end the person's life, unless the latter was physically unable to do so, in which case the physician could become actively involved. The idea that the physician would only provide the wherewithal, rather than actually kill the person, had considerable attractions for some objectors to the original Bill, since it largely removed the great problem of doctors killing their patients, rather than attempting to heal them or temporarily alleviate their suffering. The changes also included additional safeguards, requiring a specialist to attend the patient to discuss the option of palliative care. After all this, and with these changes, the Bill was reintroduced as the Assisted Dying for the Terminally Ill Bill, in January 2004.

In March 2004, there was a second-reading debate in the Lords and the Bill was sent to a select committee, and it began to look as if it might become law. At that point, Lord Joffe suggested that the select committee might wish to consider the current experience of assisted dying in the Netherlands and Oregon, in particular whether vulnerable members of society had been put at risk and whether doctor/patient relationships had been adversely affected. He also suggested it would be worth examining whether palliative care could, in all cases, enable terminally ill patients to die with dignity and free from unnecessary suffering. He further asked for the committee to look at whether recent polls showing that 80 per cent of the public supported assisted dying reflected public opinion accurately. Finally, the committee was to examine whether the safeguards contained in the Bill to protect vulnerable members of society were adequate and, if not, what further measures might be necessary. The Joint Committee on Human Rights, in its report on 23 March 2003, was of the view that they were, but the Bill's opponents were not persuaded.

The aim of the Bill was to enable a competent adult, suffering unbearably as a result of a terminal illness, to receive medical assistance to die at his or her own considered and persistent request; and to make provision for a person suffering from a terminal illness to receive pain relief medication. The main argument made in favour of the Bill was that attitudes had changed in the ten years since the possibility of helping terminally ill people to die was last considered by the House of Lords Select Committee on Medical Ethics. Ten years on, Baronesses Jay, Warnock, and Flather, formerly opposed to assisted suicide, were now supporters of a change in the law.

Secondly, it was argued that there has been a change in public opinion, particularly after the Diane Pretty case (Ms Pretty died in May 2002, three days after the European Court of Human Rights ruled that her husband could not legally help her to die). Thirdly, changes to the law in Belgium, Holland, and Oregon have apparently worked out well, with no real indication of the predicted dangers associated with assisted suicide actually materializing. For instance, the Dutch government's Remmelink Report found no evidence of vulnerable people being put at risk or of increases in voluntary euthanasia in the previous five years. (It does have to be said, however, that supporters and opponents of the Bill infer different conclusions from international experience.)

Fourthly, people are able to travel to other countries, such as Switzerland, for assisted suicide, which those who support a change in the UK legislation regard as unreasonable. Fifthly, it gives choice to the patient rather than to doctors or society, a point made strongly by Baroness Flather. Indeed, the newly published *Good Euthanasia Guide* by Derek Humphry, a former *Sunday Times* journalist now based in Eugene, Oregon, suggests that personal choice is a powerful factor.

The main arguments made against the Bill were that there is still continued opposition from the British Medical Association (BMA) and the Royal Colleges, which is a real problem since a change in the law could only be effected with the support of doctors. Secondly, it was seen as 'disastrous' for 'the terminally ill, the elderly, for disabled people, for the medical profession and for wider society' by many peers, including Lord Alton of Liverpool, whose exact words are given here. Thirdly, it is seen as brutalizing society, with some drawing parallels with the death penalty and others arguing that the Bill would put pressure on all seriously ill people to consider assisted suicide, even if they had never previously considered such an idea.

Some argued that patients might feel obliged to choose assisted suicide for the 'wrong reasons', such as to avoid being a burden to others, or because of concerns about the financial implications for their families of a long terminal illness. Some also argued that it would create a 'negative climate' towards terminal illness, and that sick, disabled, and frail people might be made to feel even more acutely that they are a burden on society and on their relatives. Other objections centred on problems of definition: what is a terminal illness, particularly when some diagnoses prove to be incorrect and patients live much longer than predicted? Then it is often the case that seriously ill people are depressed, which might impede their ability to make rational decisions. Amongst the weightiest objections was the classic one from many healthcare professionals: that the legislation might affect patients' trust in their physicians and thus alter the fundamental ethos of the medical profession – a view held by the

BMA. Indeed, doctors generally remained opposed to the Bill.

Meanwhile, some argued that the proposed legislation placed too great a responsibility on doctors and that the benefits to the individual would be outweighed by the potential harm to society at large. Many also argued that the Bill was unnecessary because physicians can already relieve the pain of their patients, even if pain relief has the foreseen but unintended effect of shortening life. It was also suggested that the Bill would be impossible to police and would lead to more involuntary killings – the slippery slope argument. Then it was argued that such legislation would be seen as unacceptable to some faith communities and religious leaders: 'Euthanasia is an act of violence, an attempt to take possession of the future ... even if euthanasia were legalised in some form and pragmatic anxieties overcome, it could not be a course of action endorsed by Christians.'* It was also argued that that the insurance industry would be unlikely to accept the provision

---

* Archbishop Rowan Williams, as quoted by the *Independent Catholic News* (2 June 2003).

that no life insurance that has been in force for twelve months would be invalidated by a doctor having assisted a patient to die. Lastly, it was argued that the Monitoring Commission proposed in the Bill would be costly and that it would be difficult, if not impossible, to detect subtle coercion, pressure, or clinical errors after the event.

These were the arguments put forward over the debate, the longest re-examination of attitudes to assisted suicide in the UK in recent years. Meanwhile, many key organizations put in their views at the same time. For instance, Help the Aged strongly opposed any change in the current law related to assisted suicide. It argued:

The prohibition on assisted suicide is designed to protect some of the most vulnerable members of society, including many older people. Any change in the law would run the risk of abuse and would fundamentally change the doctor/patient relationship. Planning and taking decisions around the end of a life are deeply personal issues and, like any other adult, older people have a right to retain control, autonomy and choice. This choice includes the right to choose to refuse medical treatment. All too often, older people who wish to exercise such control are denied the right to be involved in decisions about the end of their lives. This debate highlights the lack of clarity and safeguards around decision making for very vulnerable people who may be unable to make or communicate their own decisions at any stage of their treatment or care. Help the Aged calls on the Government to introduce legislation to strengthen and support older people's ability to make decisions about their own care, to ensure that their wishes are respected, and to allow them to retain choice and control over their lives at every stage.*

At the same time, the National Council for Hospice and Specialist Palliative Care argued that:

---

* Kathryn Wilmington, Policy Officer, Community, Health and Social Care (6 June 2003).

The principles of palliative care affirm life whilst regarding death as a natural process to be viewed neither with fear nor a sense of failure. Death may be impossible to postpone but should not be hastened. Respect for the dignity of the individual is important, and regarded by many as paramount. Such respect is not manifest in the act of killing the patient which would merely serve to confirm the individual's falsely devalued sense of self-worth. We recommend that there should be no change in the law to permit euthanasia.†

The Voluntary Euthanasia Society, unsurprisingly, supported Lord Joffe's Bill, whilst the Disability Rights Commission opposed it, not on moral grounds, but because it believed that until disabled people are treated equally, with their lives accorded the same value as those of non-disabled people, their access to necessary services guaranteed, and their social and economic opportunities

---

† From the website of the National Council for Hospice and Specialist Palliative Care (10 May 2004).

equal to those of non-disabled people, the 'right to die' legislation might jeopardize people's right to live:

> The bill would open the floodgates for people who are not just terminally ill but for those with long term physical illnesses to be helped to die. The safeguards included in the bill are simply not good enough to guard against many disabled people being included.
>
> There is simply no system of safeguards that can detect the hidden pressures and strains from relatives and carers that may drive a disabled person to seek an assisted suicide.
>
> The absence of support services on the ground and high quality palliative care means that there cannot be a real choice. In this context, rather than ensuring the right to die, the bill would quickly translate into a duty to die for disabled people.*

---

* Liz Sayce, Director of Policy and Communications, DRC (6 June 2003).

The Royal College of Nursing also came out opposing euthanasia and assisted suicide: 'The RCN is opposed to the introduction of any legalisation which would place the responsibility on nurses and other medical staff to respond to a demand for termination of life from any patient suffering from intractable, incurable or terminal illness.'†

But that was not a totally universal view from the RCN. In a personal capacity, Karen Sanders, who chairs the RCN's ethics forum stated: 'I feel strongly about euthanasia because I believe that competent adults who have incurable or insufferable diseases should have the right to make their own choices about their own lives.'

Despite those supporting or opposing Lord Joffe's Bill who claim public opinion is on their side, it is actually extremely difficult to establish precisely what public opinion is on this issue. There is little independent information on how the public view assisted suicide, although it is clear that most major organizations concerned with the welfare of older and disabled people oppose changes to

---

† Beverley Malone, RCN General Secretary.

the current legislation. The Voluntary Euthanasia Society claims that 85 per cent of the population supports them, although it does not specify what, precisely, the support relates to or how it can be so sure. Many other polls ask questions that are so vague as to be almost worthless. For example, the *Sun* newspaper's 1997 telephone poll asked whether terminally ill people should have the right to die with dignity; unsurprisingly, 97 per cent said yes. But the mood is shifting and Deborah Annetts, Chief Executive of the Voluntary Euthanasia Society, is right to argue that, as an increasingly secular society in which more people are living longer, our demography will itself be a catalyst for change.*

Whilst all the debate around Lord Joffe's Bill was taking place, the Christian Medical Fellowship recommended a letter-writing campaign for people to express opposition to the Bill, but it is not clear what the response to this was. An *Independent on Sunday* poll in 2001 asked, 'Should people have the right to die when they choose?' and

* Jamie Doward, 'I don't want to plan my death ...',
  The Observer (19 September 2004).

found – unsurprisingly, given the vagueness of the question – that 85 per cent of respondents answered yes and 15 per cent answered no. Meanwhile, a survey by the Disability Rights Commission reported that 63 per cent of people felt there should be new laws to make euthanasia or assisted suicide legal. However, more than eight out of ten respondents said measures were needed to protect disabled people from the use of 'do not resuscitate' notices and the withholding or withdrawal of treatment.

Much of the debate in the media has related to people dying of 'terminal illness' such as cancer or motor neurone disease. It is not clear whether some of the common diseases of old age, such as heart failure, dementia, or strokes, or even the natural processes of ageing itself, are typically viewed as terminal illnesses. Consequently, with the exception of some age-related organizations such as Help the Aged, the possible implications for older people of proposed changes in the law are not addressed as frequently as those for younger people. Yet it is the fear of living after a massively disabling stroke, of being completely dependent and unable to exercise one's autonomy, that has driven the Bill's supporters to try to get legislation through. Despite the public discussion being focused to a considerable extent on younger people, support for this legislation is at least in part about the fear of being very old and dependent, in both existential and economic terms.

There is certainly an argument for personal self-determination, to allow older people, and others who are terminally ill, to decide when they have had enough. According to that view, it is morally acceptable, for old people – or anyone else, for that matter – to be able to decide they have had enough and to exercise their autonomy. Test cases suggest that the public is increasingly sympathetic to this argument. The classic example is the 1992 case of Dr Nigel Cox, who acceded to a patient's request – he had known her well for years – to put her out of her misery. Though charged with homicide, he was not in fact convicted and it was clear that he had the support of the patient's family. He was not 'struck off' the medical register but was required instead to go on palliative care training, the argument being that, with more specialized knowledge, he might have been able to improve his patient's pain control.* There has also been major debate on these issues in the House of Lords (Select Committee on Medical Ethics.) But the arguments need spelling out.

First, it is one thing to kill oneself because one cannot bear to continue living. Suppose one were suffering unbearable pain, or extreme depression. Although it is terrible for those who are left behind, whose guilt is never assuaged because they feel they could have done more, there is a strong case for saying such suicides are not sinful. I say this despite the teachings of almost all the religious groupings. Historically, religions have argued that suicide is a sin. Those who committed suicide were often not buried in the same cemetery as those who died naturally; they might even be buried with a stake driven though their hearts, as consummate sinners. The argument was that God had given life and it was not for human beings to decide when life should be ended. Yet judi-

---

* *GMC News* (December 1992).

cial killing was somehow permitted along-side this view, and the 'just war' was also permissible. So the logic barely stands up.

Japanese culture, and some others, have taken a different view in particular circum-stances. Certainly there is also a strong ar-gument for discouraging suicide. It is, after all, too easy to do, and the waste of oppor-tunity, talent, and expectation is palpable. Nevertheless, with all the reservations about acute depression being a mental illness and the desire for suicide it some-times engenders therefore being the result of an abnormal psychological state, it does have to be said that for some people life is intolerable. If that is the case, there may not be a strong argument to prevent them from committing suicide, or even for criticizing them post-humously if they succeed. In other words, there is a moral dimension to the argument that suicide, in these circum-stances, is not necessarily wrong and that attitudes towards it should change.

It is therefore not necessarily wrong for someone to whom life has become intolera-ble, for instance through continual pain, to commit suicide. What is wrong is to expect them to do it in order to relieve the obligation of their care from their family or from society at large, or to ask someone else to help them to do it. And therein lies the rub, for it is not easy to commit suicide if one is already very frail. This might encourage people who had not yet reached this condition to contemplate suicide *before* they became too incapacitated to carry it out.

That is a problem answered to a considerable extent by the idea of having legalized euthanasia. Obviously real safeguards would have to be put in place. Doctors could not act without another doctor, or health professional, or some other person, witnessing the request and formalizing it in some way. People of sound mind would then be able to take control of their own lives and deaths. What argument can there really be against such a system, properly designed with protection in place for individuals and protection, legal and ethical, for health professionals?

The answer has to be that it is simply wrong to ask someone else to kill you. If an individual wants to commit suicide, sad though it is, that is understandable. One could even argue that it is their right to do so, especially if they are terminally ill already and however traumatic for everyone left behind. But to ask other people to do it for you, because you lack the determination or because you want to wait to the last possible moment when life seems truly to have nothing more to offer, seems very hard. Suicide may not always be wrong. But murder – even with the best of motives, and by request – is. The role of a doctor is to heal and to care, not to kill. Crossing that line is very difficult to justify. It asks doctors and other health professionals to go against everything they have trained for. However critical we may be of the tendency within our healthcare systems to preserve life in all circumstances, asking health professionals actively to seek the death of another human being is asking them to lose their respect for human life in a quite fundamental way.

Yet it appears that public opinion has gradually been moving towards favouring mercy killing. From the beginning of the 1990s, attitudes began to change in the Western world. According to polls carried out for the *Boston Globe* (November 1991 and onwards), 64 per cent favoured physician assisted suicide for those terminally ill patients who requested it. Of those under 35, 79 per cent were in favour. Question 119, the Washington initiative to legalize physician assisted death, was not in fact carried. But it raised questions about the role of doctors in keeping patients alive unnecessarily, and in an undignified way, as well as issues about whether it was a major conflict for physicians trained to preserve life to assist willingly and knowingly in procuring death. Yet the physician who assisted in the suicide of two women (painfully but not terminally ill), Dr Jack Kevorkian, who was arraigned on charges of murder but without specific charges being brought against him, had a preliminary ruling in his favour in Michigan in February 1992 and continued to 'assist' patients commit suicide thereafter. In the UK, we are beginning to see newspaper reports about people going to Switzerland to receive physician assisted suicide, because they cannot get it here. So the pressure is there. Many people want to be able to request euthanasia 'when the time comes'.

Although there are considerable moral dangers in such a system, I believe that we will see limited euthanasia in Britain in the next decade unless a real moral debate takes place and those who are opposed to it argue hard against it. Even if this happens I believe that we will still see physicians being allowed to give terminally ill patients the wherewithal to commit suicide if they are convinced that this is what they want. The climate of opinion is changing. What we need to think about is to what extent this is because of people's fear of growing old and helpless, their fear of the disintegration of self in old age, and society's increasing unwillingness to accept that it has to pay for the care of the extremely frail and dependent.

Advance Directives

The arguments against the projected changes include, firstly, the view that asking doctors and nurses actively to kill patients is wrong and creates the wrong value system for a healthcare service of any kind. It may be the case that healthcare professionals do not need to strive to keep patients alive, but that is very different from actively killing their patients. Secondly, that suicide itself is not wrong and that an elderly or very frail person committing suicide is not necessarily to be disapproved of if it is done by their own hand rather than by another's. Acceptance of this view should lead to a change of perception which might allow people to realize they can do it for themselves, and even be helped by being given the means in particular circumstances, without having to ask someone else actually to kill them. Thirdly, a rider to all this is the need for us as a society to develop a system of advance directives, whereby people can make choices for themselves about whether they want to be treated if extremely ill or when they can no longer make decisions for ourselves.

Such a system is in place in the USA. The PSDA (Patient Self Determination Act), a piece of federal legislation, came into force in December 1991. This requires all health-care institutions, HMOs and services in receipt of federal funds to ask patients the question upon admission or enrolment about whether they have any kind of proxy or advance directive for what is to happen to them in the way of healthcare decisions if they become incompetent. At the same time, there is legislation in most US states that covers either healthcare proxies or advance directives, recognizing them in law and therefore in a sense approving their use.

There has been, rightly, increasing pressure to have a universal system of advance directives in the UK. The UK government has finally signalled, after a ten-year campaign, that there will be legislation to enforce so-called living wills via the draft Mental Capacity Bill, published in June 2004. This would apply both to those nearing their deaths, such as those who are frail and elderly, and to those who are or might become incapable for other reasons, such as those with enduring mental health problems, so that they can consent in advance to the treatments they might choose to have, or decide not to have, if they were well enough to make a decision. Some of the American evidence suggests that two separate factors are at work here. The first is a genuine desire to see self-determination for the very old. People must take responsibility for themselves, and must be encouraged do so before incapacity sets in. The other factor, which is certainly echoed in the UK debates, is the vast cost of paying for healthcare of the very old. The general view is that everything that can be done for a patient must be done, and there is a corresponding fear of being sued if any stone is left unturned, or any intervention left untried. If people could be persuaded to use advance directives, or appoint agents, there might be less use of expensive resources by the very old and very sick.

The fear of litigation in the USA is real and is growing in the UK. Though actual litigation is less common than the fear of it might suggest, it does have a powerful effect on behaviour. In the USA it is that pressure that has led to an increasingly strong argument for individual patients to have their own advance directives. State statutes on treatment directives give physicians a guarantee of civil and criminal immunity if they withhold or withdraw life-sustaining treatment relying in good faith on a patient's advance directive. So, the argument runs, encouraging the use of advance directives will lessen the chance of litigation, allow for real patient autonomy, and arguably save costs.

But, if we are to move to a system of advance directives, then, as a society, we have to think quite differently about our health and social care systems. For the first time, with the exception of palliative care and hospice services, we will have to give far greater thought to the question of suffering, for despite the success of the hospice movement, suffering is barely part of medical training in Britain. Public debate on these issues needs to be encouraged, and public standards established. The idea that patients could set out for themselves, perhaps on a standardised form, what they want to happen if they are too frail, or mentally incompetent, to make a decision, is an attractive one. It would take away from healthcare professionals the need always to make decisions 'in the best interests' of the person involved, since it is often hard to tell what those interests might be. And many people simply do not want, at the end of their days, someone striving officiously to keep them alive.

Yet the system is not yet established that would allow us, as standard practice, to make our views known to our GP or to the person acting on our behalf in the healthcare setting. It is remarkably good practice at present if GPs and healthcare professionals ask us our views and make a note of them for future use. A system of advance directives seems sensible, practical, and easy to organize once a decision has been reached about what questions should be asked. The courts already recognize living wills, but the new mental capacity legislation will enshrine the right to draw one up in law and make it possible to appoint a healthcare proxy, in exactly the same way appointing someone to look after one's financial affairs. As well as enshrining the right to make a living will in law, the Bill creates a new criminal offence of neglect or ill treatment of a person who lacks mental capacity, but it met criticism early on from the Making Decisions Alliance, a grouping of charities including Age Concern and the Alzheimer's Society, who argued that the provisions lacked teeth and did not give advocates a central role in representing those affected by mental incapacity. In June 2004, the numbers affected were some 700,000 with dementia, some 145,000 with severe and profound learning disabilities, and some 120,000 suffering from the long-term effects of severe brain injury, quite apart from those with episodic severe mental illness.

At this point, it might be worth returning to the story of the donkey, the dog, the cat and the cock– all of whom had outlived their usefulness to their owners. Evidence is mounting of the rationing of healthcare by age in the United Kingdom. Is this because the elderly are seen as being too old to be productive? Or simply that they are felt to have had their turn and are taking up re-sources that should be used for younger people? A King's Fund study in 2001 found that three out of four senior managers be-lieved that age discrimination existed in some form or other in services in their local area. Discrimination included policies re-stricting access to particular units or treat-ments, although age-related policies were thought to be on the decline.*

---

* E. Roberts, J. Robinson, and L. Seymour, *Old Habits Die Hard – Tackling Age Discrimination in Health and Social Care* (King's Fund, 2002).

Discrimination And Rationing

The cost of caring for older people can only be contained if the general view is that it is morally right to do so, and that requires a public debate and a willingness to change on the part of the medical profession. Older people must not feel they are being denied care. But care in the future might be different from what they get at present. It could mean more palliative care for the relief of pain and suffering, more holistic and less scientifically driven care. Indeed, it might mean that care – rather than often futile attempts to cure – goes higher up the agenda.

This is the nub of one of the key issues facing the frail elderly and those of us concerned about their welfare. For what quality of life do patients enjoy after all the hi-tech healthcare? At present, nearly 29 per cent of all healthcare costs are concentrated on people in their last year of life (and, obviously, death rates rise with age). More dramatically, when looked at by age group, of all healthcare spending devoted to those aged 65–74, 43 per cent is devoted to those in their last year of life; for those aged

75–84 the figure is 56 per cent and for 85+ it is 65 per cent.*

It is hardly surprising that costs should be heavy in the last year of life, but if our true aim were to be the preservation of life at any cost, then we could certainly do more to keep old people alive than we do at present. For instance, are we keen to prescribe un-pleasant chemotherapies for as yet incur-able cancers, on the basis that our success rate is improving and one day they will work, as with the childhood leukaemias? Are we willing to say we will spend more on the life of a premature baby, a child or young person than on older people? Should we ration healthcare by age? Evidence exists for the rationing of care of people with coronary heart disease and cancer. Until recently, screening for breast cancer stopped at the age of 64. Now, women aged between 50 and 64 are routinely invited for breast screening every three years, and work has been carried out to extend the programme to women up to and including the age of 70 from the end of 2004.

---

* Seshamani, M. and Gray, A. (2004).

One might argue that age criteria in breast screening have been in place because of lack of occurrence (in fact, incidence goes up with age) or because the life of a woman of, say, 70 who has advanced breast cancer has not been thought worth making an effort to save. Many experts argue that the cancer grows so slowly in older women that they will probably die of something else. But perhaps that is no longer the case with increased life expectancy. A woman of 70 is likely to be no longer economically active, yet it is also likely that she will be caring for an elderly husband or sibling – thus saving the state the cost of care. Is this not an economic activity? It may not increase GDP, but it certainly saves the state increased expenditure on social care.

The resource allocation arguments about rationing on the basis of age are well argued. The two positions are beautifully spelled out in the work of Professor Alan Williams of the Centre for Health Economics at the University of York, who is in favour of the use of age as a determinant for rationing decisions, and Professor Sir Grimley Evans, Professor of Clinical Gerontology at Oxford,

who is strongly opposed. Williams argues*
that there is a vain pursuit of immortality
(true) and that people over 65 are a far
larger proportion of the population than
they ever were. That is a point well taken.
He argues that as we get older we accumu-
late a 'distressing collection of chronic incurable conditions'. Some are a nuisance,
but some are serious, involving disability
and pain. Though most are incurable, that
does not imply that they are untreatable. We
also get more problems with acute conditions such as pneumonia and flu, and find it
difficult to recover from what younger people take in their stride, like a fall. Hence
healthcare expenditure on older people is
comparatively so large.

Yet we know that much can be done for
older people that is not hugely expensive, in
terms of alleviation of symptoms and
improving the quality of life in an unglamorous way. But, Williams argues, these
unglamorous down-to-earth activities tend
to lose out to hi-tech interventions which
'gain their emotional hold by claiming that

---

* Williams, A. (1997).

life threatening conditions should always take priority'. (This is, of course, a separate argument.) Taken to its logical conclusion, this would suggest that no one should be allowed to die until everything possible has been tried. That in turn suggests that we will all die in an intensive care unit (as many people in the USA do).

But this is not sensible. For all of us, there should come a time when we realize that a reasonable limit has to be set upon the demands we make of the system – and on our fellow citizens. What principles should determine that limit? Williams argues that the objective of the NHS should be to improve the health of the nation as a whole – the utilitarian argument. If that is so, then the people who should get priority are those who will benefit most from the resources available. So, if the concern is for the health of the nation, the older person is likely to lose out against the younger. If those are the values of the system, then the interests of a particular interest group are less important than the interests of the whole. So age will matter in two ways. It will affect the individual's capacity to benefit from healthcare, making the relative cost of a procedure more expensive for older people, and it will incorporate the idea of a 'fair innings' by which older people are somehow thought to have had their share of living.

Grimley Evans* argues the opposite. He says that each of us should be treated as an individual. He argues it would be unacceptable to disadvantage people on the grounds of race, gender or national, or social origin. How, then, can it be justified on the grounds of age?

He then suggests it is easy to do so because older people in Britain, unlike in the United States, have not traditionally been organized politically. They rarely complain, refuse to pay their taxes, or cause riots. Militancy is virtually unknown amongst older people in Britain. Yet things may be changing, despite a slow start. Ageism remains legal thus far in the UK, and there is a growing body of evidence on age discrimination in a whole variety of services, particularly in health and social services as they affect the very old. Older people are begin-

---

* Grimley Evans, J. (1997).

ning to complain. But Grimley Evans reserves his real scorn for prejudice. The old are seen to have less worth than younger people. Public attitudes in some surveys suggest this to be true. Survey interviews are rarely confidential. It is unlikely that people would say that one should discriminate on the basis of colour – even though there is racism in British society. But racism is publicly unacceptable. Ageism, on the other hand, is acceptable, and palpably so, and it is this that has led to a society in which there are so many frightened old people.

Grimley Evans then attacks the health economists. He suggests economists should restrict themselves to finding the most cost-effective way of distributing resources and that the ideology of efficiency, markets, and cost containment is no more valid than the ideology it replaced – of common purpose, collaboration, and social purpose. In the current NHS system one's viewpoint depends on whether one is a user or a provider. The professional providers, one way and another, look for the best return on their investment of time and money. Users of the service, on the other hand, see the NHS as a sort of AA or RAC, there for use when they want/need it. Citizens as taxpayers might agree with Williams, but British citizens as patients would ally themselves with service users, whose desire is to have their needs/wants met. Grimley Evans suggests that the users' perspective provides a rationale more consistent with national values and with the explicit intentions of the NHS at its foundation. That is, in my view, having examined the earliest documents about the foundation of the NHS, debatable to say the least.

Do we then believe that all service users should be treated equally, however old? The measurement of outputs in units based on life years indirectly (or directly) puts different values on people according to their life expectancy. Older people are disadvantaged and, more generally, people are no longer reckoned equal. Secondly, the economists' view assumes that the value of a life can be measured by its length. But if we assert the unique individuality of the person, then the only person who can put a value on a life is the person living it. Grimley Evans' conclusion is that lives of people are not formally comparable; it is 'mathematically as well as

ethically improper to pile weighted valua-
tions of them together as an aggregable
commodity like tonnes of coal'. He continues
by taking a swipe at nations who value their
citizens only for their use to the state. Yet
the NHS was at least in part set up to create
that healthy workforce for the state, and
people were not expected to live on into frail
old age and lengthy retirement. He also suggests that the UK has a different set of values about individual human life from the
economists' outlook. He may be right, but it
is as yet untested. He argues that we should
not create, on the basis of age or any other
characteristic over which the individual has
no control, classes of *untermenschen* whose
lives and well-being are deemed not worth
spending money on.

But however the argument is played out, it
has influenced older people. My father, who
had his first heart attack at the age of 51 in
1965, survived to be 82. He was plagued with
coronary heart disease for the rest of his
life, but managed, despite a second coronary,
to continue working until he was seventy
years of age and to survive, with considerable determination, two coronary heart

bypasses, one endarterectomy to prevent him having a stroke when the carotid artery became narrowed, and several other minor bits of surgery. Towards the end of his life, when he was over eighty, he would often say to me, as some other intervention or new drug was proposed, that perhaps he should not be having all this attention lavished on him. Yet he had a considerable quality of life. He carried on writing and thinking until just before he died. Determination made life, for him, very much worth living. And it did so for us, who did not want to lose him.

It is against that background that I think every day about the question of rationing on the basis of age. Can it be right? Is age the only determinant? Is it, indeed, a determinant of the kind of care one should receive? Pensioners make up a quarter of the bottom fifth of the income distribution. Householders aged 75+ are more likely to have housing that is unfit or substandard. Over 250,000 are on council waiting lists for sheltered accommodation. Isn't the test of a civilized society not only how it treats minorities, but also how it cares for its older people who are dependent on it? Do we send them to the knackers' yard, drown them in the well, cook them up for a stew like the cock? At least we'd get some last bit of use out of them. Or do we value them for who they are? Is there an inter-generational obligation?

Can we calculate what people should be entitled to? Should families have to look after their older relatives? What does that mean as families change? Should an ex-daughter-in-law look after her ex-parents-in-law? If so, this tells us a lot about older people and families generally. Can we judge other people's families and what they do? Or is it a state duty to provide? Our four animals ended up living happily ever after in a house that had been taken by robbers, which they then took by force from them. We have no equivalent, unless we argue that being denied care when the NHS promised to look after them 'from cradle to grave' is a kind of robbery. But, whatever we feel about that analogy, the point has to be made that caring for older people properly is expensive. Someone has to pay, and it may be older people themselves. Even so, is it acceptable to treat them so poorly? Or is there truly a lesson to be learned from the Bremen town musicians: that older people will only succeed in getting decent care if they extract it by force? And what would that suggest then for the nature of our society, if groups had to become violent to get noticed?

Nursing Homes And Care Provision

The nearest we have seen to this kind of public anger was over the Royal Commission on Long-term Care, chaired by Sir Stuart (now Lord) Sutherland, which was set up when the Labour government came to office in 1997. Its members were chosen from a variety of areas, with a heavy weighting given to nurses. Its conclusions were, essentially, that the government, with restrictions according to nursing assessments, would have to pick up the cost of the long-term care of older people.

The Commission's basic argument was that, in an NHS that was free at the point of use, there was no distinction to be drawn between the kind of long-term care a person needed when very old and frail and the kind of help and care they needed when acutely ill in hospital. This was the majority view, though the debate over the distinction between nursing care and social care demonstrated the impossibility of the position we had got ourselves into, historically speaking. There were two dissenters, the aforementioned Joel Joffe, now Lord Joffe, who was worried by the rising and unsustainable costs of long-term care for the elderly, and David (now Lord) Lipsey, who realized that the Commission was moving towards a conclusion that would be entirely untenable as far as the government was concerned. He did everything in his power to make the other members change their view. His final minority report made it clear that he believed that older people themselves would have to pay the costs of long-term care.*

Both the government and the Royal Commission missed a trick here and caused deep resentment amongst older people and their families that has not gone away, at least in part because people feel a grave injustice has been done. Indeed, it is in this area that

---

* Chris Price, 'Who Pays for Grandma?' *The Stakeholder* (1999); the Royal Commission on Long-Term Care (1999).

real political action by older people might still become a reality, in a society where grey power has been a long time in coming. The curious thing is that this was, and is, an entirely unnecessary outcome. The Royal Commission ended with a recommendation, essentially, that long-term care should be paid for by the statutory sector. The implication was that the tax rates would have to rise to pay for this. They never quite got to the bottom of what was nursing care and what was social care, a problem that has bedevilled the care of older people for all my working life and which has caused much unfairness.

The classic question is that of the bath. Is giving someone a bath because they smell a nursing or a social task? If they smell, it is argued, it is a social bath. If they have sores or the possibility of them, then it is a nursing bath. On those grounds, the same bath, given to the same person, could either be given for free, for medical reasons, or be paid for, for social reasons.

After the government decided to reject the Royal Commission's recommendation of requiring statutory payment, it came up with the worst of all settlements. According to assessments made by nurses, older people would get a weekly payment according to need, but this was not enough to pay the cost of a care or nursing home.

This has led to some bizarre results and is a good example of the politics of unintended consequences. Relatively wealthy older people, already in nursing homes and deeply dependent on nursing and social care, are getting help with the fees for their homes, usually allowing the nursing homes to raise their fees. Poorly off older people, not quite so dependent but without the children and relatives who might provide a some care, do not get enough help to allow them to be in a nursing home or care home, unless their dependency becomes so severe that the reluctant local authority decides to pay. Meanwhile, for many nursing home owners the fees provided by local authorities are so low that they have decided the whole area is uneconomic. They can make more money by selling the properties, especially in the booming southeast, and pocketing the profits. Staff costs have been rising and the availability of staff generally declining. The government settlement of help with nursing care has done nothing except raise costs and give a bit of help, often to the better off who are already paying their way in nursing homes.

In Scotland, where the decision was made to go the other way and to pay the full cost of care, the nursing homes are now deluged with older people and the system is cracking under the strain. Despite the strong feeling within the Scottish Parliament that this was the right direction, the total subsidy of nursing home care makes it virtually impossible to choke off demand. And in parts of Scotland where there is low employment or where property prices have not risen very rapidly, there has been an epidemic of nursing and care homes opening, simply because the income – though not huge – is assured.

All of this has been horribly unfair and has disappointed older people, who greatly fear the need for nursing home care and the giving up of independence. And it was unnecessary. Few older people and their families feel that it is essential that the whole cost of long-term care should be borne by the state. Approximately one in four older peo-

ple will need long-term care of some kind –
a proportion so high that it might seem like
the kind of risk we should expect people to
take on for themselves. Supposing the settlement went rather differently. Supposing
older people themselves were required to
take on part of the risk – perhaps paying for
up to two years of care, which is the average
time older people spend in long-term care.
Beyond that period the costs would be fully
covered by the state. One major advantage
of such a scheme is that it would deal with
the issue of unfairness. Though there is still
a one in four chance that long-term care will
be needed, it is reasonable to ask people to
plan ahead for such an eventuality. But the
cost would not be open-ended and, if prepared for by saving or by taking out an insurance policy, would not require people to
realize major assets, such as selling their
house, which is currently a cause of huge resentment. Though many people might not
like such a system, they could not say it was
unfair. Nursing contributions could then be
restricted to those who elect to stay in their
own homes – a further discouragement, if

one were needed, to going into a nursing home.

The reason for the anger on the part of older people was so predictable and so unnecessary. The government was trying to choke off the cost of long-term care to the statutory sector, which is what governments do. But to older people, as well as their carers and children, it seemed as if the government thought people were going into nursing homes for fun, as if it was some kind of luxury item, like going on exotic foreign holidays. But for most older people, going into a nursing home is the last stage on a journey to death, much resented, much feared, the last thing most of them want to do. It was completely unnecessary for older people to become distrustful of a new government that had come in promising to do something about a situation that was generally agreed to be appallingly unfair. All the accusations were thrown into the ring: older people had paid their taxes, older people had given service to King and country during the war, older people were being abandoned, older people were being neglected, older people were being badly treated by the NHS and were now not even being helped when they needed long-term care. But underneath all this there was genuine resentment. Older people had paid their taxes on the basis of care 'from cradle to grave' and this under-taking had been broken without any debate, without consent from those for whom it had, apparently, been made. Older people had trusted the new promises of the welfare state from 1948. And that trust was being betrayed.

People do not choose to go into long-term care, even though their relatives sometimes think it is the best option. People want to stay in their own homes and remain inde-pendent for as long as possible. Sometimes this is not possible. Did the government not understand what an awful decision it is to have to give up one's home, to embark on a one-way journey into a care home, to sur-render one's privacy, to have no control over one's own life? Did they not understand that care homes and nursing homes are a neces-sity, not a luxury? Could there not have been some sympathy, some generosity, here? In-stead, there are cases, time after time, of the Ombudsman finding that guidance on

NHS funded care has been misinterpreted to save the NHS money, with a particularly heavy judgment in April 2000 that lead to considerable payouts by the NHS. The scandals about payment are legion, with an excellent campaign being run sporadically by the *Daily Mail*, 'Dignity for the Elderly', about the perversity and unfairness of the system. Since the government has paid out over £180 million in compensation to people who should never have had to pay their fees at all, it has been argued that 'this is just the tip of the iceberg ... The system is failing the most vulnerable members of our society, many of whom fought for our freedom and paid taxes throughout a long and productive life ... More than 70,000 are selling their homes every year to pay nursing home fees often amounting to hundreds of thousands of pounds.'* The *Daily Mail* has not been alone in taking up the cudgels on behalf of older people. No one wants to be in a care home, and this is where government has made such a huge mistake.

---

* Liz Phillips, 'Does nobody care?', *Daily Mail* (7 July 2004).

Grey Power

From the resentment caused by the government's reaction to the Royal Commission on Long Term Care, after years of surprising political inactivity amongst older people, there has grown the beginnings of a grey-power movement. It does not yet have real political teeth, but they will come. Though the organisation of the grey vote is not in the league of similar movements in the USA, the voting figures, which show that older people vote more than younger people, make governments nervous. If older people voted more on self interest, then governments would be in trouble.

And there are signs that older people, who have not hitherto voted on sectional interests, are beginning to change. They see themselves as having to bear the risk of the costs of long-term care, and they cannot see how they can trust a government that has, in their view, reneged on a promise to remove the inequities of the present system. Worse than that, they are beginning to ask whether they can trust any government to treat them fairly. The 75p increase in the old age pension in 2000 met with a furious response. As Gary Younge pointed out, in a hard hitting article in *The Guardian* shortly after that famous increase, the government's determination to keep the pension increase index linked 'was more than a mathematical calculation. There was political arithmetic there too.'* The assumption, as Younge makes clear, was that old people would complain but that they would not fight back.

But the government got it wrong. Older people did fight back. The National Pensioners' Convention is growing. On the question of council tax, some older people have simply refused to pay. In March 2002, one old lady, 102-year-old Rose Cottle, furious at the prospective closure of her care home where she had lived happily for many years, took a petition to Downing Street and caused some embarrassment – but not enough. By the next week things had moved on, and she was forgotten. Some have gone on hunger strike, and others have been moved – against their will – and have died shortly afterwards. But grey power is coming. As *The Economist*

---

* Gary Younge, 'Grey power bites back', *The Guardian* (5 June 2000).

made clear recently, the overall fall in voter turnout is largely a change in the voting patterns of the young.† The old vote as they always have done. So pensioners, who represent 24 per cent of the voting-age population, accounted for 35 per cent of votes at the last election. At the next one, the figure is more likely to be 40 per cent. So grey power will soon begin to bite.*

Long-term care has been one source of anger amongst older people. Another issue that has caused resentment is abuse.

Abuse

A survey conducted by Age Concern as far back as 1991 estimated that between 5 and 9 per cent of people aged over 65 had been abused – more than half a million people. The incidence of abuse is clearly likely to increase as the population ages: the greater the level of dependency, the greater the risk of abuse. In 2004 Jennie Potter, a district

---

†'The battle for the older voter', *The Economist* (18 September 2004), 37.
* Peter Riddell, 'Getting the Grey Vote', *Parliamentary Monitor* (November 2004).

nurse who is a national officer of the Community and District Nursing Association, compiled a report on abuse of older people† that suggested the problem was widespread. The CDNA surveyed just over seven hundred nurses, and found that a staggering 88 per cent of them had encountered elder abuse at work, 12 per cent of them daily, weekly, or monthly. The most common form of abuse was verbal (67 per cent), followed by emotional (51 per cent), physical (49 per cent), financial (34 per cent), and sexual (8 per cent). The most likely perpetrators were partners (45 per cent), followed by sons (32 per cent), daughters or other family members (29 per cent), paid carers (26 per cent), nurses (5 per cent), or other persons (4 per cent).‡

This suggests a huge incidence of abuse, one that until recently we did not take seriously. Though dramatic cases often make the local press, very few are reported in the national papers. The appalling case of

---

† *Responding to Elder Abuse* (Community and District Nursing Association, 2004).
‡ Liz Gill, 'Abuse is a wicked secret', *The Times* (1 January 2004).

78-year-old Margaret Panting, for instance, who died after receiving huge physical abuse that included cigarette burns and cuts from razor blades is little known. Whilst there is a major inquiry over the death of Victoria Climbié, and over every other child who dies in appalling circumstances, abuse of older people, which may also lead to death, simply does not carry the same weight, or tug at the heart strings as much. Yet there is equally a serious problem here, and some older people, as well as their carers and nurses, are now speaking up about it in a brave and forthright way. For it is not a simple issue, which, to some extent, is why older people have been loathe to raise it. Though there is some violence against older people on the wards of hospitals, most abuse is not the stuff of headlines. Much of it is score settling – often by a wife who feels she has had a rough time at the hands of her husband – when one partner becomes physically dependent on another. This may be no more than rough handling, verbal abuse, and a general lack of care and kindness. But it can still make the last years, months, or weeks of a person's life intolerable. Then there are some paid carers who take advantage of their position to steal from their employers. I well remember my own mother's fear of us confronting one of her early carers (the majority were completely wonderful, with this one exception) who was stealing from her and forging stolen cheques. That fear, that loss of the normal ability to confront an issue, makes the abuse of older people truly dreadful.

Even more complicated is the amount of abuse received from partners and children, normally due to the considerable levels of stress experienced from trying to care for someone as well as carrying on with the normal things of life. Action on Elder Abuse, a charity set up in 1993, has been campaigning for urgent official action after demonstrating in a variety of ways, including an undercover TV programme in late 2003,* the seriousness of the situation. An analysis of the calls the charity received over a two-year period from 1997 to 1999 demonstrated that two-thirds of the calls came from older people themselves or their relatives. Most

---

* 'Who Cares for Granny?', Channel Five, a MacIntyre UK Undercover documentary (October 2003).

of the calls concerned abuse in people's own homes, though a quarter were about abuse in nursing homes, residential care homes, and hospitals.* There were cases of near starvation in care homes, of helpless older people left to die because their buzzers had been placed out of reach, nurses sleeping through night shifts and dressing patients in incontinence pads so they would not be disturbed, and the attempted suicide of several people in nursing homes that were due to close. Some of the statistics are particularly concerning. For instance, abuse appears to increase with age, and therefore with vulnerability. Given that vulnerability makes it harder to complain, this is particularly terrifying. Three times as many calls to Action on Elder Abuse concern abuse of women: women live longer and are therefore likely to be amongst the very old.†

There is the additional likelihood that cases of abuse will rise as the population grows older and the number of people with Alzheimer's disease increases. Though we

---

* Jenkins, G., Asif, Z., Bennett, G. (2000).
† Action on Elder Abuse press cuttings, April 2002–March 2003.

may not be ill for any longer than previous generations, the nature of our illnesses is changing. The increase of Alzheimer's disease has huge implications for the kind of care we will need, and the amount of patience that will be required to deal with often very difficult, irrational, older people. Ironically, it will be even harder to detect abuse, for often the complainers will not be believed, even if they are telling the truth, simply because of the nature of the disease. Caring for those with dementia requires such a degree of patience and skill, and can lead to such frustration, that the chances of abuse increase and the levels of care needed will be much greater – for instance, more and more lengthy home visits will be required. Present provision is patchy at best, and often simply unsatisfactory, as Tony Robinson reported in his story in the *Daily Mail* about the care his parents received:*
'The NHS still fails to recognize the special needs of people with dementia, and won't pay for their long term care ... If we want a dignified old age for ourselves and our par-

---

* Tony Robinson, 'This shameful neglect', *Daily Mail* (13 January 2004).

ents, it's up to us to do something about it.' Meanwhile, research suggests that some 22,000 old people are being given drugs to sedate them, to make it easier for care staff to manage them, according to Paul Burstow, the Liberal Democrat spokesman.† If anything, this figure seems on the low side.

Yet on this whole question of abuse of older people there are detectable signs of change – most notably in the fact that considerable numbers of older people have raised the issue themselves. They have told district nurses, social workers and others, including friends, that they are being abused – despite the difficulties involved for those who may not have access to a telephone and the fact that those committing abuse may be close family members, as well as professional carers. Action on Elder Abuse suggests that there is a category of carers who hop from one agency to another as soon as suspicions about their abusive behaviour become known, with the result that they are able to move to another care home, to another group of vulnerable older

---

† *Daily Express* (5 November 2003).

people, and perpetrate their abuse all over again. To compound the problem it will be a long time before the National Care Standards Commission will be able to register all care workers. Action on Elder Abuse‡ argues that it may take anything between ten and eighteen years before care assistants and home helps are registered by the General Social Care Council; yet, as Gary FitzGerald, Chief Executive of Action on Elder Abuse, argues: 'Less than three per cent of the identified abusers are social workers, whilst 36 per cent are home helps. There is clear evidence that we need to look at the other end of the scale.' Despite this, the General Social Care Council is starting with the registration of social workers. Even when it reaches all care workers, registration will not give us all the answers because there will always be staff shortages and employers may well believe – understandably – that it is better to have some staff, even if a bit dubious, than none. Whilst the government wants half of all care home staff to have achieved NVQ level 2 by 2005, it must be questionable

---

‡ K. Leason, *Community Care* (6–12 November 2003).

whether care home owners will pursue that goal as hard as they might, given how hard it is to get staff at all. It must be equally in doubt whether individuals who might have thought about becoming care staff will bother to go all out to be recognized as capable and reliable in these circumstances, given the numbers of hoops they will now have to go through.

Only the worst cases of abuse make the news, such as the attack in 2000 on Lillian Mackenzie, who was kicked and beaten by two teenage girls who were befriended by her. Jean Lyons and her sister Kelly had run errands for Mrs Mackenzie, who lived in the same block on an estate in Manor House, north London. Wearing balaclavas, they kicked her, beat her with an iron bar, and robbed her of about £800, as well as stealing her handbag and some documents. They then visited friends and bragged about what they had done. Yet Kelly was able to tell the jury that Mrs Mackenzie had been 'like a nan' to her and had taken her for meals at a local café. This was, as one reporter put it, 'as mean and despicable offence as can be imagined'.*

Yet if one scans the local papers, there are hundreds upon hundreds of cases. In June 2003, the Yorkshire papers took serious issue with a nurse who took away an older person's buzzer because he was using it too much. He had to be fed by tube, as his stroke had left him unable to speak and partially paralysed. Yet he was perceived as being too much of a nuisance. As a result, he was overfed by five times the correct amount, could not let staff know things had gone wrong, and died unnecessarily.† Another nurse in Yorkshire strapped up her patients in incontinence pads so she could sleep the night shift through, resulting in blisters, sores, and burns.‡ In Leicester a care worker was given a caution for slapping a frail older person. Again in Yorkshire, a nurse was accused of running a military style 'boot camp' in a care home for mentally ill older people: she had sworn at a 90-year-old wheelchair-

---

* Sue Clough, *Daily Telegraph* (15 August and 9 September 2000).
† *Yorkshire Post* (5 June 2003).
‡ *Evening Press*, York (11 June 2003).

bound man, as well as instructing care assistants not to lift up a 78-year-old man with dementia after he had fallen on the floor with his trousers round his ankles.‡ A woman of 69, a psychiatric patient, had her bed moved away from an alarm button because she was constantly pressing it. Mrs Wootton had a long history of mental health problems, and had set herself on fire whilst in hospital. But her death was the result falling from her bed whilst trying to reach the buzzer. She sustained a broken hip and, later, bronchial pneumonia.§ And these examples are quite apart from the murder investigations and the major cases of neglect.

The truth is that we know about this in our hearts. We see it ourselves with our own eyes. Look at the fear, the terror, in the eyes of some older people in hospital wards, in care homes, in nursing homes. Listen to what they say in code. Listen to how their carers speak about them. It is not universal, by any means, but it is common. And one of the terrifying things is that we have known about it, subliminally perhaps, for many years.

---

‡ *Yorkshire Post* (11 June 2003).
§ 'This is Lancashire', BBC News (30 April 2004).

THE ELDERLY

The redoubtable campaigner Erin Pizzey, famous for her action on domestic violence, has now taken up the cudgels. She argues that abuse of the elderly has a terrible habit of being kept quiet: 'It is a bit like domestic violence amongst the middle classes – no one ever talked about it, although people knew it was going on ... If baby-boomers don't start kicking ass now about elder abuse, this will be their future – and they are a generation who are used to their freedoms. Tackling elder abuse requires a revolution – a grey revolution.'*

We know human beings are often very abusive to people who are in their care. We understand that there is a risk, but our way of dealing with it is to add layer upon layer of regulation and inspection rather than to encourage the opening up of institutions such as care homes and nursing homes so that ordinary people can come and go frequently, as part of daily life. Whether those in care are children, older people, people with enduring mental illness or learning disabilities, or even prisoners, cruelty can often

---

* Maureen Paton, 'A veteran fights a new battle', *The Times* (27 April 2004).

well up from the depths of the human personality. We know it well enough from all
the inquiries into abuse in large institutions.
Abuse occurs wherever vulnerability exists.
If we have strong legislation to protect the
vulnerability of animals, why not for older
people also? But legislation needs to go
hand in hand with opening up institutions,
for openness is far more likely to breed an
atmosphere of trust than any system of regulation and inspection.

Fear of abuse has been further exacerbated by the chaos surrounding care and
nursing homes, particularly, though not ex-
clusively, in the south and west of England.
With the rise in property prices nursing
home and care home owners find it difficult
to maintain standards and get staff. One by
one, homes have been closing. The result
is that older people who moved – often un-
willingly – into nursing and residential care
find themselves with nowhere to go when
they are at their frailest and most desperate. Though this is not abuse as such, it is a
form of mistreatment that beggars belief.
Many professionals suspect that many old

people attempt suicide because their future in such circumstances is so bleak.

Abuse exists in the NHS sector as well, as the CHI (Commission for Health Improvement) report into conditions in Rowan Ward of the Manchester Mental Health and Social Care Trust made clear. There was abuse, an inward-looking culture, low staffing levels, high use of agency staff, poor supervision and appalling management.* The report, which came after complaints of abuse of older patients by staff, found amongst other things: a ward left physically isolated when other services were moved to more modern premises elsewhere; poor reporting and clinical governance procedures that failed to pick up early warnings of abuse; regimented care; 'Patients' clothing was changed and their hygiene needs addressed according to a schedule rather than when the need arose.' They also found sickness rates of 9.8 per cent during 2002 among nursing staff; widespread use of mixed sex wards in the Trust's older-age mental health services; 'rudimentary' performance management of

---

* *CHI News* (October 2003).

staff; an aimless service; and a lack of management attention to quality of care caused by transition to care trust status.

So can the NHS do better? Its record in this area is not all that reassuring. An inquiry by the Health Advisory Service in 2000† demonstrated that older people were less satisfied with the care they received than younger people – which is surprising given that older people complain less than younger people. They experienced unacceptably long delays in admission, problems with feeding and with the physical environment, staff shortages, privacy and dignity, communication with staff, and, most profoundly, with staff attitudes towards older people. The recommendations were lengthy, but the most significant was that everyone – patients, relatives, and staff – has to take on responsibility for challenging negative attitudes about old age, about prospects for recovery, and about worth. So if the NHS has problems of this sort, will voluntary organizations take on the provision of care homes?

---

† *'Not because they are old': An Independent Inquiry into the Care of Older People on Acute Wards in General Hospitals* (Health Advisory Service, 2000).

Many already do, particularly those that are religiously or ethnically based. The mess in care home provision has come about as a result of inadequate planning and a cross-party agreement to shift the burden of care to the private sector. But the position is untenable. The risks of abuse would not be not hugely improved, and feelings of insecurity would remain.

An inquiry into the care market in London currently being carried out by the King's Fund shows that there are still concerns about a number of familiar issues. For example, there is a very limited choice of care and support for older people. While there is no evidence of insufficient care home places for older Londoners, these may not always be where people want them; and there certainly is a shortage of services for older people with mental health problems such as dementia. The King's Fund has also found that throughout London there are difficulties in recruiting and retaining nurses, social workers, therapists, and care workers. Older people's views of services have been shown to be varied; some are very appreciative of a wide range of services, but there are widespread concerns about the quality of home care and residential care services. All of this is compounded by financial pressures, for in spite of increased government spending councils have to juggle the needs of older people with other priorities.

Though inspection of care homes has led to the uncovering of some abuse, inspection in itself is not enough: in fact the burden of inspection and regulation on an already precarious nursing and care home sector may make even more owners give up. Part of the answer lies in allowing ordinary people to visit older people in nursing or care homes, as part of a daily or weekly routine. However, the Better Regulation Task Force, a government body, warned that vital care services were being withdrawn precisely because of inflexible 'no touch' rules stopping volunteers taking older and disabled people to the bathroom or feeding them.* Indeed, volunteers, often in their sixties or seventies themselves, the so-called Third Agers, are now often subjected to the same training requirements for a few hours of

---

* Better Regulation Task Force, *Bridging the Gap* (2004).

help as professional care workers. The report was the work of a committee chaired by Sukhvinder Stubbs, who argued that small local agencies who work with volunteers are being affected by 'silly regulation, bonkers regulation'. But the issue is really about the level of risk service users want to accept – for instance, the extent to which they want to be able to choose the temperature of their own bath water.

In the present climate we are automatically suspicious of people wanting to visit nursing homes and care homes on a casual, uninvited basis. Who are they? Are they would-be abusers? Are they after the older people's money? Yet this attitude of mistrust, and the now ubiquitous fear of risk, may well be leading to a greater degree of isolation for residents. The more we close off institutions, the less we know what is going on within them, the easier it is for abuse to take place and for the residents to feel isolated, hopeless, and forgotten. Some system whereby lonely older people get visited on a regular basis needs to be taken up by a whole variety of organizations, from schools and colleges to churches and mosques, from Townswomen's Guilds to Working Men's Clubs. This sense of isolation, and the fear that taking an interest in older people will be seen as perverse, must stop.

A few schemes exist, such as the excellent British Red Cross's Home from Hospital scheme, which has some 55 initiatives operating nationwide, but many more are needed. The Red Cross model gets round the issue of strangers coming in to people's homes because the volunteers are trained and supported and the service is paid for by local social service departments. This model of supported, trained volunteers who do it because they love it, supported by professional volunteer co-ordinators and a serious, respected organization like the Red Cross, gives older people the confidence to use the service, gives volunteers the feeling that they will not be rejected by the people they visit, since the Red Cross badge will be seen as a mark of quality and safety, and makes the system run as a truly voluntary service with rigorous quality and safety checks.* It is this kind of service that we need to see nationwide, with an expectation that most of us, if not in need of such support ourselves, should be taking part in providing it under the auspices of a respected, sensible organization. Such a model of practical help combined with care and companionship would make all the difference to the isolation and fear felt by many older people.

Care Workers

Another enormous issue is one that will run throughout this book: the low status, low pay, and generally poor conditions and training of those who provide care for the elderly and other vulnerable groups. Over the last thirty years or more we have seen the professionalization of nursing. Nurses are now university graduates whose training has made them technically very proficient. At the same time, they are often unskilled in basic hands-on procedures, which are in-

---

* Melanie Henwood and Eileen Waddington, *Home and Away: Home from Hospital and the British Red Cross, Progress and Prospects* (2003).

creasingly undertaken by care assistants whose training is often minimal and whose security of tenure, and relationship with other members of staff, tends to be poor.

This is a complex issue. Originally, health professionals – particularly nurses – had their hierarchy modelled on the military. After the Second World War nurses came to see themselves as being on an equal footing with doctors. The result has been that nurses' status has risen. The former slave labour demanded of student nurses has, by and large, disappeared, and student nurses are now spending a great deal more time actually studying. There has, however, been a downside to this. Nurses no longer provide the discipline and structure of a ward or a hospital in the way that they used to do; in addition, routine tasks such as emptying bed pans, giving patients their meals, or turning them and making them comfortable in bed has been handed 'down' to care assistants. Nurses are now too expensive a resource to be allowed to feed patients, make beds, or plump up pillows and are too busy giving drugs and injections to empty bedpans. Nor have they been trained to talk to patients and find out what is really worrying or concerning them.

All this is a cause for deep concern, because so many patients will be older people whose recovery rate will be slower than that of younger people and who will inevitably be worried about what will happen to them when they leave hospital. Many will not be fit to go home. Many will be classed as 'bed blockers', as if it were their fault that they have nowhere to go and not that of the system that has failed them by not supplying enough nursing home and care home beds. Nurses could be the ones who listen to the fears of elderly patients, who reassure and comfort, who try to speed up social services, who use their position to get things done – and often they are. But because they have so much less hands-on experience than in former times, because they have not been routinely talking to their older patients as they help them eat, or change, or wash, or make their beds, they often do not have the closeness, the intimacy – in its true sense – with their patients that could be used to allay some of these fears.

The people who are currently performing the most intimate tasks for the patients, most of whom are old, are the care assistants. However, they do not have the status to allow them to tell relatives and social workers what is worrying a patient. It used to be said that the people who knew most about what patients were really feeling were not the nurses at all but the cleaning staff, who would chat to patients while they mopped round their beds. The gradual contracting-out of cleaning services has removed even this degree of contact. The people who are left to hear the patients' stories are very often the care assistants. Yet many of them are largely untrained. National Vocational Qualifications are increasingly common, and many hospitals, care homes, and nursing homes encourage their care assistants to take those exams. But not all hospitals pay for the training or allow staff time off, and many do not offer more pay when a qualification has been gained. If care assistants were actively encouraged to study for NVQs and then, where appropriate, to move on to more advanced qualifications, the whole atmosphere might change. Care assistants would then be seen as embryonic nurses rather than skivvies. Though this happens to some extent with the skills ladder the NHS has in place, there seems to be a remarkable amount of resistance to letting people through the various 'glass ceilings' and allowing them to move from care assistant to nurse, and from nurse to manager.

Transferring such a scenario into the main care sector for older people, nursing homes and care homes, where there will probably be only one qualified nurse on duty, would similarly have a transformative effect on care assistants. They would no longer be seen as short-term employees doing dirty work for little money and no emotional and 'respect' reward, but people who may go into nursing eventually or who may choose to remain as care assistants, at the top of that particular tree, with all its attendant qualifications and respect. The government has set itself the target of half of all care home staff having reached NVQ level 2 by the year 2005. It is pretty unlikely that the target will be reached, but the government's intentions are good, and grants given to care home owners to help them pay for courses and study leave would speed up the process. It is, after all, well attested that training care home staff can reduce the amount of abuse, both intentional and unintentional, quite considerably.

Providing that hands-on, day-to-day care is hard work and can lead to stress and frustration. It is no surprise that nurses, who cost the system a lot to train, do not want to wipe bottoms and change beds, or feed patients or help them wash. Until care assistants have real status, recognizing them as the people who actually provide this vital and difficult hands-on care, they will not – as a group – necessarily give of their best. Until they are trained properly and achieve professional recognition there will always be the risk of deficient care, even abuse, from care assistants who have no vocation or professional dedication and who have only taken on the job because they can get no other work.

Example after example of poor care, often not abusive as such but insensitive and uncaring, emerges from CHI reports, from local newspapers, and from anecdotes from friends and relatives. And these must be just the tip of the iceberg. Typical is the case of a nursing home in East London which had a complaint against it upheld by the National Care Standards Commission because of the 'unprofessional' attitude shown towards a lady just minutes after her relative's death. Care workers did not sympathize or help her come to terms with the news of her relative's unexpected death (she had already complained about unexplained bruising on his arm). Instead, she was told that 'there was not much point' in an undertaker taking his body away that night because of the extra cost (of after-hours collection, presumably) and was told that his body would have to remain in the room he was sharing with another man – a piece of insensitivity about the effect on the other man which beggars belief.*

Insensitivity and uncaring attitudes. Yet something can be done about them, and care staff can be trained and encouraged to think differently, if employers make it worth their while. Care assistants should know that the ladder into nursing is available to them.

---

* *Wanstead and Woodford Guardian* (20 November 2003).

Nurses, and their organizations, should celebrate the contribution care assistants make and welcome those who climb the ladder into nursing to join them. There has to be another way into nursing that does not require a university degree, and there has to be recognition that caring is of equal status with providing hi-tech interventions. Equally, care assistants will have to accept that they will be regulated and checked by the police for any record of abuse and that they will be expected to work in a care home or nursing home for a considerable period, rather than hopping from one agency to another.

These would be major changes. Care assistants have been appallingly badly treated. We have allowed our most vulnerable older people to be cared for by people to whom we do not show respect. The challenge is to pay care assistants properly, train them properly, and support them properly without the cost of care becoming so prohibitive that no one can afford it. Yet without this the existing situation will get worse. As Janet Street-Porter argued fiercely in her article entitled 'I'll do anything except go into a care home':

'The whole culture of care for the elderly gives me cause for concern. If we don't value teachers, we insult carers. The pay is appalling, the job unattractive, the prospects pathetic.'* Quite so. And it is our fault.

The fact that we think it acceptable to put our old people into care homes at all is another issue that needs consideration. Yasmin Alibhai-Brown, redoubtable campaigner on race issues and doughty journalist, wrote a piece in *Community Care* back in 1998† about her mother, arguing that 'the worst luck in this country is to be alive when old'. She said it even more strongly after the death of the only other Asian resident in the housing association block in Ealing, where she lives. Mrs Pal fell before she died and had to go into residential care. All the residents were Asian, and they sat 'silently, eyes unseeing, as if they had already passed away'. Mrs Pal died after two weeks of this, and Yasmin Alibhai-Brown's mother will not forgive her son for putting her there, nor

---

* Janet Street-Porter, 'I'll do anything except go into a care home', *The Independent* (6 February 2004).
† Yasmin Alibhai-Brown, 'Age of Respect', *Community Care* (10– 16 December 1998).

'this society for the way it treats old people so that they feel they have to oblige us by dying'.

Regulation of Care Homes and Nursing Homes

The issue of care assistants, and how we value and reward them is one illustration of where we have got it wrong with regard to who most deserves respect in our society. Another area that has impacted heavily on older people has been in the attempts by government to make a difference to older people's welfare, encouraged to some considerable extent by the two main organizations representing the interests of older people, Help the Aged and Age Concern. This has resulted in regulations requiring certain standards of provision within care and nursing homes, particularly the size of rooms.

Of course, this was all very well intentioned. There were many homes in which people were crammed two, three, and four together into one not very large room. The idea that older people should share rooms in nursing and care homes is itself surprising, given that few of us share rooms with anyone other than spouses and partners at any other stage of our lives, except in childhood. There had, of course, been scandals surrounding care home owners trying to make additional money out of cramming people in, so it is hardly surprising that Help the Aged, itself formerly a provider of nursing and care home accommodation, and Age Concern should have raised this as a matter of concern. The desire to keep prices down – understandable though it may be – should not allow local authorities to get away with paying substandard fees for substandard accommodation. But the problem is that size of rooms, and facilities such as private bathrooms, important though they might be, are not all that is needed, and many smaller care and nursing homes have closed because the costs of alterations required, and the complexities of providing accommodation for residents whilst work was being carried out, were just too much.

It is of course desirable that everyone should have their own room. Most of us would contemplate nothing less. It is equally desirable for everyone to have their own bathroom. But there are two major factors that those who drafted the regulations, and those who campaigned for them, did not fully consider. The first is that for many confused older people, being confined to their own rooms all day does not provide the stimulation they might need, nor will it delay the deterioration process. They need company and activity – the social buzz that being on their own watching a television in their room cannot provide. Secondly, though many of the older care homes were not up to modern standards, some of them provided a personal quality of care that was of infinitely greater importance than a room of one's own, particularly for those who were confused and frightened. In all this, there has been a confusion between physical standards – space and the need for basic privacy – and the quality of care. Though better accommodation is undoubtedly desirable, tender care, with well supervised and well supported care assistants, has an enormous amount to recommend it. Yet again, our desire to regulate takes precedence over what really matters: the *quality* of care. Old-fashioned premises where the staff are well supervised and truly committed to what they do might well be preferable to a spanking new facility, gleaming bright, but with no soul. You cannot legislate for soul. But you can make palliative care more available to many older people.

Palliative Care

Older people who are not dying of cancer, motor neurone disease, or AIDS/HIV often fail to benefit from Britain's superb palliative care services. Yet death comes in many ways: we may die of heart disease, be it congestive heart failure or simply a fatal coronary infarct. We may die after being disabled in a severe way by a stroke, or by end-stage renal disease. We may have chronic obstructive pulmonary disease. We may have dementia. We may die of a single cause, or a combination of many, or we may simply die of old age. Yet the palliative care services are often not there for us, and whether we get access to them depends on the area in which we live.

With little trouble, and at relatively little cost, it should be possible to provide palliative care to people who are dying of whatever condition, in whatever setting. People dying in a nursing home should still get the specialist care that they would have received had they still been in their own homes. People dying in a care home should be just as entitled to a visit from the palliative care team as those who are living with a son or a daughter. If we could ensure that, as well as providing proper palliative care for those who have the misfortune to be dying in an acute hospital, some part of the fear of dying might be assuaged. Some principles could be established covering, for instance, privacy, good physical care and proper pain relief, a guarantee of not dying alone, choice of place of death, treatment choices (advance directives again), and who should be present when death finally comes. These principles would provide a kind of guarantee of respect for the person's dignity and autonomy, as well as guaranteeing diminution of suffering, and respect for their autonomy, so that, insofar as is possible, people get the services they want when they are dying.

In the working paper of the health and social services group for Age Concern's

THE ELDERLY

Millennium Debate of the Age,* which I chaired in the late 1990s, we identified twelve principles of a good death:

To know when death is coming and to understand what can be expected

To be able to retain control of what happens

To be afforded dignity and privacy

To have control over pain relief and other symptom control

To have choice and control over where death occurs (at home or elsewhere)

To have access to information and expertise of whatever kind is necessary

To have access to any spiritual or emotional support required

To have access to hospice care in any location, not only in hospital

To have control over who is present and who shares the end

To be able to issue advance directives which ensure wishes are respected

To have time to say goodbye, and control over other aspects of timing

---

* *The Future of Health and Care of Older People: The Best is Yet to Come* (Age Concern, 1999).

To be able to leave when it is time to go, and not have life prolonged pointlessly

All these principles would make a real difference if they were generally implemented. In practice, it would not always be possible to carry out all of them for every person. But the hope and expectation that they would be put into practice would help dissipate the fear of dying.

Conclusions

It is no surprise that many older people fear the future. For many of them, the future is simply frightening, and current policies have done little to alleviate that fear, whatever we may say, or whatever Help the Aged and Age Concern try to argue. The situation is not good enough. Euthanasia is not the answer. Striving less hard to keep people alive, along with advance directives, may help a few. But they will not help the majority.

So various things remain to be done.

First, there is clearly a need for an older people's movement above and beyond what Help the Aged and Age Concern now do, a movement of older people that fights hard and dirty, and that makes government wake up to what older people are feeling. There is a real need for a grey-power movement to point out to government that the present settlement is neither fair nor acceptable and remind it of older people's voting power. To some extent, this exists in the shape of the National Pensioners' Convention and the re-doubtable Rodney Bickerstaffe. But this movement needs to get much bigger and much angrier, and to show government that it really means business by being prepared to play dirty. Older people must complain.

Second, old age itself needs redefining. This not only concerns retirement age – though it is clear that we will all have to work longer, and possibly differently, in order to afford our pensions and our end of life care. It also involves the recognition that most of us are at the peak of our powers in our forties and fifties and that it is perfectly sensible – indeed, the Americans already do it – for us to switch to different, less de-manding, jobs when we reach our late sixties and seventies. Retirement and activity in older age needs rethinking, and government cannot rely on older people's goodwill for much longer.

Very old people need to be assured that they will have proper care, properly funded, when they need it – even if they have to bear some of the cost themselves. They need to be reassured about what their liabilities might be. This means accepting that we will need to pool the risk for some of their care, and old people need to know that society accepts their care as an obligation, and also that they will not be abused in care homes, or indeed in their own homes.

Care workers need to be treated with greater respect, receive more and better training, and to be paid more. It should be deemed just as honourable to be a care worker looking after older people as it is to be a doctor or nurse looking after children – and there may need to be new financial and status rewards to ensure this.

Older people need to know that they can control their own death when the time comes, and to be able to die at home, with all the information and support they require, if that is what they want. They need to know that they can make advance directives so that, if they are not able to make decisions themselves at the time, their wishes will still be carried out.

Older people need to know that there will be no discrimination against them in the provision of healthcare, that they will get what others get, subject to whether it seems sensible to them and their clinicians, and that they will be consulted every step of the way.

Finally, older people have a right to expect kindness and care from the rest of us – there are so many older people, and soon we will be amongst them. It should be part of what is expected of every citizen that, whilst he or she is able, they visit and generally look out for older people who are their neighbours.

TWO

THE MENTALLY ILL

In my years of chairing a large community and mental health trust in central London, Camden and Islington Community Health Services NHS Trust, I became sadder and sadder at what was happening to people with mental illness who accessed our services, and, still worse, to those who for some reason or other were not accessing the services they wanted or needed. I remember being taken to see the best of our then three main adult inpatient units. One of the (male) consultants said to me that in the first few weeks of being a trainee psychiatrist you cried and cried; if you did not do so, then you would be no use as a psychiatrist.

In some ways, the issue of mental health is at the heart of this book. For we are not – in the way we structure and think about the services we provide – kind. Kindness is not what we value most, nor does it drive the system. If it did, the services would look quite different and be far more responsive to what users say they want. We would be providing decent housing and trying to pro-vide employment, or at least some kind of daytime activity that makes sense and has meaning; we would be helping with money, with food, with the normal things of life, with talking and engaging with the issues that those with mental illness say bother them. Instead, over centuries now, we have provided a service that is largely based on fear and containment, on a view that those with enduring mental illness are worthless and do not deserve the level of public ex-penditure that running a series of respon-sive high quality services would entail.

This chapter is about those who have men-tal health problems, how we treat them, and how we regard them.

It looks at the stigma attached to mental health and at our lack of kindess towards people who are mentally ill.

It examines how our thinking has grown out of past experience, and tells the history of attitudes towards people with mental illness. It asks whether we are any more enlightened than our ancestors were, and whether our new drugs and other interventions make the lives of those with enduring mental illness any easier.

It looks at whether we use the mental health system as a form of social control and ask whether the experience of innumerable cases where things have gone very wrong tell us that those who work in mental health do not care for their patients.

It will also examine the increasingly risk-averse public policy climate and ask if the mental health world can ever be risk free. And it will also ask whether, if the views of service users were taken more seriously, there might not be better outcomes, with people being able to work and live comfortably, secure in the knowledge that if a crisis arises there will be proper care available from a team already known to the individual.

Finally, it will ask the essential question: if we were seriously concerned to care for, and even cure, those with enduring mental illness, would we ever have invented anything remotely like the present system?

Psychiatry As Social Control

We are not alone in our attitudes towards mental health. Many countries, many systems, are the same. How we treat people with enduring mental illness is a blot on the consciences of most of the developed nations, and on quite a few of the developing nations as well. In addition, there has always been the risk of political manipulation: in many countries those who have opposed the ruling system have found themselves confined to the asylum. This was most prevalent in the former Soviet Union, when dissidents were pumped full of drugs and left in the mental wards to rot. Nazi psychiatrists, too, took part in the most appalling destruction of people with mental illness and learning disabilities in the 1930s, long before the extermination of Jews and gypsies. The so-called T-4 programme was devised by psychiatrists alongside Nazi ideologues. The programme was finally ended in 1941, but not before an estimated 80–100,000 people had been killed, including the so called mercy killings of the 'insane' and of roughly five thousand 'deformed' children.*

This history of the use of psychiatry as a means of social control led to a critique of psychiatry in the late 1960s and early 1970s led by Thomas Szasz, Professor of Psychiatry at Syracuse University, New York. He argued that mental illness was a man-made myth and suggested that psychiatry as a discipline was a pseudoscience, comparable to alchemy and astrology. Michel Foucault, the profoundly influential French historian of culture and ideas, rather agreed. For him, and for Szasz, psychiatrists became, as Roy Porter puts it, villains, and their discipline akin to a form of magic. Martin Roth and Jerome Kroll argued precisely the opposite – that there had been real progress in the study, diagnosis, and treatment of madness and psychopathologies and that there was a real organic basis to mental illness.

---

* Burleigh, M. (1994), passim.

The truth is that there has been a terrifying and disgraceful history of using psychiatry and its antecedents as a means of social control, whilst at the same time some of the treatments, both pharmacological and psychotherapeutic 'talking' remedies, have proved beneficial and effective for some, but not all, sufferers.

To understand how we view mental illness now, at the beginning of the twenty-first century, we must look back at the history of mental illness and its treatment.

Possession by demons and other evil spirits may not be part of our intellectual armoury now, yet when we bury our dead (in Jewish ritual anyway, and in many other practices) we still stop up bodily orifices to prevent them being invaded by evil spirits, and pause on our walk to the grave to shake off any lurking demons. Belief in evil spirits is just below the surface in many of us, as we touch wood, avoid walking under ladders, and look askance at black cats. Yet all this is intimately tied up with how we view those who have mental illness. Do we think they are possessed? (Sufferers themselves often take that view.) Or do we regard them in the same way as we would do if they had a physical illness? If so, why don't we allocate them the same resources, and treat them with the same consideration, as those suffering from physical illness? Do we believe they need to be controlled, as their containment in the old asylums would suggest? If so, is that for their protection or ours? All these questions may have half-answers in our minds; but society is split, and individuals within it are confused, about mental illness and how to care for those who suffer from it.

Historical Reflections

Before the witch craze of the fifteenth to seventeenth centuries, treatment of mental illness was often kinder. Much mental derangement was viewed as being inflicted by Satan and was therefore susceptible to the saying of masses, pilgrimages, or indeed exorcism. Protestants had a different view. The Anglican divine Richard Napier doubled as a doctor and specialized in healing those 'unquiet of mind'. He thought that many of those who consulted him were suffering from religious despair (something still cited by many of those with mental illness in the twenty-first century, and less than comprehensible to many of the rationalist, post-religious, mental health professionals). They feared damnation, the seductions of Satan, and the likelihood of being bewitched. Napier's treatment was prayer, Bible readings, and counsel – the talking therapies so many people with mental illness ask for now.

The excessively religious were also thought of as mad. Many of Wesley's followers in the early days of Methodism were thought fit only for Bedlam (the Bethlem Hospital, now part of the Bethlem and Maudsley hospitals configuration), even though Wesley himself still believed in witches and demonic possession. His followers, at what might be described as revivalist meetings, would cry out and swoon uncontrollably. Many thought this must be madness. The same was said of Anabaptists, Ranters, and Antinomians. They were thought to be sick (puffed up with wind) and doctors and others who believed in social control pointed out that the religious fringe and outright lunatics shared much in common: they all spoke in tongues (glossolalia, now prevalent in much of the evangelical side of modern Christianity), and suffered convulsions and spontaneous weeping and wailing. Towards the end of the eighteenth century, with the rise of rationalism, doctors and scientists berated the Methodists for preaching hellfire and damnation, which they said led people to abuse themselves and commit suicide. Religious visions became a matter of psychopathology, and those who experienced religious yearnings and visions were thought mad.

As belief in witchcraft diminished new scapegoats appeared – beggars, vagrants, and criminals. But the idea of the rational had come to stay. Religion itself had to be rational – why else would John Locke write *The Reasonableness of Christianity* (1695), and why else would Freud and his allies later describe God as wish fulfilment? Belief was all too real. Its object, however, was not real at all; it was a projection of neurotic need, explained, as Roy Porter describes it, in terms either 'of the sublimation of suppressed sexuality or the death wish'.* Porter also points out that, in time, the medical profession replaced the clergy in dealing with the insane.

The religious view had been accompanied since ancient times with a different, scientific, view. Galen, the ancestor of modern medicine, had described melancholy and other mental illness and Aretaeus of Cappadocia (c.150–200), a contemporary of Galen's, had already identified bipolar affective disorder with his descriptions of the depths of depression and the delusions that could accompany it and the patches of mania, the rapid extreme mood swings, that define classic manic depression. Not until Richard Burton's *Anatomy of Melancholy* (1621) was a better, fuller description given of depression, as he reviews the old explanations of blood, bile, spleen and brain, whilst adding lack of activity, loneliness, and many causes. His recommendations for treatment (or possibly containment – living with melancholy rather than curing it) consist of a variety of classic later advice: exer-

---

* Porter, R. (2002), 32.

cise (still recommended), diet, distraction, and travel, as well as hundreds of herbal remedies and music therapy, also often recommended in modern practice.

But it was the French philosopher Descartes (1596–1650) who brought about the biggest shift in the rational approach to mental illness. If, as Roy Porter puts it,† 'consciousness was inherently and definitionally rational', then 'insanity, precisely like regular physical illnesses, must derive from the body or be a consequence of some very precarious connections in the brain. Safely somatized in this way, it could no longer be regarded as diabolical in origin or as threatening the integrity or salvation of the immortal soul, and became unambiguously a legitimate object of philosophical and medical inquiry.'

This was a deeply influential approach and in the late seventeenth century some began to take the optimistic view that people who are mad could be retrained to think correctly and rationally. But folk beliefs in witches and possession persisted, and the treat-

---

† Ibid., 58.

ment of the mad was by no means totally predicated on this new, optimistic view of humanity, even though there were an increasing number of private asylums where treatment was more humane and some form of talking therapy – aimed at retraining the mind – was available.

The practice of locking up people suffering from all kinds of mental illness and disability had started to grow from the fourteenth century. The religious house of St Mary of Bethlehem in Bishopsgate (Bedlam, now the Bethlem and Maudsley Hospitals in London) was founded in 1247 and started catering for lunatics in the late fourteenth century. Some time between 1255 and 1290 an Act of Parliament, De Praerogativa Regis, was passed that gave the king custody of the lands of natural fools and lordship of the property of the insane. The officers in charge of this were called escheators, and they also held inquisitions to decide if a landholder was a lunatic or an idiot. Already by 1405 a Royal Commission had inquired into the deplorable state of affairs at Bethlem Hospital, suggesting that concern has been prevalent for centuries about how people with mental illness were treated.

By the eighteenth century asylums for the insane were widespread, though from 1774 certification was instituted so that confinement in a madhouse had to be done on the authority of a medical practitioner (with the exception of paupers, who could be locked up on the say so of a magistrate.) In Catholic countries, asylums were under the rule of the Church, with care provided by religious orders. In Protestant countries, care varied, but the state gradually played a greater part. Michel Foucault regarded shutting people up in asylums, not as a therapeutic practice, but as a police measure – a divide still found in mental health treatment and policy to this very day. He describes how houses of confinement such as the Bicêtre in Paris gradually came to be seen as a source of infection and concern was expressed that this would spread to the poor ordinary decent criminals who were thrown in with the insane.* Asylums became spectacles and

---

* Foucault, M. (2001), 192 ff.

objects of fear at the same time: at the new Bethlem Hospital, a beautiful building in Moorfields, one could pay to view lunatics until 1770.

But, for the inmates of these asylums, the regimes were cruel. There was annual bloodletting at the Bethlem and general use of strait jackets and purges. There were, however exceptions. One of the most distinguished was William Battie (1704–76), physician to the new St Luke's Asylum in London, who also owned a private asylum. A small proportion of the insane did, in his view, suffer from incurable conditions; but the majority, he argued, had what he described as 'consequential insanity' – derived from events that had befallen them – and for whom the prognosis was good. So instead of bloodletting, purges, surgical techniques (such as removing 'stones' from the brain, a particularly vile treatment), and restraint, what was needed was what he described as 'management' – person to person contact designed to treat the specific delusions and delinquencies of the individual. Battie considered that 'madness is ... as manageable as many other distempers'.†

And so a humane period – relatively speaking – in the treatment of mental illness began. Amongst others, Francis Willis (1718–1807), who was called in to treat George III, pioneered a 'moral management' school of treatment, where the experienced therapist would outwit the patient. At Willis's Lincolnshire madhouse everyone was properly dressed and performed useful tasks in the gardens and on the farm, with exercise being a key feature. Similarly, the York Retreat developed moral therapy in a domestic environment. The Quaker tea merchant William Tuke (1732–1822) started a counter-initiative to the local York Asylum, which had been bedevilled by scandal. Patients and staff at the York Retreat lived, worked, and dined together. Medical therapies had been tried but dispensed with in favour of kindness, mildness, reason, and humanity, all within a family atmosphere.

But this enlightened approach was not to last. Although from 1890 onwards two medical certificates were required to detain any

---

† Porter, op. cit., 102.

patient, the result was to close off mental institutions to the outside world. They were hard to get into – and even harder to leave. Little treatment, let alone comfort, was provided and the reputation of the new asylums began to sink as it became clear that they were silting up with long-stay, zombie-like patients. Criticism of such institutions began in the late nineteenth century but it took a hundred years before the last of the old long-stay mental hospitals closed.

Scientific thinking about madness had begun to degenerate too. John Stuart Mill criticized the operation of writs *de lunatico inquirendo*: 'the man, and still more the woman ... [who indulges] in the luxury of doing as they like ... [is] in peril of a commission *de lunatico* and of having their property taken from them and given to their relations.'* Science was beginning to believe that madness was caused by heredity, like the first Mrs Rochester in Charlotte Brontë's *Jane Eyre* (1847), and most real progressive thinking was being carried out in specialist institutions such as the Maudsley, leaving

---

* J. S. Mill, *On Liberty* (1859), quoted on the Mental Health Timeline website.

the asylums, gradually starved of resources, to become the chronic patients' permanent home. Only there could we be sure that the bad, the mad, and the other were kept away from us all. And since the newer asylums were built on the outskirts of towns and cities, or in the country, most patients were kept confined long term at some considerable distance from their homes, families, and friends, who all too quickly lost touch with them. When patients died, after being confined for life because their condition was thought to be incurable, their brains were examined in post mortems for signs of the cerebral lesions that many thought were the basis of all insanity. Psychiatry had become a tool of social restraint. In Britain this continued well into the twentieth century and remained the case until the creation in 1948 of the National Health Service, which largely took over responsibility for the asylums.

Twentieth-Century Policy and Practice

The twentieth century started with an obsession about degeneracy of the 'stock'. It was feared that a 'submerged tenth' of the population would outbreed everyone else. The Royal Commission on the Care and Control of the Feeble Minded (1904–8) suggested that mental defectives, so described, were often prolific breeders and that, if allowed, would resort to delinquency, excessive sex, and alcohol. Winston Churchill, then Home Secretary, supported proposals for the forcible sterilization of 100,000 moral degenerates. His views were thought too extreme, however, and his plans were thought so sensitive that they were kept secret until 1992. But he was not alone.

Some forcible sterilizations did in fact take place, and in 1934 the Brock Committee recommended voluntary sterilization as a cheaper means than physical segregation of separating moral defectives from the nation's gene pool. Homosexuals continued to be 'treated' in mental health units into the mid 1970s, the treatments including oestrogen therapy, electric shock therapy, psychoanalysis and behaviour aversion therapy.*

* Smith, G., Bartlett, A., King, M. (2004).

All this has to be set against a gradual change in thought. Freudian theory, as well as the work of Jung and Adler, with their insights into the importance of the unconscious mind on emotions and behaviour, was just beginning to influence the way people thought about mental health. Containment, however, was still the order of the day, and concerns that the mentally defective would affect the genetic character of the nation only disappeared gradually. Even in the 1990s there were discussions about the forcible sterilization of young women with learning disabilities, ostensibly to protect them from unwanted pregnancies but presumably also because of fears about the children they might produce. Broadly speaking, however, theories about degeneracy and contamination of the gene pool had become unfashionable because of their Nazi associations. Therefore the assumption had to be made, for want of any other theory, that mental 'defectiveness', as well as insanity, was a health issue. With the establishment of the NHS, local authority hospitals were transferred to the Ministry of Health, but there was little change in conditions.

However, the drugs did change. Largactil, along with other antipsychotic phenothiazines, appeared around 1955. It controlled symptoms without the sedative effects of the old drugs. Despite being a form of control, such drugs were widely used and community care became easier and less risky. In 1953, almost half the beds within NHS hospitals had been for mental illness or mental 'defectiveness'. However, after 1954, the number of patients in mental hospitals began to decline and moves were made to change mental hospitals into institutions like those for physical diseases.

In 1959, the Mental Health Act excluded promiscuity or other immoral conduct as grounds for detention under the Act. The idea of moral degeneracy was beginning to fade, as well as the beginning of a realisation that institutionalizing people was bad for them.

No new large-scale asylums were built after the Second World War, but hospitals for mental 'defectives' continued to be built until 1971. And the old institutions remained.

By 1966 there were still 107 mental illness and 66 mental handicap hospitals with two hundred or more beds. The following year *Sans Everything* was published, a collection of articles by Barbara Robb about how elderly people were treated in institutions, particularly in psychiatric and geriatric care. It caused a storm, and the official investigation, in 1968, substantiated most of what she said.

The Era of Inquiries

And so we come into the great era of inquiries, from the early 1970s onwards, and the gradual shaming of the institutions for the mentally ill and of those who worked in them. Virginia Beardshaw's later work for Social Audit in the late 1970s and early 1980s pulled together a great deal of the evidence from those inquiries about who blew the whistle on what was going on in some institutions for the mentally ill.

For example, there is the case of Ken Callanan and Art Ramirez, two student nurses who were forced to stop training at Brookwood Hospital in Surrey after staff and management united to discredit them. In August 1978, Callanan, a former merchant seaman aged 29, began training as a psychiatric nurse at Brookwood Hospital School of Nursing. His introduction to nursing included a lecture on nursing ethics during which his Director of Nurse Education told the class that: 'If I find that any of you have ill treated a patient or failed to report ill-treatment by other staff, your feet will not touch the ground. I will personally show you the door.'*

After twelve weeks of training he was sent for his second practical posting on Tuke 4, a ward named after that great reformer of mental health services two centuries earlier. Tuke 4 was a ward for the chronically mentally ill – in other words, a long-stay ward. Here, in early 1979, Callanan witnessed repeated abuse of patients by the ward's charge nurse, who had been at Brookwood for years and was well liked.

Callanan's next posting convinced him that what he had seen on Tuke 4 reflected systematic abuse and malpractice. A fellow stu-

* Beardshaw, V. (1981), 25.

dent, Art Ramirez, told him that he had seen the same charge nurse kick a patient. So, in a confidential letter, Callanan told his unit Nursing Officer about the ill treatment he had seen. The investigation was delegated to the Senior Nursing Officer, who knew the charge nurse well. The investigation continued for about a month, but even before its results were known feelings against Callanan and Ramirez were running very high and staff threatened a walk-out unless the pair were suspended. Management 'compromised', as Beardshaw puts it. The two were sent to the training school, with nothing to do.

After the SNO's investigation, the charge nurse was completely exonerated. Callanan's 'inexperience' had led him to 'misinterpret' what he had seen. Despite the official exoneration of the charge nurse, the other staff continued to threaten to walk out if Callanan and Ramirez were allowed back and the local branch of COHSE (Confederation of Health Service Employees, as it then was) voted to recommend Callanan's expulsion from the union.

Callanan and Ramirez were offered a deal: they could return to work if they were prepared to accept, sight unseen, the internal investigation's findings and a new procedure for making complaints. The students agreed to the complaints procedure in principle, but could not agree to accept the internal investigation's results without having seen it.

On the Royal College of Nursing's advice, the pair took their concerns to the Beaumont Committee, which Surrey Area Health Authority had set up to look more widely at conditions in mental institutions. A string of staff witnesses defended the charge nurse, both to the Beaumont Committee and to the General Nursing Council Disciplinary Committee, to which Callanan had referred the case. But the strength of the students' evidence did convince a lot of outsiders. In February 1980, a year after the abuse was first witnessed by Ken Callanan, the charge nurse was finally struck off the General Nursing Council's register, after five charges of ill treatment and drug abuse were found proven. He was dismissed from Brookwood. In April, the Beaumont Committee upheld the students' allegations, saying that the pressure they had been put under by fellow and senior staff and the union was deplorable. Art Ramirez left Brookwood and trained elsewhere. Ken Callanan became an ambulance man, a great loss to mental nursing.

We see the same pattern in inquiry after inquiry. A few brave staff members – people of great conscience, who are prepared to take risks with their own livelihoods and reputations for the sake of others – tell the authorities what they have seen and heard, but it rarely does them any good. Few of them ever reach any kind of senior position, even after allegations are proven.

The late 1960s and 1970s were filled with inquiries about the state of things in the old psychiatric hospitals and the hospitals for people with learning disabilities. Virginia Beardshaw cites inquiries at Ely Hospital, Cardiff, (1969), Farleigh Hospital (1971), Whittingham Hospital (1972), Coldharbour Hospital, Sherbourne (1972), Napsbury Hospital (1973), South Ockendon Hospital (1974), Brockhall Hospital (1975) Warlingham Park Hospital (1975), Memorial Park

Hospital, Darlington (1976), St Augustine's Hospital, Chartham (1976), Psychiatric Department, Bolton General Hospital (1976), Mary Dendy Hospital, Great Warford, Cheshire (1977), Normansfield Hospital (1978), Brookwood Hospital, as above (1979), Church Hill Hospital, Bracknell (1979) St Mary's Hospital, Gateshead (1979) Brookwood, again (1980), and Sandhill Hospital, Somerset (1981).

Some of these inquiries are famous because of the very strangeness of them. At Normansfield, for instance, the medical superintendent had a view – not shared by anyone else apparently – that it would be easier to keep the patients quiet and controlled if they were fed a diet that was largely a form of porridge. In fact, they were being slowly starved. It was, as ever in these cases, a concerned member of staff who blew the whistle – and who lost her job as a result.

What emerges from these inquiries is a picture of a culture in which it was extremely difficult for members of staff to raise concerns. For instance, in the case of St Augustine's Hospital near Canterbury, it took the resignation of Ollette Weston, an experienced psychiatric nurse, and Brian Ankers, a nursing assistant who was doing the work to support himself whilst writing his Ph.D. thesis, finally to convince the Regional Health Authority to stop believing local management and to read, and take seriously, the critique of policy the two had written. This was a large hospital where many of the senior staff had been in place for far too long and where many people on the staff were related to each other, whilst the long-stay wards were starved of resources. There had been a critical report in 1971 by the independent Hospital Advisory Service, which had been treated with disdain by the senior management, and Weston and Ankers' report was simply treated as a laughing matter by the senior staff. Reaction at the Area Health Authority level was inept, even though thirty-four other members of staff had endorsed the critique by this stage and the head of the Regional Advisory Team had found most of the comments to be basically true.

Weston and Ankers resigned and decided on shock tactics. In February 1975 they produced 'The Critique Part 2 – The Evidence' in which they cited seventy or so instances of neglect, ill treatment, and mismanagement on long-stay wards. Management again re-acted with defensiveness and complacency. But by now it had gone too far. The Regional Health Authority, having failed to take things seriously at an earlier stage, set up an independent inquiry which found that the whole of the first part of the Critique and a large proportion of the second part to be well founded. It made detailed recommen-dations for change, putting monitoring ar-rangements in place and special provisions for the long stay wards. But the whole story shows that it needs courage and determina-tion in quite exceptional quantities to with-stand the pressure from fellow staff and management when making complaints about poor or abusive treatment of vulner-able patients.

Beardshaw's work makes for depressing reading, for one is forced to the conclusion that few of the people who participate in such appalling treatment are bad people. Somehow, being in these institutional caring roles makes them lose the sense of what is proper behaviour. As a student at Cambridge, I spent some time volunteering in a big hospital for people with what was then called mental handicap, many of whom were in fact quite elderly and suffering from dementia. I remember then, in the early 1970s, being absolutely shocked by what staff thought was quite normal. Everyone's false teeth were taken away in the evening and put into a bucket of Steradent or some other cleaning agent, and the volunteers went around in the morning trying to fit sets of teeth into people's mouths – they were not labelled, and there was no means of working out whose teeth belonged to whom without simply trying time and again. It seemed both time wasteful and astonishingly degrading at the time, but I am convinced the staff did not see it like that. It was simply the way it had always been done, in the same way that one face flannel was used to wipe everyone's faces. Everyone's clothes were held centrally and nobody had their own space at all. Institutions can breed an atmosphere that diminishes any kind of individuality, and those who work in them become institutionalized themselves. This, in itself, is a powerful argument for opening up any kind of institution to public gaze, or at least to some kind of regular monitoring.

None of these explanations and observations, however, makes sense of the real and repeated physical abuse and neglect that emerges from all these inquiries. Kicking patients, threatening them so that they do not tell the true stories, stealing their money and possessions, beating them with damp and often urine-soaked towels around the buttocks and thighs, knocking their heads against walls, tying them to the toilet – these and other brutalities are far too common to explain as simply the effect of institutionalization. It seems, from examining these and later reports, that a small proportion of people are attracted into working with the vulnerable because they somehow get a sense of power from that relationship. Though we tend to see those who want to work with vulnerable people as being motivated by good instincts, is there a question to be raised about the ability of some people to resist the attractions of this power in favour of enabling the people they care for – however handicapped and vulnerable they are – to live as independent a life as possible?

Alongside the inquiries of the late 1960s and 1970s, some of which were never published and many of which were only published in a thoroughly sanitized form, there were inquiries into the deaths of individual patients. By the late 1990s attention had turned to examining what had gone wrong in the community in inquiries relating to people who had either murdered or attacked violently someone else, or who had simply committed suicide. By the beginning of the new millennium people were beginning to ask whether it was sensible to hold an inquiry every time something went wrong when, depressingly, the conclusion was always the same: that all the services involved in looking after someone in the community had failed to work together.

The Blofeld Inquiry into the Rocky Bennett Case

Of all the inquiries that have taken place in recent years, perhaps one of the most concerning is that of David Bennett, known as Rocky, who first entered the mental health system aged 20. He then spent eighteen years in a number of hospitals, including spells in prison, and was given numerous diagnoses of schizophrenia and cannabis-related psychosis. In all that time, he experienced racist abuse from other patients and was a deeply disturbed and unhappy man. But the climax came when he died after being restrained for twenty-five minutes by between four and five nursing staff (the number was never absolutely clear.) There had been a struggle on the ward at the Norvic clinic. Rocky Bennett had wanted to use the phone and when he went to make a call from the patients' phone, another patient was using it. After asking politely how soon the phone would be free, Mr Bennett went off but then returned in an angry mood. A struggle developed as he tried to seize the receiver. He threw a punch at the other patient's face, making his lip bleed. The other patient responded with a torrent of racist abuse, calling Mr Bennett 'a black bastard' and saying: 'You niggers are all the same.' The staff tried to calm the men down, but after less than an hour decided it would be safer if one of them was sent overnight to another ward. It was Rocky Bennett that they moved.

According to the report of an inquiry led by Sir John Blofeld, a retired High Court judge, the nursing staff did not recognize that Rocky Bennett thought he was being shifted because he was black, while the white perpetrator stayed on the ward. The staff had treated Mr Bennett as 'a lesser being ... who should be ordered about'. They were unaware of the 'corrosive and cumulative effect of racist abuse upon a black patient'.

He was taken to another ward and was calmer for a while, but then he punched a female staff nurse who told him he was staying overnight, landing three 'horrendous blows' on the left side of her face. That led other staff into control and restraint mode, and they held him face down on the floor as he thrashed about trying to break free. For a few minutes, five nurses (later reduced to four) were involved in pinioning his limbs. The inquiry found that was one too many throughout the procedure. The injuries he sustained under restraint were 'consistent with excess pressure being used'. There was no evidence of deliberate misbehaviour, but the male lead nurse was 'negligent' in not acting to support Mr Bennett's head to spot signs of distress. The nurses did not release Mr Bennett until he 'went quiet'. By then it was too late. Staff tried in vain to resuscitate him with oxygen. By the time an ambulance arrived, he had been unconscious for ten minutes. Shortly afterwards he was pronounced dead.

Remarkably, the senior nurse on duty declined to give evidence to the inquiry, which concluded: 'The restraint was mishandled by the nursing staff.' Mr Bennett's capacity to breathe was restricted and the restraint 'continued for substantially longer than was safe'. This was due to 'a serious failure of training', common across the NHS at that time. There was also inadequate resuscitation equipment in the ward, whilst a doctor who might have been able to help took more than an hour to arrive at the clinic, due to a mix-up at the taxi company sent to fetch him. The inquiry team said foolproof arrangements should always be in place, wherever a mentally ill patient is detained, for a doctor to be available within twenty minutes. More than five years after Mr Bennett's death, these are not yet in place.

The report went on to castigate the authorities for their 'inhumane' treatment of Mr Bennett's family. Some of its most disturbing findings concerned deficiencies in the treatment given to Mr Bennett over the eighteen years of his mental illness. He had worked as a signwriter for three years before his health began to fail. Initially his doctors thought his mental health problem was cannabis-induced psychosis, but he was eventually diagnosed with schizophrenia in 1985. His progress through the NHS was marred by persistent failure to recognize the difficulty he faced as a black man in a largely white medical establishment. The inquiry found the NHS did not try hard enough to engage his family in his treatment. He was managed 'at times with intolerance and at times as if he were a nuisance who had to be contained'.

The inquiry found no evidence of deliberate racism at the Norvic clinic. Individual nurses were kind and generous with their time and money, taking Rocky regularly to Norwich City football matches. But insufficient attention was paid to his cultural, social, and religious needs. In 1993 he wrote to the nursing director pointing out: 'As you know, there are over half a dozen black boys in this clinic. I don't know if you have realized there are no Africans on your staff.' Before his death a black Zimbabwean nurse became his key worker. But the inquiry concluded: 'There was evidence of institutional racism from time to time through the lengthy period Mr Bennett was suffering from mental health problems ... They indicate that institutional racism has been present in the mental health services, both NHS and private, for many years.'

So the Blofeld inquiry concluded that the NHS was 'institutionally racist'; that the NHS Trust responsible for the Norvic Clinic in Norwich had failed to offer a culturally competent service, and that Rocky Bennett's death was the result of negligence by staff. It also recommended, among other things, a three-minute limit to restraint techniques, which would certainly have saved Rocky Bennett's life, and urged ministers to acknowledge the degree and extent of racism in the NHS and to ensure cultural awareness training for all mental health workers.

This was not the only inquiry to come up with some pretty horrifying findings. There was also the case of Michael Abram who attacked and injured severely George Harrison, the former Beatle, in 1999.

The Michael Abram Case

Abram had become obsessed by the Beatles, and indeed probably believed he was the fifth Beatle. At age 33, he had a ten-year history of mental health problems complicated by the taking of drugs (the so-called dual diagnosis), and he was inseparable from his Walkman, the noise of which he used to drown out the voices in his head. He used to wander around the streets of Huyton, Liverpool, humming Beatles' songs, and his obsession with the music led to an obsession with the Beatles themselves. So he travelled to Henley-on-Thames, believing he had been possessed by Harrison and sent on a divine mission to kill him. Three psychiatrists examined him after the crime and were unanimous in saying that he had a 'complex delusional system'.

The sound of breaking glass alerted the Harrisons to the presence of an intruder. George Harrison went downstairs to investigate and received a near fatal stab wound, causing his lung to collapse. Olivia Harrison hit Abram with a brass poker and a heavy table lamp before the police arrived. Harrison was taken by ambulance to hospital, had emergency surgery to repair his lung, and made a full recovery. Abram was arrested and charged with attempted murder but was acquitted on the grounds of insanity, which infuriated the Harrisons, and was ordered to be detained in a secure psychiatric hospital.

The independent inquiry commissioned by the St. Helen's and Knowsley Health Authority, published in October 2001, concluded that there had been serious failings in Michael Abram's care. In particular, he had not had a managed care programme and each of his episodes of mental ill health had been treated as a one-off isolated incident, when they were, of course, part of a pattern. Each time, he was dealt with by different agencies, and only a month before his attack on Harrison he had been discharged from hospital and left to walk home in the early hours of the morning after he had apparently punched a member of staff.

The inquiry report described the decision to discharge him because of the punching incident as 'unacceptable' and that was made still worse by the fact that the mental health services had made no attempt to contact him subsequently. But the inquiry also said – alongside its considerable criticism of the system – that the attack on Harrison could not have been foreseen. Abram had never suggested to any staff or to his family that he had any harmful designs on George Harrison, nor had he a significant track record of violence. His three forensic psychiatric reports, which were used at the trial, did not suggest a risk of violence, but they did identify a moderate suicide risk, which was neither acknowledged nor acted upon. However, his mother, Lynda Abram, was extremely critical of the support he had received from the relevant services after all this. She argued that getting help for him had been 'like walking into a brick wall'* and said: 'I tried doctors, psychiatrists and they don't want to know. You tell them he was a drug addict and they just switch off.' All of this suggests that, although there was no indication of Abram's obsession with Harrison, he did have a (recent) track record of violence, as evidenced by punching a nurse before being discharged, and he did have long-term problems that had been ignored within the system.

Dual Diagnosis

Dual diagnosis, when people have drug and mental health problems combined, is one that vexes the mental health services. The fear engendered by the Abram case, and the fact he attacked someone as high profile as George Harrison, has led to an even stronger call for people like Michael Abram to be locked up because of the risk they pose – even if it is not possible to define or predict the risk in advance. So, as a reaction to such front-page stories, the mental health services become increasingly cautious, leading

* Laurance, J. (2003), 47.

to a situation where, in order to contain risk, some of those who would be quite well enough to live independent lives with some support are kept in inpatient units – not for their own sakes, but because the system has been so criticized in newspaper and media reports.

This is not a small issue in economic terms. The cost of mental illness in England 2002/03 has been estimated at £77.4bn, of which £12.5bn was in care (formal and informal), £23.1bn lost economic activity, and £41.8bn human costs of suffering.* Public spending on mental health services has risen in recent years, from £2,849m 1997/98 to £4,006m in 2001/02.† The Sainsbury Centre suggested that the total spend in 2002/3 on mental health services in England was £7,928m, which includes £754m on drug prescriptions, a further £898m on GP consultations, with local authority services at £1,389m, of which £418m was for the el-

---

* *The Economic and Social Costs of Mental Illness* (London: The Sainsbury Centre for Mental Health, 2003).
† Written Parliamentary answer by Rosie Winterton (15 January 2004).

derly, £695m for adults, and £267m for children. This left some £4,887m for NHS hospital and community services, of which children got a paltry £312m, even though we know that much acute mental illness and its ensuing misery starts in childhood or adolescence. Of the remainder, £4,349m went to adults, and a mere £226m to older people, again a small amount given the incidence of Alzheimer's disease and other forms of dementia affecting the elderly. But the rate of growth in spending is in any case below that of the NHS and social services as a whole. In the year 2003/04, a cash rise of 6.3 per cent in English mental health services reduces to just 1.6 per cent when pay and inflation are taken into account.*

The many inquiries into mental health care, and the engendering of fear of people with mental illness by individual high-profile cases, has led to huge staff shortages. These affect the whole healthcare system, but mental health services are amongst the worst affected. Three-month vacancy rates

---

* *Money for Mental Health* (London: The Sainsbury Centre for Mental Health, 2003).

are currently (2004) estimated at 11.5 per cent for psychiatrists, 3 per cent for nurses, 5 per cent for allied health professionals such as occupational therapists, and 6–9 per cent for qualified social workers.† Spending on locum and agency staff exceeds £1m in some south of England NHS mental health trusts.‡ Compulsory treatments are increasing both in number and as a proportion of consultant episodes. In 1991/92, there were 20,636 formal admissions (11.6 per cent of adult mental health Finished Consultant Episodes); in 2001/02 the number rose to 26,256 (17.7 per cent).§

The 2003 Audit Commission report on progress in implementing the NHS Plan looked seriously at mental health services and concluded mental health trusts were lagging behind other parts of the NHS on overall performance. Almost two-thirds of mental health trusts were 'at high risk' of

---

† Personal communication from the Sainsbury Centre for Mental Health.

‡ Goldie, N. (2003); *Money for Mental Health* (SCMH, op. cit.).

§ *The Draft Mental Health Bill: An assessment of the implications for mental health service organisations* (NHS Confederation, 2003).

failing to achieve financial balance and recruit sufficient doctors, while 58 per cent of mental health trusts were at high risk of not achieving the National Service Framework.* The Commission for Health Improvement (CHI), the government's own independent watchdog, looked at mental health trusts and concluded: 'The historical legacy of the neglect of mental health services is still regrettably evident in the findings of CHI's investigations. CHI has found that factors such as the isolation of services, institutional environments, low staffing levels and high use of bank and agency staff, closed cultures and poor clinical leadership and supervision have caused the neglect of patients. While these instances are rare, CHI cannot be confident that other examples of poor quality care do not exist.'† The CHI report also found that staff work in difficult conditions in often unacceptable environ-

---

* Achieving the NHS Plan: Assessment of current performance, likely future progress and capacity to improve (Audit Commission, 2003).
† What CHI has Found in Mental Health Trusts (London: Commission for Health Improvement, 2003), 9.

ments; that there is little evidence of feed-back of reviews of adverse incidents; that staff lack any degree of confidence in the systems in place to manage violence and ag-gression; and that there are inconsistent risk assessment procedures. All of this ex-ists in a service that is held up for public scrutiny on a regular basis because of the interest in and high profile nature of some of the attacks by people with mental illness on ordinary members of the public, rare though they are.

In addition, the CHI also found that, in acute wards, there were wide variations be-tween those in new buildings containing ex-cellent facilities and 'old Victorian buildings, mixed sex wards with shared bathroom fa-cilities and poor security between dormito-ries ... Child friendly visitor environments are rare. While uncommon, CHI has found examples where service users do not have access to fresh air either because of insuffi-cient staff escorts or because of unsafe external environments.'* So much of the service is said by those who examine at it to

---

* *What CHI has Found in Mental Health Trusts,*
  op. cit., 21.

be unsafe and inquiries are still happening, though they will be replaced by a new system under the National Patient Safety Agency, arguably even more complex.

Staff nearly always bear the brunt if anything goes wrong. If someone with mental illness becomes violent, staff are blamed. If they kill someone, staff are blamed. If they get lost to the system, staff are blamed. This makes staff very unwilling to take risks. So, rather than worry about their patients and how they are cared for, increasingly they worry about the risk they might pose to others. Homicide, not suicide, is the main concern. Yet the homicide rate *against* people with mental health problems is six times higher than the general population, as well as there being a much higher suicide and accident rate.†

A brief look at the inquiries relating to those who were not on acute wards but were living within the community shows that the concern is still largely for the safety of the public. There is relatively little concern for the individuals concerned, or even for the

---

† Louis Appleby, *British Medical Journal* (22–29 December 2001).

staff looking after them. Indeed, in 1992 the government commissioned the Royal College of Psychiatrists to undertake the first national investigation into homicides committed by people with a known mental health history. The remit of that inquiry was extended to include suicides, expressly at the behest of the psychiatrists.‡ The main recommendations included the development of services for people with mental illness and drug or alcohol dependency (the so-called dual diagnosis), a recommendation that has been extremely slow in being implemented, despite there being a government publication on the subject (Department of Health, 1999).

The RCP inquiry showed that 'people with schizophrenia are one hundred times more likely to kill themselves than others'. In other words, perhaps the real public concern should be for schizophrenia sufferers rather than for the occasional homicides, terrible though they are. It is also much more dangerous – if one is simply calculating risk – to be the relative of someone with severe

---

‡ Boyd, W. (1996).

mental illness than to be a stranger on the street. But services are increasingly designed to protect the general public, not the people who bear the brunt of the illness – the carers and the people who are mentally ill themselves.

Margaret Reith, in her excellent compilation of the conclusions and policy implications of the main inquiries,* suggests that the fascination with homicides carried out by people with mental health problems mitigates against a concern about the much larger number of homicides and murders carried out by people with no known mental health problem – surely a greater cause of concern to most of us. Added to that, she argues that the sheer number of inquiries, as a result of government requirements, has probably led to them no longer being used to change policy and practice sufficiently. Though she does not herself suggest that an assimilation into one set of guidance for practitioners is likely to be more useful, that is clearly a conclusion one could draw from reading her excellent work.

---

* Reith, M. (1998).

The Carol Barratt And Kevin Rooney Cases

Two other conclusions can be drawn from an examination of all of the various inquiries. The first is that, despite the view, gaining currency, that they are expensive in human and cost terms, inquiries have already led to changes in policy and practice – changes that are largely for the good, but some of which may be regarded as being for the wider public benefit rather than for the good of the individual. The second is that they tend to apportion blame, sometimes inappropriately, so that doctors who make critical errors of judgement are likely to be disciplined or even dismissed, as in the cases of Carol Barratt or Kevin Rooney, described below.

Carol Barratt killed an 11-year-old child in a shopping centre on 16 April 1991. She had been discharged from the Psychiatric Unit of Doncaster Royal Infirmary a mere two days earlier, having been detained under the Mental Health Act (Section 2) after threatening a young woman with a knife in the same shopping centre about two weeks before. Five days after this admission, she tried to strangle a visitor and was put on one-to-one observation. Despite such close supervision, she managed to abscond and attacked a girl outside the hospital the same day. Seven days later, the Mental Health Review Tribunal heard an appeal from Carol Barratt for discharge but refused it, saying she still needed supervision. Three days later, Carol Barratt's mother complained to nursing staff about her care and demanded that she be discharged from compulsory detention. At that point, the Responsible Medical Officer (RMO) agreed to her discharge. The report concluded: 'The RMO's decision to terminate her Section thus enabling Carol to discharge herself, and the circumstances in which this decision was made, constituted a serious error of clinical judgment.'

The case of Kevin Rooney, who killed his girlfriend Grace Quigley at the age of 28 and was found guilty of manslaughter on the grounds of diminished responsibility, is another case in point. He was detained under Section 37 of the Mental Health Act, with a restriction order. He had a history of mental illness dating back to 1985 and had been in hospital on several occasions, most recently a two-day stay the week before he killed his girlfriend. He left hospital on that occasion against medical advice but, because he was not then compulsorily detained, he could not be forced to stay. The picture that emerges is one of a relapsing mental illness, with some personality disorder, and subsequently recurring paranoid schizophrenia further complicated by drug use. But despite all the attempts made to get him adequate housing, Rooney's state was exacerbated by inadequate accommodation and bouts of sleeping rough. He had a chaotic behaviour pattern and often refused to take his medication. Though he often displayed threatening behaviour, he was not considered a risk because he never carried out his threats. Though the criticism of the staff was far less pointed in this case than in Carol Barratt's, nevertheless there were serious criticisms of the lack of cover and communication over the weekend, and the lack of a regular system for informing a patient's General Practitioner about admission, discharge, and, perhaps most importantly, when a patient has gone missing without leave. However, the inquiry into Rooney's care and the death of Grace Quigley focused largely on the question of the lack of ability of doctors to force patients in the community to take their medication. The Mental Health Act 1983 makes no provision for compulsory treatment in the community, and the evidence that Rooney's illness could be well controlled in hospital but that he lapsed as soon as he left suggested to many, including the inquiry team, that some provision for compulsory treatment in the community must be made.

The Christopher Clunis Case

This argument is brought into even sharper focus by the Clunis case. In December 1992, Christopher Clunis killed a total stranger, Jonathan Zito, on the platform of Finsbury Park underground station in London. He was convicted of manslaughter and detained under Section 37 of the Mental Health Act, with a restriction order placed upon him as well. Clunis was 29 when he killed Jonathan Zito and he had been in contact with mental health services in Britain for some five years, though he had been known to services in Jamaica, having been diagnosed there as suffering from paranoid schizophrenia in 1986. He had a number of admissions for in-patient care, but the report reveals how poorly linked up his care was, how frequently he disappeared from view, and how deficient his aftercare was.

One criticism from the inquiry was of the care he received at Dulwich North Hospital. He was treated there as a homeless person, but no contact was made with social services in the area he thought of as his home. Nor could the inquiry team understand why the psychiatric social worker had come to the view that Clunis had not presented any behavioural problems on the ward, as it was clear from the clinical and nursing notes that there had been problematic incidents. The inquiry suggested that the social worker's desire was not to stigmatize the patient, or label him in any way as violent or difficult, because that might have been to his disadvantage. But the inquiry was disturbed by this: 'While we understand the humanitarian considerations that may prompt this attitude, we find that time and again a failure to assess properly or describe his condition properly did not present an accurate picture to those who came to care for him afterwards, which ultimately served Christopher Clunis very badly.' It then considered the matter of Clunis's disappearance: 'We have been unable to discover, despite our investigations, where Christopher Clunis lived or what treatment he received between September 1988 and April 1989. During all that time, he should have been receiving careful planned aftercare under S 117 Mental Health Act 1983. He was effectively lost to the health and social services for 7 months.'*

All this was complicated by a chronic bed shortage in London at the time, which I remember well as I was chairing Camden and Islington Community Health Services NHS Trust at that time, which had responsibility for mental health services for the area and where we were frequently running at 120 to 130 per cent bed occupancy, which was, in my view both then and now, not a safe way to run a service. If people went on weekend leave, as they were preparing for discharge

* Ritchie, J. (1994), 9.3.4.

from a section (being compulsorily detained under a so-called 'section' of the Mental Health Act, for their own benefit, or to protect others), they would frequently return to find no bed available. If there was no bed available in a locked ward, then people might receive high doses of drugs on a general ward, because there was little else we could do. At the same time, the health authority, which picked up the tab, had serious worries about the amount we were spending on mental health services, even with such a high occupancy rate, and we had frequent recourse to the private sector, outside London, with medium secure facilities.

Things have improved somewhat since that time, and the introduction of the practice of assertive outreach has made a significant difference. Nevertheless, the need for more specialist and intensive services remains, but the resources are simply not available for them. So it might still be the case that someone like Christopher Clunis, sick and lonely and homeless, but with links to an area of North London, might be sent to a bed in a South London unit because no bed could be found for him in North London. In

Clunis's case, this exacerbated the sense that his care regime lacked coherence and focus. To add to that, he was removed from the list of the GP he had registered with because his behaviour had been abusive and angry, but his subsequent GP, whom he only saw once, was not told of his behaviour. Nor was he sent a list of other GPs in the area when he was first removed from the list.

Clunis continued to be treated by many different units and became increasingly violent. He missed hospital appointments and was clearly failing to cope with life. Just one social worker, Ursula Robson, tried desperately to pull it all together and even went around to Clunis's flat unaccompanied, potentially very dangerous for her, because she was so worried. The inquiry team said she had done more in one day to try to pull it all together than anyone else had done in the previous two months. When she went round to Clunis's flat one evening, to put a letter through his door asking him to come and see her the next day, he had already murdered Jonathan Zito. Her concern was well placed, and her readiness to work beyond the end of her shift was commendable.

But she was rare. It was not that people did not do their jobs. It was just that the need to keep closely in touch with one another, across disciplinary, borough and health authority boundaries, was insufficiently recognized. These were not bad people, or even – on the whole – people who fell seriously short of what could be expected. But they were simply disinclined to put in the extra effort, to go the extra mile for someone who was so difficult and unrewarding, when they were already overworked and open to criticism and abuse.

The Clunis case once again brought to light failures that had occurred many times before. Above all, there was a lack of communication between the professionals involved – consultant psychiatrists, nursing staff, GPs, community psychiatric nurses, social workers, the police, the Crown Prosecution Service, the Probation Services, and people providing care in the private and voluntary sector. There was also a general failure to inform or involve his family, and also to obtain an accurate and detailed history. One of the most significant lapses recognized by the Clunis report was the failure to identify the needs of homeless mentally ill patients on discharge from hospital, to keep track of such persons, and to provide for their care even when they cross geographical boundaries.

The problem is that the services are simply not adequately staffed to achieve this level of tracking. To accurately and properly keep track of people in the community, a caseload of some twenty patients is the maximum a community psychiatric nurse could manage. Yet I have rarely met a CPN with a caseload of fewer than fifty to sixty, especially in London, where keeping track of vulnerable and difficult patients, as people criss-cross local authority boundaries, is made all the more difficult. Nor is there sufficient accommodation for people on discharge from acute care. We tend to place people temporarily in hostels. Some will be moved on to 'step down' accommodation, others will leave and take to the streets, which are often perceived as a friendlier and safer environment for those on drugs who do not want to be bullied by hostel workers into taking their medication – something that the advocates of compulsory treatment in the community fail to recognize as a problem.

The Clunis inquiry recommended that young black males should not be typecast as suffering from schizophrenia unless their clinical condition warrants it, nor should any odd behaviour be ascribed to illicit drug use without good reason. It also recommended that young black people should be encouraged to become general practitioners and psychiatrists, so that health services are not perceived as being dominated by white or other ethnic groups. Once again, this is incredibly hard to achieve, but there have been important initiatives with some medical schools deliberately going out to schools in heavily black neighbourhoods and providing access courses for children from relatively deprived backgrounds.

The issue of race in mental health care is perhaps best analysed in a piece of work produced by the Sainsbury Centre for Mental Health in 2002, *Breaking the Circles of Fear*, which examined the state of the relationship between African and Caribbean communities and the mental health services. I shall return to this issue later.

The Michael Buchanan Case

Another well-known inquiry was into the case of Michael Buchanan, who killed Frederick Graver, a stranger to him, in 1992. He was found guilty of manslaughter and sentenced to life imprisonment. Buchanan was born to parents of Afro-Caribbean origin in 1964. His mother left the family and he was in residential care at eighteen months old. He returned to live with his father at the age of seven or thereabouts, but his father was unable to cope and he went back into residential care. His childhood was dominated by institutionalization and characterized by a lack of stability, and by the age of 13 he already had a criminal record for theft. He was first detained under the Mental Health Act in 1983, aged 18, and his mental health problems continued to build, as did his offending behaviour. He was admitted thirteen times between 1983 and 1992, and was obviously seriously distressed. His drugs habit meant he stole in order to get the funds to pay for his drugs, whilst his drug use interfered with his treatment – when he was prepared to take medication at all – and he was difficult to manage both in hospital and in the community.

All this was made much worse by inadequate aftercare and lack of discharge planning, so that he rarely had appropriate accommodation and rarely saw a community psychiatric nurse. Indeed, if he was not to be found, the CPN would simply discharge him from the books. The inquiry's recommendations were strongly in favour of properly supported, supervised accommodation for people like Michael Buchanan, and close supervision by a CPN. It also said that some review of the reasonableness of a CPN's caseload, and his/her ability to discharge patients from the list should be made – picking up on an earlier point in relation to the Clunis report that caseloads are unmanageable. But the lead recommendation, perhaps, was that meetings to discuss the discharge of patients under a Section 117 or the Care Programme Approach should be attended by representatives of all disciplines involved in the care of the patient. If the person is a mentally disordered offender, this means including the police and the Probation Service, where there has been contact with the patient in the past, as well as social workers and community psychiatric nurses in all cases.

Michael Buchanan's early childhood suggests he was marked out from the beginning for a poor future. He was abandoned by his mother, rejected by his father, and then institutionalized from a very young age. What kind of future can such a child expect? The point I am making is not that Michael Buchanan's illness and behaviour was bound to happen, but that he never really had a chance to deal with whatever life was to throw at him because of his early institutionalization and the absence of love and stability. Nigel Eastman, a leading forensic psychiatrist, gave evidence to the Buchanan inquiry suggesting that personality disorders, like Michael Buchanan's, range from being untreatable to being treatable largely through psychological and psychotherapeutic regimes. He also argued that people such as Buchanan should be detained for a much longer period – two or three years – in a secure setting. However, his view that some personality disorders are treatable is at odds with the view of many psychiatrists, who do not see such disorders as a reason to detain someone under the Mental Health Act. But while the professionals dispute, those who have these disorders suffer increasingly from prejudice and poor care.

The Andrew Robinson Case

There are many more inquires of failures in care in the community. Another example from a long list was entitled *Falling Shadow: One Patient's Mental Health Care 1978–1993*, chaired by senior lawyer, Sir Louis Blom-Cooper. This was the case of Andrew Robinson, who killed an occupational therapist at the Edith Morgan Centre in Torbay. Robinson was actually an inpatient at the time he killed Georgina Robinson (no relation), but he had been in the care of the community for many years. He was 35 when he committed the homicide, having already committed a serious offence in 1978 when he threatened a girl with whom he was infatuated with a loaded shotgun. It was this offence that led to him being diagnosed as having schizophrenia and he was sent to Broadmoor for three years, after which he was transferred to a local psychiatric hospital, and conditionally discharged in 1983.

Over the next ten years, Andrew Robinson received care both as an inpatient and as an outpatient, including a guardianship order from 1989 to 1992. It was after this order was removed that his health began to deteriorate rapidly, since he now had relatively little support from a multidisciplinary team and was no longer having regular depot medication. He was readmitted to hospital in June 1993 and detained on a section, but he managed to leave hospital without authorization and then bought a kitchen knife which he later used to stab Georgina Robinson.

Blom-Cooper highlights many disturbing features of the fifteen-year history of Andrew Robinson's care. What stands out, however, is that his parents, who had expressed frequent and growing concern about their son's mental state, were not drawn into the discussions about his care. One of the key recommendations was that the Trust should develop a clear policy about the values, principles, and practices that govern relationships between staff and the patient's close relatives and recognize relatives' right to information, practical help, and involvement in care and treatment plans. Parents and other relatives also need to have emotional and practical support. The key task in working with relatives is to engage them in the overall care plan so that they become partners with the clinical team in the care of their relative. This may seem obvious, but it is a relatively recent phenomenon. Yet if one drew a parallel with the hospice movement, it would be inconceivable not to involve a terminally ill patient's relatives in decisions about their care if they were unable to make decisions themselves; the idea that relatives of people suffering from mental illness should not be similarly consulted on the package of care seems eccentric in the extreme. Yet this was commonplace until just a few years ago, and is still to be found.

The John Rous Case

The last case I want to feature is the murder of Jonathan Newby, a young volunteer working in a hostel run by the Cyrenians in Oxford, by John Rous. Newby was untrained and was working alone in the hostel on the day he was stabbed by Rous, a man with a history of severe mental illness with a diagnosis that changed from schizophrenia to personality disorder. Rous had spent at least part of his childhood in foster care and was known to the criminal justice system by the age of 17. At 18 he was admitted to a psychiatric hospital for the first time. He had serious drug and alcohol dependency as well as his mental illness and lacked stable accommodation for many years, which led to him living in the Cyrenian hostel. This in turn led to him not getting access to all the services that might otherwise have been available to him. However, one reason the Cyrenians offered accommodation was because the local social services in Oxford took no responsibility for housing people with a history of mental health problems, leaving it all to the housing department, which had failed to deliver. Rous got support from his probation officer and intermittent help from social services, but no one took overall responsibility and his mental health deteriorated, culminating in the killing of Jonathan Newby.

The subsequent report was tough on the social services department and on the housing department, arguing that they, and the NHS, had both a statutory and a moral duty to ensure provision of proper care to people with serious mental health problems. But it also criticized the Cyrenians and its management committee, arguing that they should have required proper accounts of what was going in the hostels and that leaving one unqualified volunteer in charge of a hostel with people suffering from severe mental illness was simply inappropriate and wrong. But the criticism went further. The voluntary sector needed to realize that it was no longer providing exceptional care to people for whom the social services could not find a home. Increasingly, the voluntary sector was providing mainstream care and needed to maintain professional standards and be professionally accountable.

So Where Does All This Lead Us?

What conclusions can one draw from these and the many other inquiries that have been held into failures of the system?

One is certainly the need for community psychiatric nurses to have reasonable case loads; another is the necessity for proper communication between professionals. The voluntary sector has to be serious about the risks it takes on, whilst the statutory sector should not ask it to take on the impossible. Time and again evidence has shown evidence that mental health professionals failed to take seriously the view of patients' relatives and close friends, even though these are often the people who know the person best, and who may have most to contribute to their treatment.

One of the problems in looking at mental health inquiries – important though they are – is that the serious nature of the incidents they examine can lead public and professionals alike to take their eyes off the wider picture. For most people, mental health problems result in far less newsworthy anguish, although the suffering of individuals and communities can be very great.

Most people with mental health problems, such as depression and anxiety, are treated by their GPs, if they are treated at all. Looking at it from another perspective, it has been estimated that about a third of GP consultations have a mental health component but that 30 to 50 per cent of these are not acknowledged during those very consultations.*

Inquiries will continue in some shape or form, partly because we feel, as a society, that 'something must be done' about these failures in care. Yet, though we are willing to hold an expensive inquiry into care failures where a homicide has taken place, we seem less inclined to worry about the death of a close relative at the hands of someone with mental health problems than the death of a stranger. It is as if we feel that the relatives, who are often the carers, of people with severe mental health problems are less deserving of our care and concern than the complete stranger.

---

* Cohen, A. (2002).

The Race Issue

As the Clunis case demonstrated, the issue of race in mental health care is a serious one. When the Sainsbury Centre began work on its report *Breaking the Circles of Fear* (2002), there was clear over-representation of young black men on acute inpatient wards. The introduction to the report argued that black service users are often sectioned under the Mental Health Act, rather than coming into the service voluntarily. There is likely to be police involvement; medication is often forcibly administered; and the relationship between staff and patient can be contentious, to say the least. Black people are the most disaffected of all service users (though users report favourably on black-led services provided by the independent sector) and, to quote *Breaking the Circles of Fear*, such is the 'level of disenchantment with services amongst service users, and their families and carers, that there is the feeling that services no longer have the best interests of clients at heart'.

It is worth looking at the reasons for this. First, there is the aforementioned over-representation of black people in the most restrictive end of mental health services. Second, the black community has been asking for decades why it is that mental health services continue to fail black people but they have not yet been given a serious answer. Third, of the twenty-eight inquiries Margaret Reith studies in her survey *Community Care Tragedies* (1998), nine – just over a third – investigated people from ethnic minorities, which seems astonishingly high. Fourth, black people are more likely to be readmitted to the services. Fifth, there is an arguable over-diagnosis of schizophrenia and an under-diagnosis of depression or affective disorder. Sixth, there is an over-reliance on medication and an unwillingness to prescribe psychotherapy, psychological treatments, and counselling.

The first inquiry into community care to examine the race dimension was in 1988. It concerned the care and treatment of Sharon Campbell, who killed Isabel Schwarz, a social worker. It concluded that a deliberate policy to establish services for minority groups would be inadvisable because it could hamper integration. The inquiry also suggested that such a policy would lead to disputes about allocation of resources between different groups. It did, however, recommend that community mental health services should take account of the needs of ethnic minorities, which is hardly generous, but at least was a nod in the right direction.

The Buchanan inquiry (1994) recognized that it was important to involve black mental health organizations in its discussions and regretted that the organizations approached had declined its invitation, which suggests just how angry black voluntary organizations involved with mental health were at the system. The Grey report (1995), on the case of Kenneth Grey, who killed his mother after absconding from an open psychiatric ward, virtually ignored Grey's ethnicity and the impact this might have had on his diagnosis and treatment or on the variety of services offered. However, the same year, the Woodley report considered the issue at some length, at least in part because the chairman was himself black and understood the anger of the black community. In the report's words: 'The lack of access to, and appropriateness of, preventative and support services to black/ethnic minorities, compounded by socio-economic disadvantage, leads to over-representation of black/ethnic minorities in the psychiatric hospitals system.'*

Meanwhile, the NG inquiry (1996)† virtually ignores the ethnicity issue, by dismissing the suggestion of any racist prejudice in the provision of services to NG, and without questioning the attitudes or simply the ethnic composition of the staff concerned. Two other reports (Mabota 1996, and Nicholson, also 1996) highlight – amazing though it is – the failure to provide adequate interpreting services in the mental health services. Kumbi Mabota came from Zaire, with English as his fifth language. The psychiatrist who assessed him said it was difficult to get a history from him because of the language difficulty. Yet since communication is so vital for mental health services, you might have thought that interpretation services would be freely available. In the case of

---

* Quoted in Reith, op. cit., 144.
† *Report of the Independent Inquiry Team into the Care and Treatment of NG* [chair: J. R. Main, QC] (Ealing, Hammersmith and Hounslow Health Authority and London Borough of Hounslow, 1996).

Maria Caseiro, who stabbed a local GP (not fatally), the Nicholson inquiry report makes the point that Caseiro, who was Portuguese, herself drew attention to the need for inter-pretation but that there was no service available despite her requests.

There have been many reflections on what it is like to be a black service user, and to have survived. Devon Marsten works for Sound Minds, a South London charity help-ing black youngsters with mental health problems. He was a teenager when detained under the Mental Health Act:

I was young, I was smoking dope and my hair was long. I was a Rastafarian – it was my religion then – but my mother was worried that I wasn't eating and I went home for something to eat and they had a doctor there. They said I was ill so they detained me, without my permission, un-der a section. When I got to the hospital it was like Colditz Castle, a terrifying place to be. On a ward, the doctors and nurses were talking about me – not to me – and I heard them saying: 'The police say he's taking drugs.' That night I said to the nurse: 'I'm OK, can I go home now?' Before I knew what was happening, five or six big geezers – they seemed like bouncers – came out and jumped me and put me in an arm lock. I couldn't escape. They held me down and injected me with tranquillisers. I woke up about four days later and was a different person. My mind was blank. That experience made me part of the system and when you are a black man in that system you get the worst. The people in there didn't know how to deal with street people. I was a Rasta, I didn't eat certain foods but they still gave them to me. They seemed to say: 'You are a black man who has been smoking ganja, you must be a paranoid schizophrenic.' I am through it now and work with black kids with mental health problems, but what you hear of their experiences it is just the same. They get put into pigeonholes or stereotyped.*

---

* Taken from 'No holding back' by Mark Gould, Raekha Prasad, and Alison Benjamin, *The Guardian* (11 February 2004).

Fiona Bloomfield was sectioned, aged 18, after seeking help for depression:

> I was given huge doses of medication – 10 times that of most white people. The left side of my face was paralysed and I was dribbling. I've been in and out of hospital ever since. Once I was known to services, I was harassed by police and accused of having drugs on me. I was refused counselling and told it wouldn't be beneficial, that I was not well enough and that I'd be incoherent. It was drummed into me that I shouldn't have sex, because I shouldn't have children. They thought my child would be a burden on the state. I twisted my hair and the consultant said I should change it because I had a religious delusion. The assumption was that I'd become a Rastafarian.†

Paul Grey was diagnosed as a manic depressive at the age of 20. He now runs his own company, working as a plumber and mental health consultant. He argues that none of what he experienced as an inpatient was

---

† Gould, Prasad and Benjamin, op. cit.

about care. The focus was always on the effects rather than the cause:

> What I needed was space, cheerleaders and support. Compassion not containment ... Although there's a lot of misinformation about how the black community operates, communicates and how respect is gained, this isn't a black or white issue. There are white folk in my neighbourhood who also get stuck in the system. When I was being injected, there were black nurses holding me down. It's about valuing everyone and seeing every life as precious.

Or there is Desmond McLean, who was raped at the age of 14. He would not speak about his ordeal, but his family became worried about him and, after an argument at home, he was admitted to an adult psychiatric ward:

> Whenever I showed any resentment to what was happening to me, four or five adults would jump me and pull my trousers down and put a needle in my buttocks. Having that needle gives them

a lot of control over your emotions. Whenever black people show any signs of psychiatric problems they are labelled paranoid schizophrenic or psychotic. It's because they don't understand where black people are coming from and how we express our frustrations.

These are just a few examples of how black people feel about the mental health services. The sense that emerges is that they are being perceived as somehow 'riskier' than white patients. As a result they are given a higher dose of drugs and are refused counselling (though that is a common complaint throughout the NHS mental health system, where the use of drugs is the standard and counselling and psychological treatment are in very short supply).

The evidence is growing that black people's perceptions of inequality are well founded. Some studies show that psychiatrists are more likely to see black people as violent and that racism and prejudice could account, at least in part, for the different experience.* Later studies, such as Minnis et

* Lewis et al. (1990).

al. (2001), have a more mixed view, arguing that this stereotype is no longer valid, though they agree that racism is still present and evident in mental health services. When Rachel Spector* reviewed the various studies that had examined the relationship between race and coercion, both in the United Kingdom and the United States, she found that racial stereotyping and perceptions of dangerousness particularly influence how patients are treated and managed. Stereotyping has also been compounded by publications suggesting that black people are over-represented in the mental health services because of a predisposed genetic disposition to schizophrenia.† But there is little evidence to support this, despite a growing interest in, and fashion for, neuro-biological explanations for mental illness, rather than social ones. A number of experts have roundly condemned the genetic predisposition argument,‡ but this view is still held, and with it goes the tendency to over-medicate and under-treat

---

* Spector, R. (2001).
† Selten et al. (2001).
‡ Fernando et al. (1998), Jenkins (1998), Sharpley et al. (2001), Rose (2001).

with psychological interventions and counselling.

When the Sainsbury Centre began its work on the *Circles of Fear* report, one might have expected a high degree of enthusiasm from both health professionals and from service users. The opposite was true. Senior management of services failed to engage with the project to any great extent whilst users and carers were sceptical. Although a high response rate was achieved from mental health professionals, psychiatrists, almost always the team leaders, were noticeable by their absence. The scepticism expressed by service users included the view that black people are over-researched and never see any benefit from taking part in such projects.

The views of service users quoted in the *Circles of Fear* report bring us back to the question of fear:

'Coming to mental health services was like the last straw ... You come to services disempowered already, they strip you of your dignity ... you become the dregs of society.'

'I remember when I first went into hospital ... I feared that I was going to die.'

'When I heard the word schizophrenia I was so afraid of what was going to happen to me.'

These reactions have to be set against professionals' fear of violence, often deriving from previous physical assaults by patients:

It's of great concern to us because we've got a small team, we might have 20, 25 patients, some of whom have had psychotic episodes, and virtually all of whom will have had a diagnosis in some form of acute psychosis with personality disorders, because that's what we specialise in ... I think I'm more wary of size. If someone's big, that actually worries me ... we tend to get out of the way, which I think is the best route, avoidance ... If the whole team are fearful for example of someone, we would put that as a greater risk than if somebody's not. If someone says, 'Oh no, he's fine with me', we might think that reduces the risk a bit, because it's likely that that person might be able to talk to them if they're so agitated they may become violent.*

In 2003, there was a dramatic case of a member of staff at one of London's most prestigious mental health units, Springfield Hospital in south west London, being killed by a patient. Jason Cann killed Mamade Chattum, a nurse at the hospital, on 17 June 2003, leading to yet another inquiry and to considerable anguish amongst staff and managers alike. So the fear of some patients is not wholly misplaced; nor, if you walk through the wards, can you fail to be aware of a suppressed level of violence and anger amongst patients, unless they are too medicated to respond much at all. Patients are often angry, staff are wary, and this breeds a very unhealthy climate in what is supposed to be a place of care. The more those who are less acutely ill live in the community, the sicker those remaining in hospital acute wards are likely to be, and therefore the more threatening and difficult the atmosphere. It rarely feels like a therapeutic environment.

---

* *Breaking the Circles of Fear*, 26.

The term 'Circles of Fear' becomes more and more accurate. Everyone is scared – of each other, of what is going to happen to them, of what they are going to be asked to do. This is a whole system driven by fear, as Jeremy Laurance makes clear in his brilliant book *Pure Madness*. So what can be done to lessen fear?

One way forward is to try assertive outreach and crisis resolution, to treat people with respect, and trying where possible to keep them out of hospital by means of a genuine community care model. John Hoult piloted the use of the technique of assertive outreach combined with crisis intervention in his native Australia and then brought it to Britain. I first saw his work in Birmingham, where, by intensive work with people in crisis and those who needed treatment, he managed to keep the majority of them at home, with the consent and support of their carers where they had them, by having people stay with them when they were in a crisis. His no-nonsense approach involves the use of drugs, but it also involves the giving of help in a whole variety of other ways – with food, with money, with accommodation. The results, though not always perfect, are far lower bed occupancy, less distressed service users, and a sense that the issue of homelessness amongst this very needy group can be dealt with in a planned way by those who are also concerned about the mental health status of the individuals.

John Hoult's can-do approach impressed me, and I was determined to recruit him into the Trust I then chaired. Despite Camden and Islington being a tougher proposition than Birmingham, he made huge inroads into both bed occupancy rates and the satisfaction rates. The crisis team, paired with the community mental health teams over which he had an oversight role until recently, tries to keep people out of hospital and at home; if people are too unwell or too disruptive for their family and carers to cope with, then they can be admitted to a crisis house or some other accommodation. Hospital is used as the last resort. 'If you are admitted to a mental hospital, what would you think? "Oh my God, here I am in mental hospital." If you go to a house that's different. We are talking about normalising the situation. The reason that such arrangements are not more widespread is that they are time consuming, hard work, and involve more risk.'* John Hoult still uses medication, but he offers other things as well: respect, negotiation, and a way of engaging with people that seems to bring better results.

Although this approach is not cheap, the evidence in Camden is that the cost of the assertive outreach and crisis teams is offset by the saving on private sector beds. Another crucial element is the whole user and carer movement in mental health, people who are articulate, demanding, and highly critical of services as they presently exist. The service user movement has largely come into being in the last ten to fifteen years. When surveyed by the Sainsbury Centre in 2003 it consisted of some 900 organizations nationally, of which 300 were surveyed in detail. Of those, 75 per cent consisted of less than a hundred people, and 75 per cent of the user groups had been established within the past ten years. Amongst the most common functions of the user groups were self-help and social sup-

---

* Quoted by Laurance, *Pure Madness*, 113.

port; consulting with decision-makers; and education and training. But the key factor was the increasing role for these groups in mental health service user involvement (more than two-thirds of them are now engaged in this), although there is a worrying growth in evidence of burnout among representatives. There is also a smaller number of national networks which have developed, such as Voices Forum and UKAN (which now has 270 member groups), but there is no single national voice to speak for people with mental health problems.

Critics of such groups can be surprisingly harsh, perhaps because their very articulacy seems threatening. Marjorie Wallace, chief executive of SANE, argues that survivor groups only speak for their members and not for the silent majority who are not in the least interested in the politics of mental health but simply want decent services. But she fails to recognize that articulate service users have brought about change in maternity services, in some cancer services, and in the treatment of children in hospitals. Why then would articulacy not bring similar benefits to mental health? Diana Rose, co-ordinator of service user research at the Institute of Psychiatry in London, is dismissive of the negative approach to articulate user groups: 'This argument says that if you are articulate you are not representative. Therefore, you can only be representative if you are not articulate. Therefore, you can't have any representation at all. It is nonsense.'*

The relationship between service users and mental health professionals has to be a credible one, so that services will be seen to be more attractive and so that a willingness to engage with services by users becomes a marker of the next stage in the development of safe, secure, and effective services for people with mental illness. To achieve this, mental health professionals must take seriously the voice of users and their genuine opposition to the way the services mostly work now. Another important, but difficult, issue here is the understanding of what causes mental illness. Most psychiatrists have a strongly biological model of mental illness – people are sick, and they need

---

* Laurance, op.cit., 77.

drugs to enable them to be well. Though there is clearly some validity to this, most of the user groups argue that social factors, early history, psychological issues, oppression and poverty have a major part to play. There is also the dual diagnosis group, those who use illicit drugs and alcohol as well as having a mental illness, where social factors are clearly a major component of their condition. If the relationship between the two groups – professionals and service users – is to work, there needs to be an understanding between them of how each views mental illness.

The Irish Community and Mental Health

A relatively recent addition to the mental health services user movement focuses on the Irish community – another group who have a disproportionate experience of the mental health services. In an article entitled 'When Irish eyes aren't smiling',* Herpreet Kaur Grewal argued that Irish people are a virtually invisible minority within Britain's mental health services and that their suf-

* *The Guardian* (11 February 2004).

fering tends to be neglected as a result. She cites the story of one Gavin Walsh (a pseudonym), 56, a first-generation Irish immigrant with severe schizophrenia. He lives alone in the Midlands, where he was raised, and has been in the British mental health system for twenty-four years. His problems grew as an adolescent:

'When I was 14, my mother kept a lodging house and I was molested by a man who did charitable work for the Catholic Church. I was sexually assaulted twice by another man who used to take me to the pictures,' Walsh says in his still strong Irish accent. He believes the abuse destroyed all his relationships as he could not face telling his partners what he had suffered. He had no children because he harboured irrational fears that he might become a child molester himself. As Mr Walsh grew older his father developed an alcohol problem and his mother began to go blind. 'My mother was suffering, which made her nervous and afraid to be left alone, so she lived in her blindness and I looked after her. We lived in a rat-

and cockroach-infested place with no bathroom. In those days, with the trouble with Northern Ireland, people were very cruel towards the Irish and there were prostitutes living next door who threw used condoms into our garden and my mother didn't know what they were. It made me angry,' he says. Although he completed mathematics A-level within a year and wanted to study at university, he worked as a carpenter because education was too expensive. As life became unbearable he found solace in alcohol.

Mr Walsh was admitted to hospital for three months, diagnosed with severe anxiety and stress and then depressive paranoid schizophrenia. 'They just kicked me out of hospital and pumped me with injections. Then I took an overdose because I couldn't bear it – it was a cry for help.'

First-generation Irish people such as Gavin Walsh make up 1.27 per cent of the population of England and Wales, the country's third largest ethnic minority. According to a report launched in 2004, funded by the Department of Health and commissioned by the Federation of Irish Societies, many Irish people say they experience discrimination. It shows that 40 per cent of Irish people within mental health services rate their experiences negatively. The report also illustrates that the Irish are more likely than black, Asian, or Chinese people to see lack of cultural awareness in staff as a problem.*

There are other groups of people who have been largely ignored and under-treated. For example in 2000 the suicide rate amongst young Asian women aged 15–34 was twice as high as for their white counterparts. Unfortunately, depression in groups such as Asian women is often not recognized. Where it is recognized, the view has all too often been that some minority ethnic communities 'look after their own' and do not need or want support from public services. But we have known for a long time that this is not the case. As long ago as 1993 the Commission for Racial Equality funded a research

---

* *Consulting the Irish Community on Inside Outside: Improving mental health services for black and ethnic minority communities in England – The community response and its evaluation* (FIS, 2004).

study of Asian women in Bristol.* Most of the women mentioned six or more symptoms, such as weakness, listlessness, tearfulness, inability to sleep, inability to cope with simple tasks, loss of self-confidence and the sense of meaning in life, even contemplation of suicide. Although there is now more appreciation of the existence of these reservoirs of misery, it remains true that some mental health conditions – and some communities – are likely to have their needs overlooked because they do not conform to the stereotypes of risk that is reflected in almost all of the major inquiries. It is possible to remain mentally ill and hidden from view – as long as one remains quietly miserable.

The problem about the wider public taking the user movement more seriously is that government is increasingly punitive and controlling in its attitude to people with serious mental illness. At the same time as implementing assertive outreach and crisis resolution – two of the really great leaps

---

* Steve Fenton and Sadiq Azra, *The Sorrow in my Heart: Sixteen Asian women talk about depression* (London: CRE, 1993).

forward in thinking about mental illness and key components of the National Service Framework (1999) – government wants to make treatment with medication in the community compulsory, making it harder than ever for mental health professionals to engage with people on a voluntary basis and more likely that people will shun the services altogether. If they feel that they can be given medication in the community by force, without any other services being offered to them, they will feel that the only thing on offer is a form of social control without any promise of care, help, and support. The user movement is unanimous in being highly critical of such moves; but government has been disturbed by some of the high-profile cases discussed above and wants to avoid the risk of violence committed by people with a history, or diagnosis, of mental illness, even though there is no evidence that such an approach will succeed in reducing the risk.

This is yet another example of being averse to risk, rather than putting care first. Far more violence is committed by people who have consumed too much alcohol than by people with mental illness, yet the desire to control these people in any serious way is limited – no one sections the person who is over the limit with alcohol when driving, though it might be considered to be an irrational act to drive in such a state. Nor does anyone section – though they might face a criminal charge – the person who consumes so much alcohol that he becomes violent and picks a fight in which people get seriously hurt. Instead of curtailing drinking hours, indeed, the government is moving to 24-hour licensing, as if this will somehow discourage binge drinking and its associated violence. The user movement in mental health never tires of pointing out this anomaly to government, but to no avail. As a result, those who are mentally ill feel stigmatized.

Inpatient Care

Beyond the issue of engaging with service users, particularly with users and carers from ethnic minorities, there is a further area where real improvements could be made: the conditions of inpatient wards.

The picture here is mixed, but in my experience many wards are gloomy, with little in the way of activity in the daytime and little in the way of engagement between staff and patients. Staff seem far more concerned with security and safety than with well-being. In my time as Chair of Camden and Islington Community Health Services there was a major refitting of one of the worst settings for people with mental illness I have ever seen in my life – and that includes the days of the old asylums. The old mental health unit of the Whittington Hospital, now the Waterlow Unit, had been designed with no outside space for patients, no decent windows, and too many exits from the wards, which meant that staff had to sit at the ends of the wards rather than engage with the patients. In terms of a therapeutic environment, it was truly terrible. But fresh paint, pictures on the walls, decent flooring, and better lighting – pretty minimal changes – changed the atmosphere. It wasn't perfect, but it improved hugely. All the evidence of the environment having a powerful effect on how patients feel had formerly been disregarded, and it was an object lesson for me and the other members of the Board to see the change. Indirectly, it led to the Kings' Fund, during my time as Chief Executive, extending its Enhancing the Healing Environment programme to mental health trusts in London. I was convinced by my experience at Camden and Islington that one could achieve major changes by involving nurses and patients and the estates teams in thinking differently about space, light and art.

Jeremy Laurance tells of several famous professors of psychiatry and other well-known mental health professionals finding the state of inpatient units so scandalous that they would not want to be treated there themselves, or any member of their family either. Locked wards with no outside space are a disgrace, and where there are no single rooms – which means no privacy and nowhere to keep personal belongings – it becomes desperately depressing, which is hardly helpful for people who have a diagnosis of serious mental illness. But it is not only the physical state of inpatient units that still cause concern, but also what happens in them. Survivors express a mixture of emotions, from acknowledging kindness received to desperation that they never see the same psychiatrist or member of staff twice. Staff members themselves often complain about the uncaring culture and the terrible abuse of patients that still takes place. Here, for instance, is one account:

I have just finished an 18-month stint working at a home for people with long-term mental health problems ... residents had often quite large sums of their money spent for them by staff on items they repeatedly said they didn't want. One resident ... would protest that he had no need of the item he was being pressured to buy, but every time his protests were ignored. And every time he eventually gave in to demands that he produce the money, sometimes with tears in his eyes.

Some residents were also bathed by staff on the grounds that when they bathed themselves they did not do it properly ... Indeed the personal hygiene of the residents was the most popular topic of conversation among the staff – and the word 'stink' frequently cropped up here. Staff would also complain constantly of the laziness of the residents, mimic their table manners and mock their families.

But reports by local authority inspectors described the home in glowing terms.*

Conditions are also often bad in acute and locked wards. Food is often poor, there is no activity, people watch television all day, and staff seem disinclined to engage with patients, particularly with younger patients. The result is pent up-energy and frustration.

But it is possible to do things differently. A senior nurse, Peter Dodds, at Lynfield Mount Hospital in Bradford, has managed to achieve major change in some three years. He started in one ward and was desperately shocked by what he found. 'It was like a war zone. Patients lay in bed all day, there was no routine, the staff didn't do anything – it was a disaster. You can have a nice beautiful building but unless you know what you are doing with the patients all during the day

---

* Ina Heffernan, 'Diatribe', *Mental Health Today* (October 2003), 37.

you have poor care.'† He started engaging with the patients, getting them up in the mornings, banning loud music from radios etc., and ensured each patient got at least fifteen minutes a day of meaningful contact with a member of the nursing staff – going shopping, playing a game, or just talking. There is an active art therapy department (though other patients and survivors have criticized art therapy), as well as yoga and relaxation classes. Contrast this with the commonplace drug dealing on open wards in parts of inner London, and the atmosphere of aggression and violence experienced by many inpatients.

Continuity of Care

Another area where a real difference could be made is by ensuring that people who use services see the same team each time so that a level of trust can be built up on both sides. It may not always be possible to see the same individual on every visit, but the same team, whether in inpatient care or in the community, is essential. The widespread

† Quoted by Laurance, op. cit., 104.

practice of constantly changing staff has to change. Making it change ought to be part of the professional responsibility of all psychiatrists and nursing staff. No one wants to be left in the situation Rachel Studley experienced, of which she writes in her impassioned plea against locums, entitled 'Locum Shmocum':

Here in The Locum Zone continuity of care is a dirty word. Here you can be admitted under one psychiatrist and, two weeks later, discharged by another (the previous one having found a tastier position, perhaps). Here you tell your life story to one amiable shrink, repeat it to another (who seems not that interested) at your next appointment, repeat it again to someone new (who seems very interested) and then have to go over it all again to someone new (by which time you are understandably fed up with it all and are perceived as 'resistant' and 'aggressive'). I can repeat my psychiatric history backwards, standing on my head whilst juggling flaming torches with my feet (well almost – you get the point

though, don't you?). In a 15 minute appointment (I'm being generous here)
there isn't much time to do anything
else.*

Without continuity of care there is not a
chance that mentally ill people will use the
services willingly. If they then think they
will be forced to take medication or, worse
still, could be compulsorily detained over
the long term with inadequate rights of appeal, they will become less and less inclined
to use services that already have a poor
reputation.

This is clearly difficult for mental health
professionals. They tend to get blamed
when things go wrong, and rarely get praise.
They work in an area of great risk: things go
wrong simply because they do, and professional judgement can never be perfect. But
more can be done to minimize staff changes,
to provide continuity of care, and to listen to
the voices of users who desperately want
someone to understand what is bothering
them, and who want one-to-one psychological interventions and counselling instead of

* Rachel Studley, © 2003.

medication. There is a great deal of good practice out there – such as the 'Enhancing the Healing Environment' programme, which has involved service users in changing the physical environment in which services are provided, and the wide range of daytime activities organized by voluntary organizations up and down the country. But good practice is by no means universal and the general impression of the services amongst most user groups remains one of poor understanding and lack of kindness on the part of professionals.

Activity and Employment

Lack of daytime activity is a huge concern to many people with mental health problems. Some art and pottery workshops are excellent, such as Heritage Ceramics in West London, for black Africans who have had severe mental health problems, where they produce pots of a quality and beauty that are in high demand. But for many people with enduring mental illness, such therapeutic opportunities do not exist, whilst finding employment can be even harder. Working-age people with severe mental health problems have a lower rate of employment than any such group except those with severe learning disabilities. The reasons for this include the pessimistic attitudes of mental health staff and GPs towards their patients who have mental illness. Professionals tend to lack confidence in their patients' abilities and also want to avoid the risk of exposing them to the stresses of a working environment, for good positive reasons. But if work is what people want, it seems curiously counter-productive to make it more difficult – yet another example of professionals failing to comprehend what it is that users actually want.

To make matters worse, users are also caught in the classic British benefits trap. If they work a small amount, they may earn less than the benefits they lose. An even more worrying fact, given the government's desire to cut incapacity benefit payments, is that people with mental health problems are the only category of incapacity benefit claimants that is still growing. The appalling truth is that a person who signs off sick for six months or more with a mental illness has a 50 per cent chance of never working again.* For the incapacity benefit system makes it hard for mentally ill people to gain financially from employment unless they work fulltime. It also makes it difficult to leave work temporarily if they fall ill, which does not fit well with the episodic nature of mental illness.

Homelessness

Homelessness is another huge issue. All the evidence from the inquiries suggests that housing and support services need to be a key part of services for people with mental health problems, yet even now mental health workers spend huge amounts of their time trying to sort out housing and benefits for people because other staff, in other agencies, seem to have given up. Elaine Murphy makes the point very tellingly in her book *After the Asylums*, in which she argues that people with mental disorders are no different from anyone else in wanting to live in

* *Vocational Rehabilitation: The Way Forward* (London: British Society of Rehabilitation Medicine, 2000).

good, decent housing. But it does not work out like that. Too many of the homeless are people with mental health problems, which is no coincidence. Estimates of the number of homeless people with mental health problems vary between a third and a half, but the figures probably only represent those people known to the mental health services. People who came out of the old asylums only make up around 1 per cent of the mentally ill homeless. Younger people who come out of the acute inpatient wards are particularly vulnerable since many of them probably have a lifetime of episodic mental illness ahead of them. The estimates suggest that around half of people who go into acute wards are homeless, but that the proportion is nearer two-thirds when they come out. Accommodation when they leave is of varying quality, from excellent hostels offering care and support and with a commitment to getting people into their own homes as soon as it can be managed, to poor quality bed and breakfast accommodation where the care is non-existent and the population transient, making it hard for aftercare services to find them at all.

Yet there are some excellent models for supported housing, such as the Times Square Hotel in New York City, which has excited great interest in the UK for the reason that it does not try to put people with problems into sharing accommodation only with people like themselves. Half of the hotel's residents are people who have, or have had, mental health or other health problems; the other half consists of people who want low-cost accommodation in central Manhattan. The result is that people with problems see others who get up in the morning to go to work; they see people living ordinary and normal lives, and live in a building where social space is mixed. The support services are present, but not obvious. And everyone works. If they can, they work outside the building; if not, they work in the hotel itself.

There has to be a lesson here for the UK. The mixed population stops people from being categorized. The fact that half are living perfectly ordinary lives means that the other half have an example and a pattern to follow. The mixed space means it is possible to build a community. The 24-hour security and concierge service ensures the building does not get trashed. And each person has their own front door, and their own assured tenancy, provided they pay the rent.

It is a magical place. More importantly, it is part of a nationwide supported housing movement. There are also examples in the UK, though not on the same scale and not with the mix of residents. It is now to be tried here by involving key workers, for whom low-cost housing in city centres is essential, as co-residents. But there is also the option of housing people in different ways. In New York, CUCS, the social care agency that provides the social care support in the Times Square Hotel, also supports increasing numbers of formerly homeless people with mental health problems in apartments located all around the city.

The UK has been less keen to address this problem of homelessness in a positive, pragmatic way. Our predilection is for treating people in silos, in which services have made things worse for the most vulnerable people of all. The inquiries all show that. Christopher Clunis was shoved from pillar to post. The mental health services did not take charge of his housing, as they might have done in the USA. Such combined services are still rare, though there are some signs of attempts at a similar approach: in North Birmingham, for instance, the assertive outreach and crisis service deals with housing and homelessness issues.

People with mental health problems are automatically perceived to be bad tenants and neighbours. Equally, the tendency to give people with mental health problems flats no one else wants in high-rise blocks or on sink estates is likely to exacerbate a tendency to relapse. It is essential that people with mental health problems have decent housing, in an area where they can go out easily and integrate. But Elaine Murphy makes the point strongly that housing for people with mental health problems must not be seen as the only answer. It must be the home to which people return, not where they spend 24 hours a day. They need to go out to work, to the shops, to the library, to the gym. That need for social integration into the community is vital and to achieve it requires them being in accommodation, supported or otherwise.

Money can be another huge issue. In *After the Asylums*, Elaine Murphy reports that a study of the work of mental health professionals in the London Borough of Hackney in 1990 demonstrated that a quarter of the time of a community team working with people at home was spent on working out welfare entitlements. One said: 'Being articulate and diplomatic and having saintlike patience and dogged persistence have become key attributes needed to prise money out that should be available as right.'* Social workers make huge efforts to fight the system in order to get the money to which their clients are entitled; but often what their clients want is just ordinary help – someone to talk to, early intervention, daytime activity, and so on. Time after time clients talk of how difficult it is to access ordinary help, before things become violent or worse.

When Jeremy Laurance toured the UK he met more and more mental health professionals who were longing to provide greater help but could not, because the system is

---

* Murphy, E. (1991), 151.

rationed and because the main concern is whether or not a person was dangerous. If you are not dangerous, you will have huge difficulty in getting the help you need. 'There is a sea of distress out there,' said a manager in Norfolk. 'If we have open access we will be overwhelmed.' 'You can be as mad as a meat axe,' said a psychiatrist, 'but if you can live independently – cook, clean and look after yourself, and you don't frighten the neighbours – then no one is going to take the slightest notice of you.'† It is public order that still drives the service through containment and confinement. Mental health professionals are barely allowed to use their own judgement to offer help to those who need it but who are not likely to be a nuisance, or worse, to others. What kind of therapeutic service is this? What has happened?

Two things. First, mental health professionals are becoming agents of the government's – and, arguably, the public's – desire for greater social control. As a result, they, like the general public, are becoming in-

---

† Laurance, op. cit., 8.

creasingly unwilling to take risks. But there will always be risk – life itself is risky; but killings by people with mental illness have not increased over the last twenty years. Second, mental health professionals are inevitably blamed when things go wrong. This needs to stop. We need to give our mental health professionals a sense that they are not there just for social control, but to help people feel better about themselves, and not only when things get to a crisis stage.

Yet attitudes are changing. Mental illness is a part of our society and it hits many of us at some stage in our lives. For some of us it will be very serious. When Frank Bruno, the former boxer, was admitted to mental hospital in September 2003, the *Sun* newspaper began the day with one headline – 'Bonkers Bruno locked up' – and finished with another – 'Sad Bruno in mental home'. It is clear that the public will no longer tolerate the use of derogatory language around mental illness, and yet media stories that perpetuate public fears about mentally ill people living in the community still persist, as the 'Murder in the Park: Mental Patient Seized' headline from the *Evening*

Standard about the stabbing of a 40-year-old cyclist in Richmond Park in September 2004 makes clear. The accompanying commentary suggested, without stating it categorically, that the series of attacks around London over a six-month period might all be blamed on people with mental illness, despite the lack of evidence. Even the leader article on the same day suggested that 'this case suggests that the weight given to even a small risk that a patient will prove dangerous needs to be increased and, with the Mental Health Bill now being considered, the procedures for approving a release rewritten to protect the public better'.* Madeleine Bunting, writing in *The Guardian* in 2004,† looked at the portrayal of mental health in the media: 'The public association of mental ill-health with violence is reinforced almost daily in the British media. One study found that two-thirds of all references to mental health in the media included an association with violence; in the tabloids, 40 per cent of such references are liberally sprinkled with

---

* *Evening Standard* (3 September 2004).
† Madeleine Bunting, 'The Last Taboo', *The Guardian* (5 July 2004).

derogatory terms such as "nutter" or "loony". In fact, for every murder by someone with a psychiatric disorder, 70 people are killed in car accidents. Men between 16 and 30 are more likely to commit a murder. Yet no one suggests that cars be banned or young men be locked up, unlike the extraordinary "lock 'em up" response to those with mental disorders.'

Nevertheless, the summary report on attitudes to mental illness published in 2000 by TaylorNelsonSofres shows that the vast majority of the public do in fact have a sympathetic and caring view of mental illness. Some 90 per cent of respondents thought we should adopt a far more tolerant and caring attitude towards people with mental illness in our society, unlike government's less tolerant, risk-averse attitude. The same survey showed that 90 per cent of respondents disagreed with the statement that increased spending on mental health services is a waste of money, whilst 85 per cent agreed that people with mental illness have been the subject of ridicule for far too long.

So public attitudes appear to be changing, though not fast enough. The image, for some, of the frightening Big Black Beast is still there. For the person with mental health difficulties, the Big Black Beast is the representative of the mental health services system who will compulsorily pump him full of chemicals he does not want, and confine him physically and pharmacologically in an unkind and repressive environment. At the same time, the general public still fears those with mental illness, though we do not fear the potential murderer in the family, or the gratuitous violence brought about by drinking binges.

Mental health workers are also often afraid. They have to conduct risk assessments – itself an uncertain business. Yet, just as in the 'age of reason' of the eighteenth century, reason escapes us and we are driven to lock up and confine mentally ill people, physically and by medication, with a lamentable absence of kindness and care. Fear is rising. Risk is seen as avoidable. If we lock them up, cosh them with medication, they will not hurt us.

But people with mental illness are part of us. They are part of our society, part of our world. They need to be with us, in our communities. For we too go mad, one in every six of us. We too take risks, and expose ourselves to danger – far greater than any mentally ill person could expose us to – by driving cars, by drinking alcohol, by walking through city centres late at night.

How we treat people who are mentally ill will come to be seen as the ultimate test of the twenty-first century. As Vincent Browne put it in the *Irish Times*:* 'What is it about our society that the most vulnerable – whether they be people suffering from mental illness, Travellers, refugees, the homeless, lone parents, people in poverty – are the most disregarded?'

Are we reasonable? Scientific? Kind? Caring? Prepared to assess danger and act upon it? Or are we happier with the strange stories, with the fear, of the myth of the big monster out there? If it is the latter, then it is because we do not want to face the truth that the violence we face is not, to any great extent, at the hands of strangers. But perhaps that is too difficult and the myth helps us to forget what it is we should really fear:

---

* 'Benefits in presidential campaign', *Irish Times* (1 September 2004).

the relationships in our families, our streets, our homes, and what makes them go wrong, with violent endings.

So what do we need to do?

First, we need to recognize that we cannot get rid of all risks, and that locking up large numbers of people with severe personality disorder is probably not going to avoid any, or many, terrible deaths.

Second, we need to enthuse those who work in mental health with a new zeal to really support and help those in their care. This means more than simply giving out drugs, with all their side effects. It means far more cognitive and other psychological therapies and interventions. It means ensuring the provision of decent housing, daytime activity and work, and ways of having and keeping a social life.

Third, we need to recognize the episodic nature of much mental illness, and be prepared to allow those who experience it to work when they are well enough, and to admit to a crisis, and get instant help, when they need it.

Fourth, we need to support those who care for those with mental health problems, recognizing that they bear a huge burden and often need a break from the constant pressure.

Fifth, we need to understand that most people who suffer from enduring and severe mental illness are not violent to anyone else, and that they are far more likely to kill themselves than anyone else – which is an avoidable tragedy.

Lastly, we need to encourage the attitude – which seems to be growing – that shows a greater understanding and sympathy towards the mentally ill, and encourage the befriending of people with enduring mental illness, whose lives are so often painfully isolated. Instead of fearing them, we should be befriending them and making sure that they can cope.

THREE

THE YOUNG AND VULNERABLE

As a congregational rabbi in the late 1970s and early 1980s, I came into contact with the care system for children more often than I would have believed possible in a middle-class congregation. Partly, it was over individual children within the congregation, and in most cases when there was a question there turned out to be no case to answer. But in a few cases, it was quite different. We had, within the ambit of the congregation, children who were seriously neglected, children who were physically and sexually abused, and children who were desperate about their circumstances. As they moved towards adulthood – so called, at 16 – and knew they could leave the care of their foster parents or children's home, they made a break for freedom, though what lay ahead of them was quite unclear.

I also met, at that time, some remarkable people who were acting as foster parents to difficult and troubled teenagers. In one particular case, a couple had fostered children, and adopted some of them, for nearly thirty years, ending only when they were in their late fifties and the husband began to lose his hearing. But their 'kids' kept coming to see them until the end – a dramatic demonstration of how good, continuous foster care can form relationships for disturbed kids whose natural parents were unable to cope or wanted nothing to do with them.

This chapter is about how we treat children who are troubled and in our care, and why their achievements are generally so low. It looks at the history of child protection and asks whether the decision to take children into care is a sensible one in all circumstances.

I shall look at how social workers are increasingly ground down, and argue that all of us need to take some responsibility for the children who are collectively in 'our' care. I shall also look at child sexual abuse and suggest that this has made it virtually impossible for any ordinary, decent outsider who is not a professional to take an interest in the care of children, with the result that children are all the more exposed to the possibility of abuse within the system.

I shall ask what we think we are doing when we allow children and young people to leave 'our' care if we are unable to maintain the contact with them they need until they are way past their twenty-second birthdays and gradually acquiring the life skills to see them through.

I shall question whether the present care system works to anyone's benefit and, if not, how best we might change it. Finally, I shall ask why we do not appear to like children and young people much in the UK, why we are prepared to tolerate Anti-Social Behaviour Orders for troubled young people, and why society in general is disinclined to stick up for the young.

We have a strange attitude to children in Britain. Children were given legal protection relatively late in the UK, and we still prefer children to be seen and not heard. Our obsession with the conventional family leads to us blame single mothers of unruly children for not 'controlling' their children without asking what happened to the father.* The stranger who might prey on our children is feared, yet the absent father, the mother who abandons her children, or the family that just can't cope, are blamed rather than feared. We want ASBOs (Anti-Social Behaviour Orders) for unruly teenagers, taking power away from parents and leaving them feeling inadequate and unsupported, yet we still relish the thought of the family – if it is the two-parent conventional model, of course. At the same time, many of us are now loathe to have children at all and increasingly see children as a nuisance. Britain is not a family friendly country, and parents often see themselves as pariahs when out

---

* Celia Brayfield, 'The death of the family?' *The Times* (12 October 1998).

with their children.* Indeed, we are so negative about children in Britain that our fertility rate is below China's, which has a one-child policy. We bear 1.64 children per couple, which suggests that children are deeply unpopular, even though there are many reasons why people may choose not to have children as well as for not liking them. Yet the question we keep asking ourselves, if we think about children at all, is whether children make us happy, as Mary Riddell put it so well.† The question, she argues, should be the other way round: 'Do we make children happy?' And the answer is that we do not. Families are stressed, and messages about children are mixed. You are supposed to control your own children, yet, when you need a break, you fear leaving the children, with a stranger. Family friendly policies are welcomed by some but resented by others. The strain all this puts on families, including financial pressures, particularly on one-parent families, is huge. Children get beaten

---

* A. Frean, 'Parents are pariahs of modern Britain', *The Times* (20 October 2000).
† Mary Riddell, 'Childhood betrayed', *The Observer* (16 November 2003).

and abused in their families, but often we cannot intervene if the family is not considered to be problematic in any way. Even where intervention occurs, social workers get blamed for what goes wrong, and receive little praise for their efforts to help. And we still see one or more murders a week of children by their parents.

As government promises us a reorganization of children's services in the wake of the horrific Victoria Climbié abuse case, one might be left asking what this will achieve if there are too few social workers who have too little respect and are too undervalued by government and by the public. Most social workers I have ever met have been remarkably devoted people, truly committed to serving the least able and the most vulnerable. Yet their role has become less that of a friend to those in need more akin to that of a policeman. At present we have a risk-averse society more concerned with stopping one child murder – however awful – than with supporting dozens if not hundreds of vulnerable youngsters via a system that places full trust in the judgement of professionals. The more that the need for independence of thought and judgement is removed from social workers, the less truly committed people are likely to want to do the job – no matter how many re-structurings are attempted.

Since the 1980s social workers have taken a heavy battering as details of child murder after child murder become public and sensationalized. Yet the publicity never deals with the hundreds and thousands of children whose interests have been well served by these very social workers who are held up to scorn and ridicule. An opinion survey carried out by Gallup after the Jasmine Beckford and Tyra Henry cases of 1984, but before the Heidi Koseda case came to court in 1985, demonstrated that 45 per cent of those questioned had read or heard something to make them view social workers less favourably.* As with mental health professionals, social workers respond by making greater efforts to cover themselves against criticism by being even more governed by bureaucratic procedures, rather than relying on their own judgement. Indeed, some argue

---

* B. Deer, 'Panic is not a solution', *The Times* (29 September 1985).

that they are so concerned with their own reputation and well-being that they may neglect precisely the vulnerable individuals they are there to protect.† The sensitive – and by no means easy – task of social workers and others involved in child protection is giving way to procedure-driven practice – and still there are disasters, because this is not, and can never be, a risk-free business.

The public is disturbed and upset by the abduction and murder of children by strangers, as in the case of Jessica Chapman and Holly Wells. But when a murder is carried out by the child's own parents – and these run at something like one a week – we are somehow less disturbed. Sarah Payne's death led to a campaign for the death penalty for those who commit such crimes, and the then editor of the *News of the World*, Rebekah Wade, renewed calls for 'Sarah's law' in the wake of the Soham killings. Soham itself became a place of pilgrimage for thousands of people, who brought flowers and signed special books of condolence. It was a bit rich when the *Sun*

† Anne Dempsey, 'Too scared to keep children safe?' *Irish Times* (26 July 2004).

233

also asked rhetorically, 'What kind of people can treat such a terrible tragedy as a peepshow?' after all the publicity it had given to it. But there are no peepshows for the children who die at their own parents' hands, and we rarely call for 'something to be done' about the parents – often fathers – who kill their children. Social workers often get the blame for not knowing a family was at risk. Yet how can they always know? That is a particularly difficult call if we continue to believe, as we do, that the conventional two-parent family is a safe haven for children.* Yet the father in a conventional family who kills his children is as much a murderer as the stranger who preys on children playing alone.

Meanwhile, the blaming of mothers in one-parent families is matched by a readiness to accuse men of child abuse, something that is increasingly deterring young men from a career in teaching or in other careers where contact with children is the norm but which will not deter the determined paedophile. It has reached the point where, in her

---

* Dea Birkett, 'If it's daddy, we don't care', *The Guardian* (20 July 2000).

advice column, the usually sensible Virginia Ironside advises a young man who enjoyed working with children abroad not to train to become a teacher in the UK because of the risk of accusations of child abuse.* So men are perceived as risky, but children need fathers. Two-parent families are safe, but fathers in them sometimes kill their children. This cannot be a sensible view of the world, and it is certainly not a coherent one. Children are innocent, but they are also tearaways who need Anti-Social Behaviour Orders served on them. It does not make sense.

Concepts of Childhood

Some would argue that we do not really believe in childhood at all, and that the whole concept of childhood developed relatively late. I find that hard to believe, given the attitudes to maturation ceremonies in the earliest of societies. If you have a maturation ceremony, suggesting you are now ready to join the adult world, the assumption must be

---

* Virginia Ironside, *The Independent* (17 November 2003).

that you were hitherto not an adult but a child. Even when people point out that children were dressed in miniature adult clothes, I think they forget the absolute abundance of what appear to be children's toys and babies' rattles from the earliest periods. And there have been rules about what one might and might not do with one's children for millennia – including a duty to feed one's children (to be found in the Talmud, Ketubbot 49a–b), an obligation to educate one's sons (Mishnah Avot 5.21), and questions about how – and whether – one could force one's daughter into marriage. (Talmud Kiddushin 44b, though some of the rabbis were opposed to child marriage in Talmudic times, and thought marriage should wait till the girl was grown up and could express an opinion. That view did not prevail.)

Philippe Ariès, in his *Centuries of Childhood*, suggests that the concept of childhood is a cultural invention. He argues that children were not considered different in kind from adults in the medieval world and were moved into adult society as soon as they could function without their mothers. Children certainly had to work – all evidence points to adults and children working in the fields together. But there did not seem to be any difference between them except strength and endurance.

In the Renaissance period, things changed. Children were seen, in the Christian West, as products of the original sin of adults in sex, as well as evidence of God's creation, and thereby innocent. So children began to be separated from the adult world and, especially boys, placed into schools, the view being that they should be kept secluded from society and trained – often with cruel discipline – to become part of adult society.

In the seventeenth century, Puritan parents often treated their children harshly as a way of correcting their ignorance and natural sinfulness. Educating them out of ignorance and beating their evil propensities out of them were the two parts of parental duty towards children. But with the Enlightenment in the eighteenth century came a new way of thinking about children. Both John Locke and Jean-Jacques Rousseau believed, in slightly different ways, that children were born innocent. The same view is held by Judaism and Islam, and may explain a slightly less punitive attitude to children in those faiths. John Locke argued that children were born as a kind of blank slate and that if you could improve the environment and the experience of children you could improve what they would become in adult life. It was the ultimate statement of optimism, in accord with the Enlightenment view of the perfectibility of human beings. Locke had strong views about what constituted good child rearing practice: 'Plenty of open air, exercise, and sleep, plain diet, no wine and strong drinks, not too warm and strait clothing, specially the head and feet kept cold.'

For Locke, parents were both nurturers and teachers, and the teaching needed to start early with a gradual introduction to what is lovable and praiseworthy in order to encourage 'vigour, activity and industry'.

Rousseau took things further. Locke wanted to teach children to control their natural impulses through reasoning and education. Rousseau gave pride of place to the child and his/her natural instincts. He thought children would know intuitively what is right and what is wrong, and that they would discover what was possible through their interaction with nature and natural powers. Children are adaptable, and can compromise between what they want and need and what their environment demands of them. For him, the child would adapt to the outside world, but the outside world would also be changed by the child. He wanted children to be free, within certain limits, and rejected parental sanctions. This view of the child as naturally good and able to discern what is right and wrong was proved misguided all too quickly. During the Victorian period, though children were still regarded as miniadults, able to work as soon as they could leave their mothers' apron strings, the idea that they should be treated with kindness, and that they should have a well regulated life, was beginning to take hold.

The history of the children no one wanted is very different and starts in post-medieval times with the foundling hospitals. Before that, as John Boswell makes abundantly clear in his masterly work on the subject, *The Kindness of Strangers*, unwanted children were abandoned as a matter of course. It was in the late medieval period that foundling hospitals began to be established. Children were taken in off the streets and given to nurses to be looked after. The boys were taught a trade, the girls prepared for a life of service, or even marriage. The hospitals were paid for by city authorities and private philanthropy, and no one looked too closely at the appalling death rates of the infants in the early foundling hospitals. In the fifteenth century this ranged from 25 to 60 per cent; but as the centuries went on, the mortality rates rose. In Rouen in the eighteenth century, 91 per cent of infants and 84 per cent of all children admitted to the foundling hospitals died, whilst in Paris 77 per cent of children in foundling hospitals died before the age of 12, compared with around 28 per cent of children growing up in their own homes. The life of the foundling hospital was, as Boswell puts it, 'neatly organised, modern, civic, discreet and deadly'. Children were surplus to requirements. It was better if most of them died. And die they did. Even Rousseau gave five of his own children, apparently quite casually, to a foundling hospital, though he is thought to have regretted doing so later on.

But the mood was changing. Children were dying like flies in the foundling hospitals and they were working hugely long hours, first in the fields and later in the factories of industrialized Britain. However, change came about as the result of the efforts of a few enlightened campaigners, notably Robert Owen, who, in 1811 got the Cotton Mills and Factories Act through Parliament, which prohibited children under the age of nine from working in cotton mills and restricted other children to a twelve-hour day, as well as the 1825 Act, which gave the children half an hour for breakfast and an hour for lunch, and stopped any magistrates who employed children from adjudicating on matters to do with the Act. In 1847 Lord Shaftesbury persuaded Parliament to pass the Ten Hours Act restricting the labour of children to ten hours a day, with a maximum of fifty-eight hours a week during the daytime. He was also successful in forbidding the underground employment of women and children under the age of 10 in the Mines Act of 1842 and, with others, got the banning of children under 16 as chimney sweeps through Parliament in 1840. Concern was growing about cruelty, and about the state of the health of the nation's children. But families still needed their children's income, or they could not feed them. Despite abandonment becoming increasingly rare, ill treatment was still widespread.

The first Act of Parliament, the Prevention of Cruelty to, and Protection of, Children Act, commonly known as the 'Children's Charter', to prevent cruelty to children was not passed until 1889. For the first time, the State could intervene between parents and children if parents were thought to be ill treating a child. Police could arrest anyone treating a child badly, and had powers to enter any home if a child was thought to be in danger. The Children's Charter also included guidelines to limit further the employment of children and outlawed children begging in the streets. It was quickly amended and extended to include mental cruelty, and to make it an offence not to take a sick child to receive medical attention (1894). But it was not until the twentieth century that juvenile courts were established (Children's Act 1908), children under 14 were prohibited from buying tobacco and alcohol, and foster parents were registered. The school leaving age went from 12 to 14 in 1918 and in the 1940s it went up to 15, rising to 16 in the 1960s. Incest become a criminal, rather than a religious, matter in 1908. In 1932, supervision orders for children at risk were introduced and in the following year all children's legislation was rolled up into one piece of legislation.

It was really in the twentieth century that the concept of childhood, with specific rights, including protection, was defined. Legally, until the twentieth century children were as accountable for what they did as adults: they were tried alongside adults and, if convicted, were jailed alongside adults, something that has not yet completely ceased, even now.

Over the course of the last hundred years children of all social classes have become more dependent on their parents for longer, even though the physical age of maturity has fallen dramatically, with girls now reaching the menarche by age eleven. At the same time, family size has decreased dramatically, so that children can often be assured of greater personal attention from parents. In the second half of the ninetieth century, the average family size for the poorer section of the population was seven or more children (of whom some would not survive). By the middle of the twentieth century, only 2 per cent of the population would be in families of seven or more children, and most children survived. Children are now the subject of study, with swathes of advice on childhood, child rearing, and child development. Sigmund Freud invented the idea that infantile experience would define the character of the adult. From seeing children as either inherently sinful or an empty vessel, by the twentieth century they had become impressionable creatures whose future happiness and prospects lay in the right start. The wrong start, the wrong sort of parents or foster parents, the wrong upbringing, the use of violence, all gradually became matters for the State as children's rights and interests grew in importance.

In 1948, in the great days of welfare optimism, the Children Act was passed, which created a children's committee and a children's officer in every local authority. This followed the outcry over the death of 13-year-old Dennis O'Neill at the hands of his foster father in 1945. Consciences were pricked. This was a child who had been in 'our' care. In 1944, the Education Act established universal free education up to the age of 15, with the division into grammar schools, which were highly selective, and secondary moderns for the rest. But the principle behind the provision of free education, alongside a health service free at the point of use, was that everybody, especially children, had the possibility of reaching the heights of society. If things went wrong, the State would be there, to help and, if necessary, protect.

Taking children into care, usually as a result of neglect, poverty, or family breakdown, has been the norm for some fifty years or more, and really started with children in the workhouse in the nineteenth century, when destitute children would be farmed out as maids or as farm labourers to local people. That attitude to children was remarkably long lived: even in the 1950s and 1960s, respectable, responsible, and apparently caring children's charities and the

State would send children to 'the colonies', largely to Australia and Canada, ostensibly for a 'better life', often without the children knowing that they had at least one parent alive. Even though doubts about this practice had been raised in a 1956 report, the numbers increased until 1967. Some of those children were desperately abused, by, for instance, the Christian Brothers in Australia, as has been documented by Philip Bean and Joy Melville in their book *Lost Children of the Empire*. The main fact, however, is that the State and children's charities sent young children half way across the world, without telling them they had families back home.

The way the State and the public have shown concern about the welfare of children has varied from period to period. In the last fifty years, it has shifted from violent physical abuse to sexual abuse in the home, from abuse in care homes to killings in foster care and accessing child pornography on the Internet. High-profile police crackdowns, such as the international Operation Ore, show that many people, from all levels of society, access child pornography. One celebrated case was the rock star Pete Townshend in

2002. He was named in a leaked list of suspects passed by the FBI to the Metropolitan Police. Over six thousand British names were netted by the end of Operation Ore, all people who had used their credit cards to access obscene online images of children. They included a judge, several policemen, and others in respected positions. Townshend confessed to a throng of reporters gathered outside his home that he had on one occasion used his credit card to access child porn but argued he had done it for research, adding that he had been sexually abused as a small child. He was lucky. All that happened to him was that his computers, diaries, DVDs and videos were removed and returned four months later, with a caution from the police. He also had his name placed on the Sex Offenders' List for a minimum of five years and had a sample of his DNA taken. Children's charities argue that some hundred or so children may have been saved from abuse as a result of Operation Ore. Teachers, lawyers, policemen, social workers ... Yet, even if these people were all arrested, charged, and found guilty, we have no idea what to do with them. Prisons are overcrowded, and treatment centres barely exist; and child protection is still relatively low on the police's pecking order of crimes to investigate, compared with murder and other crimes against the person. So the sexual abuse of children will continue, despite attempts to stop it, and so will the downloading of child porn.

Internet pornography? Child sexual abuse? Rape? Violence against children? Neglect? The measures put in place over the course of the twentieth century to protect children have clearly not always worked. In 1968 and 1970 there was a major reorganization of social work, and all the different provisions for children were amalgamated into social services departments. Social workers became generalists, rather than the specialists they had been formerly. Yet still most children at risk seem not to have been known to the authorities. Even more worrying is how children are treated when they *are* known to the local authorities.

There has been a long line of inquiries, going back over thirty years, into the failure to protect children from their own parents, step-parents and carers. The list of failures makes depressing reading. It starts with Maria Colwell in 1973. Maria was beaten to death by her stepfather when she was aged seven, despite thirty calls made by neighbours to the local social services department in Brighton. In the wake of Maria Colwell's death and the subsequent inquiry, Area Child Protection Committees were set up in every area in England and Wales, charged with drawing together efforts to protect children at risk.

Then came the case of Jasmine Beckford, in the London borough of Brent, who was killed by her stepfather in 1984. She had been systematically starved and beaten, and the stepfather had already been convicted for assaulting her younger sister. She was only seen once by a social worker, despite the fact she was only four years old and could not be checked on at school. Louis Blom-Cooper's investigation and the inquiry report argued that her social worker was at fault.

Early the following year there was the case of Heidi Koseda, aged five, who was starved to death after being put in a cupboard and left by her mother and her stepfather. Her mother, who was of very limited intelligence, admitted manslaughter; the stepfather was convicted of murder. The NSPCC did not investigate several reports from neighbours, and the NSPCC inspector concerned fabricated reports.* Her grandmother also tried to alert the authorities.

The following year, 1986, there was the case of Kimberley Carlile, aged four, starved and beaten to death, in Lambeth, by her stepfather, who frustrated all attempts to investigate her state and who obviously intimidated social workers and health workers. The inquiry found four key health and social care staff had failed to apply the necessary skill, judgement, and care. These were the terrible days of Lambeth Council, when the social services were in complete chaos. In 1989, the Children Act gave every child the right to protection from abuse and exploitation, as well as the right to inquiries to safeguard their welfare. The view then was that children are usually best looked after within their own family. It is that central

---

* Sunday Times (29 September 1985).

tenet that is now gradually being challenged.

In 1992, Toni Dales, aged three, died from head injuries after being thrown over a wall by her mother's lover. The report into her death cited failure by social services, health services, the police, the educational and probation services – everyone, in fact, who could and should have been involved with the family. The same year, Leanne White, aged three, was beaten to death by her stepfather after suffering 107 external injuries. The subsequent inquiry concluded that her death could have been prevented if social services had responded to reports from her grandmother and neighbours that she was at risk.

In 1994, Rikki Neave, aged six, was found strangled, having been on the council's at risk register for ages. His mother, who was a drug addict, had asked social workers to take her son, but they had failed to do so. She was jailed for seven months for cruelty and the report found 'a legacy of incompetence among social services chiefs'.

In 1997, Lauren Creed, aged five, died after being thrown downstairs and jumped on by her stepfather. An inquiry by the Norfolk Area Child Protection Committee showed system-wide failures – probation, social services, police and the health services.

In 2000, Lauren Wright, aged six, died from a blow to her stomach inflicted by her stepmother, who was found guilty of manslaughter, as was her father. An inquiry found that interagency co-ordination was ineffective and that social workers had not acted with due urgency. In 2000, there was also the most famous, and perhaps most depressing, case of all, when Victoria Climbié, aged eight, who had been brought to England by her great-aunt, sent by her parents in the hope that she would get a better life here, was starved, beaten, and trussed in a bin bag. The great-aunt and her boyfriend were both jailed for murder, in a case where, as will be discussed below, Victoria had come into contact with four sets of social services departments, three housing departments, two police protection teams, two hospitals, and a NSPCC family centre, not to mention numerous clergy. Yet none of them had realized how very wrong things were for her. Lord Laming, in his inquiry report published in January 2003, insisted that the weaknesses in procedures and actions that led up to Victoria's murder were not unique. It could happen again. Her death was an indictment not only of social services, but also of the two specialist child protection police teams, the hospitals which treated her injuries but did not raise the alarm, three housing departments which dealt with her aunt, and a NSPCC child and family centre which failed to respond to a referral. There were at least twelve occasions when a minor and quite basic intervention could have made a difference.

Since then there have been more cases, including in 2002 Ainlee Walker, aged two, who died at the hands of her parents, and had an astonishing sixty-four separate injuries, including cigarette burns. Her parents were jailed for a total of twenty-two years. The report said that health agencies, the housing department and the police had all had serious concerns but had not passed them on to social services. Then, in 2003, Natalie Mills, aged 15, was assaulted and killed by her boyfriend. Though social services were responsible for her, Natalie had not been allocated a specific social worker because of a shortage of staff. The review of her case criticized 'significant actions or non-actions' by social services.

In 2004 there came the Toni-Ann Byfield report, after her death, aged seven, whilst in the care of Birmingham social services. She had been with her alleged father, Bertram Byfield, a known crack dealer, in his bed-sit in the London borough of Brent. The report criticized the failure of Birmingham social services, guardians, and the Immigration service; but the biggest criticism was levelled at Birmingham social services for moving Toni-Ann, against the law, to her alleged father's girlfriend in London, without the proper checks, so she could be near her father, and for failing to maintain weekly visits. They were also criticized for failing to communicate with colleagues in the London borough of Brent. The failure to talk to the police meant that social services, who hoped eventually to reunite Byfield with his alleged daughter (it has since emerged that he was not her father), did not realize he was part of a ruthless and organized gang of drug dealers who operated between Jamaica and

London and that he had already survived one assassination attempt. The cold-blooded killing of Toni-Ann, as a form of execution, shocked even those who deal regularly with Yardie crimes and led to impassioned calls for an end to such violence at her funeral (jointly with Bertram Byfield's) in Birmingham. The bishop who led the service, Derek Webley, got a standing ovation from mourners as he begged for criminals in the black community to end the cycle of violence and drug dealing, as well as saying that black communities should not settle for the negative images of them simply because of a minority caught up in crime.* The whole affair has been a nightmare for social services in Birmingham, who have admitted many mistakes. But the things that went wrong were precisely the same as in the case of Victoria Climbié.

It was a chapter of disasters, but the most significant thing about it was that it came hard on the heels of the Climbié inquiry, when social workers were already feeling worn down by the constant attacks upon

---

* *Daily Telegraph* (25 October 2003).

them and by a lack of public support. After the Climbié inquiry, the Secretary of State for Education admitted that pressure on staff was enormous and many have said the caseload social workers carry is unmanageable. A national survey reported in *The Observer* in May 2004 revealed that 17 per cent of children's social worker positions are vacant, rising to 60 per cent in some areas. In Birmingham, the authority so roundly criticized by the Byfield report, things were so desperate that they hired fifty Zimbabwean social workers in 2003. The Secretary of State, Charles Clarke, argued that 'Professional social workers have felt very battered about as a result of terrible events that have happened – of which Victoria Climbié's case is obviously one. Morale in the profession is and has been low, and there is a feeling that they are bearing the responsibility for some of the toughest problems in society.'* Yet we need to attract senior, responsible, and able social workers into child protection work, encourage them to stay in front-line work, and reward them appropriately. Yet

---

* Quoted in *The Independent* (30 April 2004).

two-thirds of local authority social service departments were struggling to recruit the social workers they needed to implement the measures required of them to tighten safeguards for children in care after 'Quality Protects' came into force back in 2000, because 40 per cent of posts remained unfilled.† To add to this, the government now has new powers to take over failing social service departments and hand them to more competent managers, which presumably would have happened to Birmingham had these powers been in place when the Byfield tragedy happened.

Yet some political leaders have praised Lord Laming for putting the responsibility for the tragedy of Victoria Climbié on senior managers. All too often it is junior staff who are disciplined and sacked, as happened in the Climbié case, whilst senior managers protect themselves from attack by laying the blame at their staff's doors. In the Victoria Climbié case Haringey council, with its senior paid managers and its senior local politicians, came in for severe criticism, es-

---

† David Brindle, 'Staffing crisis hits child protection plan', *The Guardian* (31 January 2000).

pecially for the ways, once the inquiry started, it failed to produce relevant papers. Lord Laming was scathing about the lack of responsibility taken and shown by those who should have been accountable, though the Chief Executive of Haringey council at the time, Gurbux Singh, did finally accept 'corporate responsibility' for the failures of the council. But he did not believe there was anything he could have done to prevent the tragedy. Counsel to the inquiry, Neil Garnham QC, said: 'There is continuous moving of responsibility and nobody has said, "Sorry, I messed up."' The Laming report, furious at this, called for a fundamental change in the mindset of managers, arguing that the failure of Haringey's senior managers and councillors to carry out their duties to protect children adequately was an important contributory factor in the mishandling of Victoria Climbié's case. The report continued: 'Never again should people in senior positions be free to claim – as they did in this inquiry – ignorance of what was happening to children.'* Haringey council's

---

* Climbié Inquiry (January 2003).

leadership seemed pleased that the independent report by the former Chief Executive of Enfield Council had concluded that its poor performance was the result of incompetence rather than deliberate obstruction. But, as the former deputy leader of Haringey council pointed out in an article,† that very same report, published in December 2002, had noted that the Council was seen as 'not apologising, not taking responsibility, individually or collectively, attempting to transfer the blame to others and withholding information'.

To add to that, Haringey council was accused of attempting to rig a government investigation into the state of its children's services, when Department of Health inspectors sent a confidential questionnaire to a random sample of parents in the borough who had had experience of dealing with the council's social services department. But a council official got the names of parents in the sample and wrote to them all, offering to help fill in the forms and saying 'we have employed a team of administration staff to

---

† Ian Willmore, 'Passing the buck', *The Guardian* (4 February 2003).

help you complete the questionnaire at your home address if required'. It was only as a result of a parent telling opposition local councillors that this was happening that this came to light. The council argued that its officials had only offered to help parents who had difficulty understanding the questions.

Nor was it the council alone. Denise Platt (now Dame Denise), then Chief Inspector of Social Services and Lord Laming's successor in that post, decided not to send confidential Department of Health documents to the inquiry until after it finished cross examining witnesses. Lord Laming invited Denise Platt to attend the inquiry in July 2002 to explain herself, but she sent a barrister instead to read a statement apologizing for her mistake and denying any attempt at a cover-up. But Lord Laming was not satisfied and accused the government of withholding evidence that might have linked the child abuse tragedy to mistakes by the government's own Social Services Inspectorate. The point at issue was the quality assessment of an inspection of social services in Haringey, where staff were supposed to be monitoring Victoria Climbié's well-being. The inspection, by the Social Services Inspectorate and the Audit Commission, declared in November 1999 that service users were 'generally well served', but an internal review, in April 2001, said that the inspection presented an 'overly optimistic picture of Haringey's children's services'.

Cases like these have led to a call for children like these not to be left at home but instead to be properly taken into care. Instead of being 'at risk', they should be in children's homes, we are told, despite the clear evidence of systematic abuse of children in many children's homes over the years. We are caught between a rock and a hard place. The present system – of checks, care workers, protection and so on – does not seem able to protect vulnerable children, but removing them into children's homes does not seem to succeeding in doing so either.

The statistics are pretty depressing. There are around 79,000 children and young people in public care at any time in the UK, of whom 62 per cent live in 37,000 foster families. 'Looked after' children in England amounted to 68,000 in March 2003, a

2 per cent increase on the previous year. Of these, 3,400 children were placed for adoption, 5 per cent fewer than the previous year, but a significant (19 per cent) increase on five years before. Of the children in care, 41,100 children were in foster care in about 32,000 foster families in England, with a further 10 per cent in children's homes, including secure accommodation for the most troubled. There was some regional variation, depending presumably on the enthusiasm of local authorities for getting children fostered. Two-thirds of fostered children return home within six months, but that may well not be the end of the story. Children may return home, where care may be inadequate or neglectful or cruel, and then go back into foster care, very likely not to the same family.

But fostering is not without its problems either, despite the truly wonderful people who take it on. People who foster often have huge numbers of children going through their homes, such as Karen Lawry, whose story was told in *The Observer* in April 2004 and who has fostered 136 children so far. A recent study of foster parents by a leading charity, the Fostering Network, in April 2004 said that half of Britain's foster parents are paid nothing for what they do, and a further 40 per cent get less than the national minimum wage for a forty-hour week or more. The Fostering Network suggested that the poor financial recompense contributed to the shortage of foster families, which leads to vulnerable, and often difficult, children being moved too often and too far from their natural families. It also means the splitting up of brothers and sisters, and it might get worse. Although foster families are supposed to get allowances to cover the cost of caring, 63 per cent said the amount was inadequate; others said that even if the allowances were sufficient, it did not make up for the lack of a salary.* (A late government addition to the Children Act 2004 was the proposal to establish a national system of fostering allowances, but the rates were not determined and official imposition of these rates will be delayed until at least 2007.) The Fostering Network's findings should disturb govern-

---

* The Fostering Network, survey October 2003–April 2004, published May 2004.

ment greatly, as the shortage of foster parents looks set to grow as the number of children who need to be looked after increases.

Children often go through many foster placements, as in the case of one young adult called Jay Sweeney,† who had been in twenty-two placements in children's homes and foster care. His story makes depressing reading. At the age of nine he was mentally and emotionally abused. 'I was made to believe that anything that went wrong in the house was all my fault. I ended up having a nervous breakdown at the age of 10. The services didn't really do anything about it.' In a patchy, complicated childhood, Jay was not only unhappy and unsettled; he was also bullied, especially in a children's home. He slit his wrists – a powerful cry for help – and was diagnosed as clinically depressed at 14. After a placement that worked for eighteen months, he had a relationship breakdown and attempted suicide. Jay's story is not unique.

---

† 'I was bullied. It was like a prison', *The Guardian* (9 October 2003).

There are literally hundreds of stories of young people who have been in care, fostered, or in children's homes, to be found on websites and in books and magazines. It is as if some floodgates have opened and people can now talk about it in a way that many could not when they were younger. Indeed, many of the people writing about their experiences record how they were unwilling to tell people at school that they were in a children's home because they would be bullied and because there was real stigma attached to it. The children were often patronized by teachers, told they had no brains, and were without a social life because other children's parents were nervous about kids from 'that home', or were simply prejudiced against 'bad kids'. Even worse, in some children's homes, as recently as the late 1980s and early 1990s, the children did not have their own clothes and had to take their daily clothes from a communal store, which meant all the other children knew who they were. It caused a kind of shame and embarrassment few of them can forget.

On the BBC website (www.bbc.co.uk/parenting/takingcare) there are stories of children who adore their foster parents, such as Matthew, who plays for Grimsby Town Football Club and still lives with his foster parents at the age of 18. For the actor Neil Morrissey, the experience of being fostered was more mixed; but, like all the others, the experience of going into care was traumatic, whilst being with foster parents offered a degree of freedom that seemed inconceivable to someone from a children's home. James Gooding, presenter and photographer, also records being with foster parents who were 'very giving and caring', but believes that no one made enough of an effort to find out how he felt. He still feels there is not enough support for children who have been through the care system, a view that is echoed time and time again.

Yet in most of the stories, good foster parents are the ones who are remembered, plus a few social workers and volunteer mentors. Having good foster parents and then having to move on, when you have begun to feel loved, is one of the most often recorded traumas. But in the happiest of cases, children who had to leave foster parents, often to go back to their own parents, and then suffer another family breakdown, do tell stories of being reunited with loving foster parents and getting a second chance at life. There are several stories on the BBC website of people who went on to university, or became professional singers, dancers, or footballers, as the result of skilful, patient, loving fostering – often second go around. Not a few of these people end up as social workers and care workers, or adopt or foster children themselves, trying to repay the kindness and care they received.

In all the accounts, there are two defining themes. The first is the importance of being treated as an individual: good foster parents, social workers, or mentors could make you realize your dreams. Second, there was the feeling that you were on your own and had to do the best to make a life for yourself. That comes out strongly in the advice some of the people recording their experiences give to others who may be in care or about to leave care. But many of them may not realize that it was the foster parents, the social workers, or the teachers and mentors who believed in them and that this enabled them to have this strong sense that they could do anything. There is one classic example of this in an account by Shirley, who was in care for ten years after her parents split.* 'I believe my life is a success because of three issues ... [first of all it's down to] the auntie, Mrs Topping, of the children's home, who instilled this: "If you want it, go out and get it ..." Auntie was my very first personal mentor, she was the focal point of all our lives and she would always say "whatever you want to do, do it to the best of your ability ... if you want it go out and get it ..." There was this parishioner in the village, a lady called Midge Prendergast, and she lived in a very big house and I used to go to tea with her. She taught me to play Scrabble and to sit upright, and she walked and talked with me. She showed me there is another way of life I could have if I wanted it.' Though old-fashioned, the sense of being able to do what she wanted, and being able to create her own destiny, came from the woman who ran the children's home, and from a form of mentor who lived in the

* www.bbc.co.uk/parenting/takingcare/real07/shtml

268

village and took an interest, something that we seem to have lost.

The last, and saddest, reflection is on cruelty, which is still present in children's homes, sometimes from the staff but more often from other children who have been bullied and then bully others in turn. The underlying cruelty and dissociation from everyone else – no one to go to spend the night with, nowhere to invite people to – lingers on, and it is this sense that life in children's homes is far from ideal that has made many people feel that encouraging fostering, and particularly long-term fostering and adoption, is essential.

In 2002, the government tried to encourage greater rates of adoption in Britain as one way of helping children in care and those who have had multiple placements in foster families. Yet the Jays of this world do not want to be adopted and often have at least one parent who does care for them in some way, and for whom they care. The Adoption and Children Act 2002 allows unmarried couples and same-sex couples to apply to adopt a child jointly, whilst hitherto only one of the partners was allowed to be a child's legal guardian. It also set up a national adoption register as part of the government's aim to streamline adoption processes and get 40 per cent more children adopted a year. Most children on the register are from tradition-ally hard to place groups, including older boys, children with special needs, and those from ethnic minorities. After eight months, only 8 out of 317 children on the register had resulted in a match occurring, and after two years only 75 placements were made. Vari-ous local authorities, as well as the British Association for Adoption and Fostering (BAAF), have been deeply critical of the scheme and the way it has been run. BAAF's own earlier BAAF-link used to place about a hundred hard to place children a year, and there is a feeling that a formal national reg-ister may be scrapped, whilst some people argue that a national register of some kind might in fact still be very useful. There are also doubts about whether all children are suitable for adoption. Some may be too dam-aged to cope with being adopted, or even fostered. If that is the case, then more re-sources need to be poured into the care sys-tem to attract and retain more suitably qualified and caring staff. Yet the instinct of government is always to try to save money on social workers, which is one of the reasons that social workers find life so tough.

Plans for an Adoption Support Agency were announced in April 2004 with which all organizations involved in adoption are to register. The Agency will also help as an intermediary in tracing birth relatives under the Adoption and Children Act (2004). Originally, the government had wanted the system to work prospectively only, from September 2005, but there was such a fierce lobby from adoption organizations and groups representing young people that they changed their minds. This way, birth relatives can ask the Adoption Support Agency to act as an intermediary in tracing relatives and to find out whether contact would be welcome. The new system is based on consent, so that if the person traced says they do not want to meet a child or a parent, then the agency cannot pass on any details.

This is clearly a sensitive issue, but the government is moving the right way, especially on the issue of those who were forced to give up babies for adoption in the 1940s and 1950s, when having an illegitimate child was still a cause of great shame. Some of those birth parents and their children are desperate to see each other and to make contact before the birth parents get too old to enjoy it. It is clear that parents of girls who got pregnant in the 1940s and 1950s were often very harsh, sending their pregnant daughters away to some secret place, often to convents and hostels where they were very poorly treated. That experience has stayed with many of those birth mothers, who still deeply regret giving up their babies and still hope to find them. Reunion is not without its problems. Many adopted children, whose lives have not gone easily, bitterly resent the fact that they were 'given away'. Adoptive parents, too, who have done everything in their power for 'their' children, now find that birth parents have rights that were never thought of when they adopted in good faith. Indeed, adoptive parents often find that the child making contact with their 'real' parents destroys carefully built-up relationships. But it also sometimes lays ghosts to rest. It can be a salutary experience for adopted children to meet their birth parents. As this develops, one can see the changing concept of family, and of children's rights, playing out before us. And it will not be without pain, any more than fostering is without pain and trauma.

There is also real concern about private fostering, as well as about the national shortage of foster parents. Private fostering – which is particularly common for children from West African origins, who are sent to live with a distant relative or friend in England, like Victoria Climbié – holds all sorts of challenges and is usually not known to the authorities. Being sent to live with a distant relation is presumably predicated on a different view of the upbringing of children, with an assumption that children are, in some sense, everyone's responsibility. Yet, in the UK, they have increasingly become either their parents' private responsibility, or nobody's – children are a private matter and so private fostering, without checks, runs grave risks for those children for no one else will take an interest, as was tragically demonstrated in Victoria Climbié's case. Yet in the debate about the Children Bill, there was still resistance to licensing private fostering, despite serious concerns being raised. The government is currently reviewing the situation for four years before considering registration, out of fear that some of these arrangements will go underground and be even more difficult to police.*

But here we are with some 61,000 children in care in England, plus a further 18,000 or so in Scotland, Wales, and Northern Ireland, up some 22 per cent in England since 1994. Of these, 56 per cent are boys and their level of achievement in schools is dramatically poor. Why are they taken into care? The largest category of need was 'abuse or neglect', and the second largest 'family dysfunction'. The Scottish figures for child protection give one a clue as to what goes on and who abuses. Forty-eight per cent of the children who were subject to a case conference – of those referred for child protection inquiries – had their primary known or suspected abuser as their natural mother; a further 28.9 per cent had their natural father; only 3.6 per cent had a step-parent, and only

---

* Baroness Ashton, *Hansard* (30 March 2004).

a further 6.5 per cent the parent's cohabitee. Some 7.1 per cent were abused by other relatives, including siblings, whilst other people known to the child or the family made up a further 3.5 per cent, with only 2.4 per cent being someone unknown to the child or family. Of course, these statistics need to be handled with care, but the family's failing in some way is a key factor in taking children into care, whilst death of a child seems to be more often related to a step-parent or cohabitee than a natural parent, but nowhere near as often as some have suggested. Some children are in more than one category of need, for obvious reasons.

Eighty-one per cent of the looked-after children are white, 8 per cent mixed race, 7 per cent black, and 2 per cent Asian. Some 2,400 unaccompanied asylum-seeking children were being looked after, of whom by far the majority were in London and 49 per cent of whom were aged 16 or over. Of the children leaving care in general, 44 per cent of them had at least one GCSE or GNVQ compared with 96 per cent of all year-11 children, up 3 per cent from 2002 but still desperately worrying. Further depressing details include, from the 2002 figures, that 10 per cent of lookedafter children were cautioned or convicted during the year, three times the normal rate for all children in the age group, and that 50 per cent had on average reached level 2 at KS1, 40 per cent level 4 at KS2, and 22 per cent level 5 at KS3, which compares with 85 per cent, 78 per cent, and 66 per cent for all children in the relevant age groups.

The lack of specific provision for black and other minority children in care is particularly worrying. It is almost ironic, given the amount of accusations that social services departments have to bear about being politically correct, that so few of them have any policies and good practices for making specific provision for children from ethnic minorities in care. Despite government's good intentions, and the aim of new programmes and teams under the 'Quality Protects' badge, there is still no overarching obligation for local authorities to take serious responsibility for ensuring good support for young people from ethnic backgrounds. Research by the Family Rights Group in 2000*

---

* Audrey Thompson, 'Why are we being failed?' *Community Care* (4–10 May 2000).

276

suggested that it was only when political leaders and senior managers took a real lead in this area that anything got done to help these most vulnerable of children,

Meanwhile, in 1999, the Protection of Children Act was passed, aiming to prevent paedophiles working with children and requiring childcare organizations to inform the Department of Health about anyone known to them who is suspected of harming children or putting them at risk. From this came the constant checking which is carried out if anyone is to work or volunteer in any way close to children, a change which has delayed people starting work and deterred volunteers from working with children in a variety of ways. The jury is out on whether it does in fact stop paedophiles, but it was passed in the wake of the scandal in Islington's children's homes in the early 1990s, when a large number of children were sexually abused by council employees.

In 2001, the Scottish education minister, Jack McConnell, ordered a review of Scottish child protection after the inquiry into the murder of 3-year-old Kennedy McFarlane found a whole list of procedures missed and failures in care. An audit published the following year found that half of all children at risk of abuse and neglect in Scotland failed to receive adequate protection. In March 2004, Scotland published its children's charter, making it clear how carers and professionals working with children should respect children's rights.

After the Climbié inquiry, Margaret Hodge was appointed the first Children's Minister (June 2003) to howls of protest because she had presided over the social services department in Islington during the period when abuse had been rife in some of the authority's children's homes. The story was that Hodge, whilst Labour leader of Islington council, had presided over a regime that had ignored complaints made by Demetrious Panton in 1985 about being abused whilst in the council's care in the late 1970s and early 1980s. He did not get an official reply until 1989, when the deputy director of social services wrote saying that the council regretted what had happened but believed it wasn't its fault. In April 1990 a senior social worker, Liz Davies, and her manager, David Cofie, raised concerns about sexual abuse at one of

Islington's neighbourhood forums. They asked for extra staff to help them investigate but were refused – Hodge sent a memo to the director of social services saying the budget would not allow extra staff. Davies and Cofie continued to raise concerns, sending reports to senior managers and to the Area Child Protection Committee, which decided there was no case to answer.

So in February 1992 Liz Davies resigned from her job, having been ordered to place a 7-year-old boy in a home run by one of the people she had concerns about, and she went to the police. Meanwhile Demetrious Panton raised his case again, this time with Stephen Twigg, who was a councillor in Islington at the time. Twigg has expressed regret at not taking all this more seriously. By October 1992, the *Evening Standard* began a series of reports alleging that dozens of children at two of Islington's children's homes had been or were being abused. Margaret Hodge accused the paper of 'gutter journalism' and rejected its evidence, before stepping down as leader of the council to become a consultant with PriceWaterhouse.

But she had been wrong. An independent inquiry led by the director of social services in Oxford, Ian White, found that Islington council had failed to investigate properly the allegations of sexual abuse and said that it was possible that many of the allegations were true and, even worse, that some of the abusers were still working in the field. At that time, of thirty-two named staff who were alleged to be involved in abuse, only four were disciplined. Two remained in post, including one working in childcare. The White report said that the way the council was run at the time of the allegations was disastrous.

When Margaret Hodge was appointed as Children's Minister in June 2003, a new campaign against her started. Liz Davies, the social worker who had resigned in disgust at Islington's inaction, went public with her anger over the appointment, but Hodge rejected calls for her resignation. Having acknowledged making one terrible error of judgement in the 1990s, she hoped people would understand. She then tried to block a BBC Radio 4 *Today* programme investigation into abuse at Islington's children's homes, writing to the then chairman of the BBC, Gavyn Davies, condemning the programme and accusing it of sensationalism. Mr Panton, who had spoken to the BBC, was someone she described as 'extremely disturbed'. Mr Panton said that Islington had repeatedly ignored claims that he had been abused as a child by Bernie Bain, head of the children's home he was living in, in 1978. Bain, described by the police as a 'brutal sexual abuser', later committed suicide. Mr Panton rejected Margaret Hodge's written apology for her remarks, saying they were not genuine. He demanded a public apology, a donation to a children's charity of his choice, and payment of his legal costs. The result was that, in late November 2003, Margaret Hodge issued a public apology to Mr Panton that was read in the High Court. But that was not the end of the story.

There was a strong desire, amongst a broad spectrum of opinion, to see Margaret Hodge toppled, both for what she was alleged to have ignored, and also because of the damage the row had done to her standing as the first Minister for Children. But no one could actually pin on her any knowledge of what happened to Demetrious Panton, as she had not been the leader of the council at the time, nor was she told about the abuse going on in Islington council homes when she did become leader, though Liz Davies says that she refused extra money to investigate when doubts were raised about the home and an individual. Abuse has also been reported and uncovered in many councils, from North Wales to Leicester, suggesting that it was not unusual for people who wanted to abuse children to work in children's homes during that period. Indeed, the allegations in North Wales were arguably much worse.

The Waterhouse Inquiry (February 2000) was the largest ever inquiry into abuse in children's homes, though the evidence it uncovered did not lead to further prosecutions beyond what had already taken place. The report described the children living in the Bryn Estyn home near Wrexham, North Wales, as living in purgatory. Victims welcomed the report – somewhat cautiously – and hoped it would protect future generations of children in care. After publication of the report, the government continued to search for twenty-eight former care workers, six of whom were convicted child abusers. The Prime Minister commented on the Waterhouse report saying: 'It is an appalling situation and an appalling catalogue of terror and tragedy inflicted on some of the most vulnerable children in our society', and he pledged to introduce tougher safeguards into the running of care homes. The Welsh Assembly's Health and Social Services Secretary, Jane Hutt, pledged an additional £2 million to support children in care in Wales, and argued that children should be listened to and more done to act on their concerns. The person then in charge of child care in Gwynedd, Gethin Evans, was especially criticized, along with social workers, care home staff, the local authorities of Gwynedd and Clwyd, and the Welsh Office, for failing to protect the children in his care after there was clear evidence of a paedophile ring that targeted hundreds of young people in care in the 1970s and 1980s.

In 1997, Sir William Utting, a former Chief Inspector of Social Services, described his review of the safeguards for children living away from home as a 'crash course in human (predominantly male) wickedness and in the fallibility of social institutions'.* He was investigating abuse in children's homes in Cheshire and North Wales since the 1970s and was appalled at what he found because he felt that much of what he was recommending had been recommended before, and that there had been such a long line of reports and inquiries into children in care that his should not have been necessary. But it was. Government accepted that many children had been dramatically let down by the system, leading to a series of reforms that are gradually, and not wholly adequately, being set in place now. But it was the whole system, social services, police, councils, councillors, the court system, schools, voluntary organizations, the news media, neighbours, the government's own Social Services Inspectorate, government departments, ministers, Parliament, and Uncle Tom Cobbley and all, who were held to be responsible in a speech the then Secretary of State for Health, Frank Dobson, made to the House of Commons in 1998. He contin-

---

* Utting, *People Like Us* (1997).

ued: 'Vulnerable children are the responsibility of us all.'† There was a cautious welcome for his words and for the promise of action which went with them. And action has been coming, slowly, except that much of it relies on a complex web of relationships between social workers and others.

There is also a chronic shortage of social workers, at least in part because they have been so blamed for all the child protection disasters that have occurred in recent years. Yet many of the people who have failed children worst of all have been staff in children's homes, as some of the big cases make clear and as Sir William Utting's report suggests. Indeed, as evidence to the House of Commons Select Committee on Home Affairs (31 October 2002) suggested, though the Crown Prosecution Service rejected a staggering 79 per cent of the institutional child abuse cases referred to it by the police, of the other 21 per cent that did go to trial convictions were achieved in 83 per cent of cases, the majority pleas of guilty. So the abusers knew what they were doing and

---

† Linda Steele, 'Good enough for your own kids', *Community Care* (12–18 November 1998).

could not deny it; the difficulty lay in the burden of proof, on the 'beyond reasonable doubt' test.

The Frank Beck Scandal

Leicestershire was the other area where widespread child abuse took place. Frank Beck was a children's home manager in Leicestershire who regularly and systematically sexually and physically abused around some two hundred children in his care. He was sentenced to five life sentences in 1991 and died in prison. Paul Gosling* suggested that there were similarities between North Wales and Leicestershire in that the abusers had some political influence (Frank Beck was a Liberal councillor) and he also suggested, though that is unsubstantiated, that there was a masonic presence at the top of both councils in these absolutely foul cases. But much more significant is that inspection and management of the homes was very weak in both cases, though in that of North

---

* 'The truth they didn't want to hear', *Community Care* (4–10 May 2000).

Wales some of the homes were in fact privately owned and run.

In the case of Frank Beck, however, who bullied children and staff in equal measure, it is strange that nobody ever took the complaints about him seriously. Staff may not have known about the sexual abuse, but they did know about the violent beatings, and yet they came to believe that Beck was acting in the best interests of the children in his care rather than reporting him to his line manager. Not only that, but when complaints did emerge, usually from outsiders such as students or temporary workers at the homes, Beck's managers refused to listen. Even worse, many children ran away, or tried to, from Beck's regime, but the police did not listen when they told them what Beck was like. Leicestershire social services did not follow its own rules for investigating abuse when Beck was prosecuted for an assault on a boy in his care, and did not realize (or ignored) that Beck had broken council rules by using corporal punishment. But he regularly beat the children in his care and kept a book of the punishments, which was there for his managers to see. But he was perceived – for all that – as someone who managed to control boys who were apparently uncontrollable: the drug users, the glue sniffers, the hardened juvenile criminals.

The question remains how he managed to get away with such a perverted regime, and why the children were simply not believed. He invented a form of therapy, regression therapy, where the children would be forced to dress up as babies in nappies and then bathed by adults, a wonderful opportunity for the sexual gratification of paedophiles in the name of doing good. There is no known form of regression therapy like this, yet people believed him. The sessions would lead to children throwing temper tantrums and needing to be restrained physically, often leading to sexual abuse.

In one case a child died. Simon O'Donnell, aged 12, apparently committed suicide by hanging himself, but it may well have been that he was throttled with a towel whilst he was raped. The coroner described the 'regression therapy' as 'fumbling in the dark' (without knowing how accurate he was being in his description) and suggested it should stop. But it continued, and Beck become an adviser to the social work course at the then Trent polytechnic, now Nottingham Trent University, to the Metropolitan Police Training College at Hendon, and to others.

Yet there was no basis to what he was doing, except to feed his own paedophile interests and those of others. His managers did not question the jargon he used; and the experts never argued with him since he seemed to have found a way of dealing with the most difficult of young people. He got away with it. And he got away with it because people decided not to question him, because his management was weak and trusting, because the police saw fewer young offenders coming back, and because the staff in his homes were too lily livered to report him or too cowed into believing that what went on was for the children's good. An insult to the name of care of children. But he was not alone, though almost certainly the worst case so far discovered.

Sexual abuse has become a major source of current concern – rightly so – but it has also led to a form of hysteria. Family life has been more and more the area of concern and there are many allegations of sexual abuse, not all of which turn out to be accurate or justified. There have been several well-publicized dawn raids on families, resulting in children being taken into care. In 1987, the situation in Cleveland hit the headlines when 121 children had been diagnosed as having been sexually abused and were removed from home on court orders. The inquiry into the case found that the consultant paediatrician had been mistaken in many of her diagnoses, too precipitate in her actions, and that greater consideration should have been given to the rights of parents and children. This was followed in 1991 by allegations of widespread satanic abuse on Orkney, where the evidence demonstrated that many children were, indeed, being brought up in less than ideal circumstances – hardly all that unusual – but that widespread satanic abuse could not be proven. All this smacks of the moral panic and hysteria of witch hunts. Yet sexual abuse was, and is, widespread, so the situation is far from straightforward, and without doubt some people accuse others of sexual abuse in a truly malicious way.

In 2002 the UN condemned the UK government for its attitude towards children and for its poor record on supporting them. In October 2003, the Children's Rights Alliance, a coalition of 180 charities and other organizations, warned the government and the public that Britain is still failing to protect some of its most vulnerable children from poverty, imprisonment, and neglect. For despite improvement in some areas, and despite the appointment of a Children's Commissioner for England, there are still too many children in jail, more than three thousand at any one time; parents are still allowed to hit their children, using the defence of reasonable chastisement, (one particularly criticized by the UN committee, but still defended by government); the State still labels many children troublesome and has invented Anti-Social Behaviour Orders without trying to investigate the problems underlying the behaviour. Meanwhile, too many children are being bullied and excluded from school, (more than nine thousand were excluded permanently in 2001–2 in England) and too many children are still living in poverty.

Carolyne Willow, coordinator of the Alliance – which includes major charities such as Save the Children and Barnardo's – argues that the UK has failed to protect the rights of the child in three key areas: juvenile justice, asylum, and corporal punishment. 'In these key policy areas, children's human rights are being sacrificed to adult public opinion. A human rights framework would take children out of party politics. It would put children's needs at the fore of policy development and, over time, transform attitudes towards children within and outside of government.'*

Runaways

A worrying fact is that we have a high rate of children and young people running away from home or being thrown out of home or care. There are some 100,000 a year who run away or are thrown out of home or care, of whom one in four is under eleven years old. As the government prepares to overhaul the whole child protection system, it is worth

---

* Quoted in Sarah Boseley, 'UK accused of failing child victims', *The Guardian* (9 October 2003).

remembering that there are no statutory services for children who run away, yet these are likely – especially the youngest ones – to be the most vulnerable of all. With all the worry about abuse in children's homes, and abuse in the home, it is curious that runaways receive so little attention.

A Children's Society survey showed that those children who run away before the age of eleven are more than twice as likely to be regularly hit by their parents, and almost twice as likely to be bullied at school. They are also far more likely to be in trouble with the police, to be in care, or to have learning difficulties. And those who run away early are also the ones who run away often, so that almost a quarter of those who started running away before the age of eleven ran away more than three times, compared with a mere 7 per cent of those who started running away after the age of eleven. To add to that, children who first run away before the age of eleven are likely to have an unstable home life with less than a third of them living with both birth parents by that age. Around a third of the children interviewed reported physical or sexual abuse of them or their siblings; parents' drug or alcohol problems were also common themes. Around a third of young runaways have actually absconded from placements in local authority care.

Most of those who go missing are between thirteen and fifteen, and nearly half first ran away from the family home, after a row or simply because the family was breaking down. Some run away to escape the peer pressure of children's homes, where older kids try to get younger ones to commit minor offences, take drugs, or become prostitutes. So they run, and the overwhelming evidence from the work done for *Going Missing: Young People Absent from Care* (1998) was a 'pervasive crisis of belief among many caregivers and social workers about their ability to prevent young people going missing and placing themselves at risk.' Yet the young people had been taken into care precisely to prevent them going missing and placing themselves at risk, a situation which our care system has done little to remedy even now.

Children who run away often feel that the unhappiness that drove them to run in the first place follows them into later life. Half of the early runaways experienced homelessness at 16 or 17, often as a result of being forced to leave home, and had the same sorts of high levels of mental health problems, drug abuse, and alcohol abuse as many of the most troubled young care leavers. Some had been in prison, and all had slept rough at some stage and had practised risky survival strategies, such as begging, stealing, using drugs and alcohol whilst on the streets, even selling sex. Despite government guidance saying that social services will have to agree formal protocols with the police and other agencies to combat child prostitution, no money has been made available for such measures, and this continues to be a major problem.* But because there are no statutory services for children who resist being taken into care or run away from their care placements, they tend to live on the streets until they are old enough for 'adult' agencies, such as Centrepoint, to help. Yet one in five of young people who came into contact with Centrepoint in 2002

---

* Nick Huber, 'Guidance says treat child prostitutes as victims', *Community Care* (25–31 May 2000).

had a history of running away. Some were the persistent runaways, known to outreach teams, social services, and the police, yet they could not use the Centrepoint young people's service till they reached the age of 16. This is serious. Children who come off trains from the north in London probably only wait some six hours before being approached by pimps or drug dealers, according to British Transport Police at King's Cross, and with a rash of very young prostitutes across our big cities, the danger is abundantly clear. An estimated 10,000 under-age children are employed to sell sex in the UK, according to the children's charity Barnardo's, of whom around 70 per cent are female. Two-thirds of the male prostitutes interviewed for the Barnardo's survey had been in council care. So refuges for young people can provide support, but by no means enough. Under the Children Act 1989, designated refuges can provide emergency accommodation for those under 16 without parental consent if they appear to be at risk of harm (as many of them are). But they can only stay for up to fourteen days continuously and no more than twenty-one days over any three-month period. And there are not enough of them – only one in London in late 2003, and that was rescued from closure by a combination of Westminster Council, the Greater London Association of Directors of Social Services, and others. GLADSS agreed to allocate some of the 'Quality Protects' money grant towards running the refuge, but its contribution has been reduced because the social services directors have begun questioning why they should pay the costs of runaways from other parts of the country. The Social Exclusion Unit published a report on young runaways in 2002 and recommended preventive work, yet thus far no one seems inclined to pay for it.

Meanwhile, one can read almost weekly accounts in the press, specialist and more general, about children who are carers for parents with severe disabilities, from mental illness to physical problems like multiple sclerosis. With the rise of one-parent families, the load on children has undoubtedly got greater. The Children's Society and others have tried to support young carers as much as they can, yet this is still a largely hidden issue, noticed more in schools when children fail to do homework or are constantly tired. The figures have jumped from an estimated 51,000 children providing substantial care for a relative in 1996 to more than 175,000 by the beginning of 2002.

Drugs And Poverty

Then there is the problem of drugs. Children are taking drugs from an earlier and earlier age – especially the runaways. With an estimated 4 per cent of children aged 11–15 trying a Class A drug (heroin, ecstasy, cocaine or crack) in the past year, and 22 per cent of all 15–18 year olds trying Class A drugs, and you have a a very troubled picture. The SEU report, quoted above, showed that 3 per cent of 11–15 year olds were taking drugs at least once a week, and a further 3 per cent once or twice a month, whilst at age 15, four out of ten children said they had taken at least one drug in the previous year. But a further 300,000 children live in a house-hold where at least one parent or carer has a serious drug problem, according to the Advisory Council on the Misuse of Drugs – some

3 per cent of all children. Add into that the very poor, on nohope estates where the attraction of drugs and gang life may be considerable because there is little else to do, and this rises to some 8 per cent of British children, according to Save the Children and the Centre for Research in Social Policy (September 2003). The government's own research suggests that nearly one in three children are poor, living in households with below 60 per cent of median income. By no means all of these children will get into trouble or take drugs. But it is clear that poor children are least likely to be happy with their appearance, with their lives, and with their prospects.

Anti-Social Behaviour

The activities of many children and young people give their neighbours real grief. Some, like Shaun McKerry, featured in an account by Mary Braid entitled 'Homing Pigeon Boy',* are a complete nightmare. Shaun barely went to school after primary school and carried out a series of offences

---

* *The Independent* (23 August 2000).

until he was finally sent down for four years in August 2000 for an armed raid on the post office in Leeholme, the village in which he grew up. He was brought up by his mother, Paula Hart, and though his father still lived locally, it was his mother who always accompanied Shaun to the police station or to court. Locals were celebrating the fact that she was moving away, since she had caused havoc by not controlling Shaun and his friends, who terrorized the locals and had endless parties and fights. Shaun was attacked by a vigilante group who were fed up with the authorities doing not enough, and his family say his kneecap was broken, and his ribs and skull fractured. As the locals breathed a sigh of relief as his mother and the family finally moved away, the fear is that he will only terrorize others instead. Such 'neighbours from hell' will be subject to new measures, including compulsory rehabilitation programmes in order to get rehoused, if the government has its way.* The idea is that they would live in a 'secure' council block for a few weeks or so, with

* Alan Travis, 'Nuisance neighbours face compulsory life skills lessons', *The Guardian* (1 June 2004).

other problem families, and have 24-hour counselling and family support. Some charities are questioning whether making it compulsory, rather than part of a deal to get support in exchange for better behaviour, is the right way forward. But the problem of families evicted for anti-social behaviour is certainly getting worse, and often the troubled children have had no help in the wake of the eviction.

Shaun McKerry is far from being a lone example. We read about disrespectful, amoral, wild, drug-dealing, alcohol-bingeing young people. They terrify local communities, like Shaun did, and they wreak devastation and destruction in their wake. The only thing to do about them, according to many commentators, is to get tough. A group of perfectly normal youngsters walking down the street are seen as frightening by their very presence, especially if they are boys. Yet this isolates them, and makes them frightened. They feel disapproved of, unwelcome. Many people are now seriously worried by this kind of negative stereotyping. A coalition of youth charities, from Barnardo's to the Children's Society, from the National Children's

Bureau to the NSPCC, and from the National Children's Homes (NCH) to NACRO, the crime reduction charity, have come together to try to reshape the debate around youth crime into something more sensible and positive.* At least part of this is due to the perennial fact that children who get into trouble are often the ones who have trouble at home – poor parenting, harsh or erratic discipline, family breakdown (ever more common), poverty and low educational achievement are all part of this. But perhaps most significant is the fact that young of-fenders are often victims of crimes them-selves.

Being a victim of crime at the age of 12 is one of the most powerful indicators that a child will offend at 15. The converse, sur-prisingly, is also true. A child who offends at 12 is likely to be a victim of crime at 15. So crime prevention and victim support in these age groups should be targeting the same people: simply arguing that we should get tough with offenders will not work. Indeed, it is arguable that being more compassion-

---

* P. Ennals, 'We are not criminals', *Community Care* (9–15 October 2003).

ate, and looking at the reasons young people offend, might be more helpful. Recognizing that young people are being pushed out of their communities, with nowhere to go, nowhere to feel safe, is a key part of that. Evidence is mounting that three out of four so-called problem children who exhibit classic symptoms of what we now term anti-social behaviour will turn out to be well-adjusted adults despite being written off by society.† So writing them off is not the answer: on the other hand, accepting them, befriending them, giving them somewhere they can call their own, might help.

Yet the common depiction of problem children – boys mainly, but increasingly also girls – enforces negative stereotyping. What worries many people is that the assumption is 'that the capacity to emerge as a human being from early loss or childhood deprivation seems no longer to be acknowledged as even a possibility, by anyone. Redemption (by education, for instance) is often out of

† Martin Bright, 'Most "problem" kids go on to thrive', *The Observer* (13 June 2004).

the picture.'* Yet the evidence cited above, that three out of four will turn out all right, ought to spur us into doing everything in our power to increase the proportion, to show these girls and boys other lives, other possibilities, giving them hope and a sense of a future they want to be part of.

ASBOs are not the answer – they make families resentful, like the mother of one 13-year-old, Michael Ashton, who has never been charged with a crime but who, being the subject of an ASBO, cannot stand in a prohibited street without committing a criminal offence. His mother works for the council and simply cannot believe that this can happen to a child who, she says, is 'being a child', wild and difficult though he may be. Or take the Ward sisters, who were banned from a large area of Gorton, in Manchester, and whose family had to move out of their house into private accommodation because of the ASBOs that had been issued. They were accused of using racist and foul language, threatening behaviour, and stealing. But will this help them get a job? Or live a

---

* Valerie Grove, 'No redemption for the rude girls', *The Times* (1 September 2004).

normal life? Eileen Ward does not think so: 'People won't give me a second chance. It's hard to get a job. They say, "We'll get back to you, Miss Ward." Only they never do.'†
ASBOs may make those who are terrorized by these kids feel better, but what will happen to the young people themselves? Are we simply moving a problem on to another area, instead of thinking of them as the community's children – as our children?

The other side of all this is the problem of bullying. One in twelve children in the UK are so badly bullied that their school work suffers, along with their further education prospects, their health, and their self-esteem. Bullied children are six times more likely than the average to contemplate suicide and a few actually do so.

There are examples of good practice, such as some of the Young People's Centres that have been growing up around the country, where children can talk about being bullied. The Tim Parry Johnathan Ball Young People's Centre in Warrington is one such example. At this centre, which appears like any

† Decca Aitkenhead, 'When home's a prison', *The Guardian* (24 July 2004).

youth club on the surface, there is a games room, a sports hall, an IT suite, a cyber café and canteen, plus arts, crafts, and cooking lessons. But what is unusual is the fact that there are social workers on hand who can offer advice and support for kids with problems and worries. There are several small rooms for private interview sessions and for therapy. The place is used by some 250 young people a week, increasing to double this number in the school holidays, with the age of users ranging from eight to twenty. What is significant is that the young people feel they can talk to the staff in an honest way, and those who have been bullied, or who have experienced several foster care placements, feel that they have people there who will talk to them, listen to them, and understand. Some of the young people never talk to social workers in the centre, whilst others come and talk to them regularly. In a feature published in the *Times Magazine** a young girl called Jasmine describes having had so much help from the centre that she is now thinking of a career in social work, hav-

---

* Candida Crewe, 'We can work it out', *Times Magazine* (1 May 2004).

ing come from a terrible home situation and poor relationships with foster parents. Meanwhile, Leanne, who had been severely bullied and become very difficult, has managed to turn her life round through the centre, which has helped both Leanne and her parents cope. A third of the young people who use the centre talk of bullying, a common experience for them, whilst sexual abuse affects 10–20 per cent. These, and many other, positive outcomes demonstrate that this NSPCC-run centre is the way forward. As Jasmine says: 'I'd like to have two kids, and a big mansion. But meantime I'll keep coming here. I'll keep coming here till they chuck me out.' The centre's success derives from the fact that it is a place where adults listen to children, something that is badly needed in a society where troubled children are more likely to talk to their pets than to another human being – especially if they're from social services.

The government's Green Paper, *Every Child Matters* (2003), published in the wake of Lord Laming's report into the death of Victoria Climbié, proposed electronic tracking for children at risk of abuse, neglect, or deprivation, along with 150 children's trusts, separate from the previous organizations, to be set up by 2006. Other proposals include a children's director to oversee local services, a statutory children's board to replace the old Area Children's Protection Committees, and a Children's Commissioner for England.

Debate about this last role has been heated, with some expressing the view that the Commissioner for England should have powers beyond those the government proposed – similar, in fact, to the powers of the Children's Commissioners for Scotland, Wales, and Northern Ireland, who are required to protect children using the UN Convention on the rights of the child. In England, however, where the bulk of the worst cases involving children occur, the proposal, now accepted, was to promote the views and interests of children but without legal powers to investigate, which can only be done at the direction of the Secretary of State – an approach that suggests too little independence and too much political control. In the debate in the House of Lords on the Children Bill, considerable scepticism was also expressed about how much one person can do in the Commissioner role (Lord Laming had recommended the creation of a national agency for children and families, led by a Children's Commissioner, not just a single individual): 'Much emphasis has been placed ... on the role of the new commissioner. I shall be somewhat blasphemous and confess to some scepticism about focusing all our hopes in one man or woman. There is a Childline publication entitled *Everybody's Business*, and child protection is everybody's business.'*

The issue of the Children's Commissioner dominated much of the debate, but even if the Commissioner for England were to have the same powers as Wales, Scotland, and Northern Ireland, no single individual or system can accomplish everything, or right all wrongs. At the time of the debate, the Welsh Commissioner told the BBC that no commissioner could substitute for well-run and properly designed services for children.

---

* Baroness Howarth of Breckland, *Hansard* (30 March 2004).

Most of Lord Laming's recommendations were carried forward into the Children's Act (2004), except that councils were allowed more flexibility in organizing their children's services and given a further two years to set up children's trusts. There will be greater – and long overdue – integration of services and more sharing of information (improved communications has been one of the key recommendations in 16 out of the 36 inquiries into child protection failures held since 1973). But the tracking proposals pose legal problems. Tracking would allow the flagging-up of serious concerns on an automated system, with data being entered by teachers, social workers, health workers, and the police. The idea is for the new electronic files to flash warning signs when there is something within a family that might give rise for concern, such as mental health issues, domestic violence or imprisonment. At present, a parent's right to confidentiality can only be breached if there is significant risk to the child, but this legislation allows parents' rights to be overridden. Some argue that this amounts to a gross invasion of privacy and is in breach of the

Human Rights Act. What it certainly does do is open up the family, hitherto in some way almost a sacrosanct entity, to the professional gaze; and confidentiality in a system such as this can certainly not be assured.

There will also be a greater focus on children of pre-school age, with a Children's Centre in every community. It sounds wonderful. But at present there are few staff, and no enthusiasm, and a widespread view that simply restructuring services is not the answer. Restructuring, as the NHS can attest to only too well, leads to staff having to worry about things other than their main concerns – such as whether they will have jobs, or how everything fits together. The disruption can last two years, a hugely long time when it affects the welfare of children all over the country.

Doubts also exist about whether the merging of education and children's services is a good thing – in fact, the government has given local authorities some leeway in deciding how to organize services because of these doubts. Two councils where services have been merged, Hertfordshire and Brighton and Hove, had significantly poorer

results in the last round of children's services inspections than others that kept the
services separate.* But it is worse than that.
The whole thrust of the new programme relies on schools taking the lead. But schools
often have poor relationships with troubled
and troublesome children – the ones who
truant, who are excluded, or who have difficult parents.

Children's trusts are to be the lead commissioners, a coalition of several agencies.
But will this initiative work, or is it yet again
a restructuring too far? It will do nothing
about the need for more trained staff, low
morale, and the lack of energy in children's
services. And is simply overhauling the management of child protection sufficient, or are
there other questions we should be address-
ing? What about society's responsibility for
the way it treats its children, the extent to
which the State should get involved, and
what relationship needs to exist between
the professionals, the children themselves,
and parents and carers? These are questions
and issues that remain unanswered.

---

* Malcolm Dean, 'Blurred vision of a safer future',
  The Guardian (3 March 2004).

Without a ban on smacking and corporal punishment, which the government would not fully support in autumn 2004, it is not clear how the level of physical abuse of children can be brought down. The UK government still sticks to its belief that parents should be able to use 'reasonable chastisement' and reached a compromise position before the Bill became law that allowed smacking that leaves no mark. That in itself is almost impossible to enforce.

Smacking has been banned in twelve European countries in the past thirty years, whilst in Sweden, where smacking was banned ten years ago, child deaths at the hands of their parents have fallen virtually to zero (four child deaths due to physical abuse in Sweden between 1979 and 2000: the UK still has one a week).* It really makes no sense to allow parents to hit their children when we remain shocked by the deaths of children from violence at the hands of their parents. In the most recent debates on the subject (July 2004), the government

---

* Joan Durrant, *A Generation without Smacking: The impact of Sweden's ban on physical punishment*, (London, Save the Children, 2000).

supported a compromise position put forward by Anthony Lester, a Liberal Democrat peer, which suggested that any smacking that produced a reddening of the skin was not to be allowed. But with black children, particularly, 'reddening' does not show. And if we do not make it more difficult to hit children, then we are clearly making it more difficult for social workers to investigate what is 'unreasonable' chastisement. But the newspapers were full of parents explaining, somewhat guiltily, how they had slapped their children in irritation when nothing else would work, and pointing out that a smacking ban would be absurd.† They failed to realize that the authorities would not punish parents for every slap, but that the legislation would have an educational effect, rather like sex and race discrimination legislation.

Nevertheless, children are the concern of us all – and of the State. When children leave public care, 'our' care, it is the State, in the form of social workers who represent us all, that is responsible for staying in touch

---

†'Smacking: We plead guilty', *Daily Mail* (7 July 2004), and others.

with those it has taken into its care. In 2003, councils remained in touch with some 81 per cent of those leaving care, whilst 49 per cent were known to be in education, training, or employment on their nineteenth birthdays, up 3 per cent from 2002. More than a third of care leavers were known to be living independently on their nineteenth birthday.*

Of young people leaving care in 2002–3, 44 per cent had at least one GCSE or GNVQ, which was a 3 per cent increase on the year before. Of unaccompanied asylum-seeking children who left care in 2002–3, 30 per cent had at least one GCSE or GNVQ and 50 per cent of former unaccompanied asylum-seeking children who had left care were in education on their nineteenth birthday, compared with 21 per cent of all care leavers.

In the same year, 2002–3, only 17 per cent of councils reported reaching the government target for the level of employment, training, or education amongst previously looked-after children – 75 per cent of the rate of all young people in the area, an in-

---

* Department for Education and Skills, national statistics, care leavers, 2002–3.

crease of 4 per cent over the previous year. In Scotland, the figures are even worse, with around 60 per cent of care leavers not in any form of education, employment, or training. In addition over 20 per cent of young people experience a period of homelessness in the year after leaving care. The picture for young care leavers is thus grim in the extreme. There are some bright lights of hope in the system, however, such as in Leeds, where Stepping Stones, an integrated programme, aims to motivate young care leavers and their carers to move on to further and higher education. It combines opening doors into higher education, with places reserved for young people in care at Leeds Metropolitan University's summer school, with influencing carers, including a carers' newsletter.

Unemployment

The national unemployment rate for 16–18 year olds is 18 per cent, but between 50 and 80 per cent of care leavers are unemployed. Yet even here there are examples of good practice, such as in Liverpool, which has a co-ordinated service for care leavers – a pooling of resources between Liverpool's leaving care service and Greater Merseyside Connexions, the advice and support service for young people. As seems to be the case in many other successful environments, the Clics personal advisers, from Connexions, seem to engage more easily with the young people than the social workers do. But the Clics team, which involves the kids themselves in planning its work, says it will not be judged by government targets of one GCSE. It wants to be judged by whether 'these youngsters are involved in something constructive, and getting on with their lives,' according to Steve Moutray, the policy and development officer for children.* Yet most young care leavers have nothing comparable to help them. Indeed, you might argue, as Pam Hibbert, principal policy officer at Barnardo's did in an interview, that the educational targets set for children in care are so low, at one GCSE pass compared with a national target of five GCSEs, that it is obvious that, as a society, we discriminate

---

* Graham Hopkins. 'It all clicks into place', *Community Care* (6–12 November 2003).

massively against them. After all, what can one expect of children in care?

To make it worse, many young care leavers have no idea about what they are entitled to, and recommendations, such as those made by A National Voice, in its consultation event AMPLIFY, in August 2002, do not appear to have been taken up. These included the proposal that all young people in care should be informed about the Leaving Care entitlements before their fifteenth birthdays, with a standard leaving care guide written by care leavers and made available to them, and a national minimum amount of £1,400 for the Leaving Care Grant being set, but with local weighting for areas such as London where living costs are higher. Lastly, the consultation recommended that better housing options for young care leavers should be made available, since bed and breakfast accommodation is not suitable. The consultation did not propose, though perhaps it should have done, that some kind of sheltered housing would be valuable – not restrictive, but with some adult support available.

In 1999, the average age for leaving home for young people in the population as a whole was 22,* whilst nearly five thousand young people were leaving local authority care at 16 or 17, with the numbers leaving care at 16 growing. The 1999 Department of Health consultation paper, *Me, Survive, Out There?*, proposed making local authorities give eligible 16- and 17-year care leavers personal and financial support, the financial part of which was removed during the Thatcher years of government. Every 16-year-old in care was to be given a comprehensive pathway plan to independence, and new resources were promised for 16- and 17-year-olds who were in care or who had left care. The evocative phrase 'Me, survive, out there?' was taken from a poem by Lynsey, aged 15, and quoted at the beginning of the consultation paper. The poem first appeared in *Who Cares?*, a magazine published by the Who Cares? Trust; but the title of the consultation report leaves out the answer Lynsey gives to those questions: 'I don't know how.' That is the voice of desperation that we, as a society, have failed to address.

---

* Department of Health consultation paper, *Me? Survive? Out There?*, 7.

From 2000, as a result of a House of Lords debate and finally a government amendment, there has also been a new duty on local authorities to help 18–21-year-old care leavers with education, employment, and training costs, and a new duty was placed on local authorities to continue support and help to those young people whom they have looked after at least until the age of 18. This includes providing personal advisers, pathway plans, advice and assistance, so that the young people do not feel that they are on their own. So some of what young people have asked for themselves has come to pass, but it is a mixed picture.

Mentoring

Mentoring for young people in care, and also for care leavers, has grown significantly in recent years. Several organizations have mentoring schemes for children in care and for young care leavers, and the government-backed charity Big Brothers and Sisters also provides support. These are, by all accounts, very good schemes. Young people in care and leaving care speak highly of some of their mentors, whether they are the formal advisers of the counselling and advice service Connexions, or volunteers. Indeed, from research conducted for the Joseph Rowntree Foundation,* it was clear that both professional and informal support were crucial to young care leavers' success or otherwise.

Emotional encouragement from family or substitute family members seemed to make a real difference to getting young people to remain with what they were doing. Previous foster carers, grandparents, cousins, aunts and uncles, particularly those with whom the young care leaver had lived, made a huge difference to how they felt and how stable their first year out of care was. And some mentioned social workers, who were less in evidence after a year, particularly ones they had known long term and who had taken a real interest in them.

David Akinsaya, now a BBC reporter who grew up in care, describes how one of his social workers insisted on maintaining a relationship with him and took him to 'normal' things, like the theatre or on short breaks.

---

* Maggie Allen, *Into the Mainstream* (Joseph Rowntree Foundation, 2003).

She had known him since the age of eight, and would not let go. Tenacious, she did the job we would like and expect our social workers to do, and she was truly a 'mentor' to David Akinsaya. But he says that: 'I regret that our relationship [that between social worker and client] would no longer be encouraged in today's social services.' Akinsaya has himself become a mentor, largely for young black men.

Yet there must be question marks over whether the new system, with its emphasis on formal and informal mentoring, will be enough for vulnerable care leavers who are disabled and who leave care at 16 or 17. Rough estimates suggest up to 25 per cent of young care leavers have some form of disability and may need even greater pro-tection than the others. Whilst what is now coming into force is undoubtedly better than what went before, it may well be very diffi-cult to have a proper care plan in place on the sixteenth birthday of a disabled child with communication problems. Those young people in care who are in a school or a hospital are in any case not covered by the new arrangements, yet there have already been many concerns raised about what transitional arrangements are in place for them when they do finally leave school, where they can stay until they are 19. New arrangements need to be put in place for this group, whose extra vulnerability suggests that greater emphasis on constant advice and support will be needed than at present. Indeed, the range of options is small and social services' knowledge is often lacking, so that young people, particularly those with mild disabilities, are often tossed about between services and run the risk of being in residential care or of spending their days in a day centre, or finding that innumerable training courses do not lead to a job.*

But is 18 the right age for young people to leave care? Or even 21? These are the most vulnerable of youngsters. What if they are particularly talented and want to go on to university? Or gain some other qualification or training? What if they had a rough start in life, through no fault of their own? Should we not be seeking to protect them for longer, given that the average age of a

---

* P. Rabiee, 'Mind the gap', *Community Care* (8–14 June 2000).

young person leaving home in Britain is 22? The Children (Leaving Care) Act 2000 has largely succeeded in removing the perverse incentives for local authorities to discharge young people from their care early so that they could claim benefits and no longer be the financial responsibility of the authority. There is now a statutory duty to assess and meet the needs of 16–21-year-olds in and leaving care, as well as a responsibility for the personal and financial support of 16- and 17-year-old care leavers (of whom the vast majority can no longer claim benefits) and a requirement to provide them with or maintain them in suitable accommodation. Every young person now has to have a pathway plan, and everyone also has to be allocated a personal adviser. Many of the young people themselves would like family members to be involved in this where possible, but that seems rare at present, despite the evidence that support of extended family members is very important for the well-being of young people who have left care and are making the transition to adult life. Assistance with education and training is to be provided to the end of the agreed programme, even if this takes someone beyond the age of 21, so one can see how there might be some unwillingness to agree long educational and training programmes because of the cost to the local authority. Yet young care leavers, because of their rough start in life, might well need to acquire more GCSEs, or more vocational qualifications, if they wish to proceed to further or higher education. But, as Pam Hibbert points out, the benefits system works against them, for they have to sign on for Jobseekers' Allowance if they are in full-time education other than higher education. So they might be part way through an A-Level course, but their financial support will cease at 19 if they have not finished it, and still may not be enough to help them gain a real start in life.

The provisions of the Act have resulted in an improved situation compared to what went before. But it is by no means perfect. For instance, the Act does not apply to everyone, only to those who have been looked after for thirteen weeks or more after their fourteenth birthday and who are in care on or after their sixteenth birthday. Those young people who do not meet these requirements – and there are many of them – and who left care on or after their sixteenth birthday only qualify for advice and assistance. The government has at last extended powers to local authorities to assist with the education, training, and employment of young care leavers, but powers are by no means the same as a statutory duty to assist, when asked or required. Amanda Allard's research for NCH on the effect of the new legislation suggests that the new provisions are often undermined by failures in the care system earlier on, and that until the issue of educational attainment is tackled the leaving care staff can do too little. There was also a real worry about the distrust of professionals exhibited by many of the young people in the study, making it difficult to build and maintain relationships.* Bob Broad's research† shows that a significantly small proportion of foster parents (15 per cent of respondents) and

---

* Amanda Allard, *A Case Study Investigation into the Implementation of the Children (Leaving Care) Act (2000)*.
† Bob Broad, *After the Act: Implementing the Children (Leaving Care) Act* 2000 (2003).

of professionals (44 per cent) knew much about the Act or had received significant training on what it meant for them, eighteen months after it came into force. But there seems to be a significant growth of the numbers of young care leavers in education post-16, and this may well be due to the government initiatives to keep 16- and 17-year-olds in further education and training, as well as the funding arrangements from 'Quality Protects'. Yet evidence is still there that looked-after children are discriminated against in applications for schools, whenever schools have more applications than places. Much more worrying is the extent to which ring-fenced money from the Department of Health for supporting young people leaving care is being used to support residential, fostering, or out-of-borough placements. This begs the question of whether the specialist leaving care and after care services are gradually being starved of resources to do their post-16 work in order to prop up overspent budgets on foster care and other placements. And leaving care grants still show astonishing variation, from £400 to £2000, which cannot be justified.

But there have been improvements in the amounts of resources available to young care leavers, as the research shows quite clearly.* Money was ring-fenced after the Act was passed until 2005, and that has made a difference. But the question that must remain is whether it will last, given that the ring-fencing is about to be removed? Will the numbers of dedicated professional workers who work directly with care leavers, and who have clearly made a great difference to individuals, diminish? There are already major recruitment and retention issues, which is a real problem given how essential it is for young care leavers to be able to form long-term relationships with adults they can trust. One London authority had 75 per cent of its posts filled by agency staff, hardly a good advertisement for permanence and stability in an unreliable world! Indeed, if money begins to seep away, workers believe that care leavers will go back to being the low priority they used to be, especially if children's services are being

---

* A. Allard, E. Fry, and J. Sufian, *Setting the Agenda: What's left to do in leaving care?* (Action on Aftercare Consortium, 2004).

reorganized and if the emphasis is only on preventing dramatic child deaths rather than alleviating enduring misery and poor futures.

Despite the change in the law, and the increased money, the research still shows considerable concern about access to leisure activities and to suitable accommodation. Real concerns also remain about the needs of young people who have left care and are in their twenties and still need support and advice. And there are still real gaps in the care for asylum-seeking care leavers, young disabled people, young parents, those emerging from the prison system, and those who have been totally disaffected from learning earlier in life. When it comes to education for those who do want to study beyond 19 or 21, unless government acts to make it a duty to support care leavers in this way, local authorities who are strapped for cash and whose spending is capped by government will simply observe their minimum statutory duty. Getting their fees paid, getting allowances for books, or tools, or art supplies, or media training, are all things normal young people would take for granted. But unless local authorities are required to do it, care leavers may well be in a position where normal supplies of tools and books are simply beyond their means. And where fees have to be paid, local authorities have a history of arguing that a young person of 18 belongs to some other authority, whilst there are often arguments about what a young person who has been in care is actually entitled to.

One of the most depressing documents I remember ever reading in my adult life was a 1995 Save the Children publication, entitled *You're on Your Own*, with its harrowing stories of how young people leaving care – interviewed by other care leavers – felt the whole system was full of vagaries and chance and was not predicated on a deliberate and enduring concern for them and their well-being. One of the researchers who carried out the interviews for Save the Children, Leslie Otto, was himself a former care leaver. He said at the time: 'I personally don't think this report will achieve all the recommendations, but I do want it to. I spent a long time in care and don't have too much faith in the system. But even just a little bit [of change] would be worth it.'*

There are heartrending accounts of prejudice against young care leavers from landlords, social workers (unbelievable but true), employers and people in general. The saddest thing about this piece of work, which moved me more than all the others, was that it did not say anything new. What it did was to highlight the failing public attitude towards these vulnerable young people. More than half of the people interviewed, as care leavers, said they never told anyone they had been in care, and the researchers also found that some young care leavers lost their jobs when employers found out they had been in care. There were also serious attitude problems to young care leavers taking drugs, as if young people of the same age who lived at home did not do the same; even worse, they were perceived as being constantly in trouble with the police. Yet the evidence demonstrated that fewer than half those interviewed had been in contact with the police since leaving care,

---

* Quoted by Polly Neate, 'Catalogue of disaster', *Community Care* (13–19 July 1995).

and for many of them it was because they had been victims of crime rather than perpetrators. The female care leavers got a reputation as 'dirty scrubbers, will go to bed with anyone, pregnant before they are sixteen, all high on drugs'. And, just to make it worse, many of the care workers were extremely negative about participating in the research, whilst the young people themselves were thrilled to be involved. Despite some professional reluctance, it was this piece of work that shifted government attitudes and led to a changed perception of care leavers as being truly vulnerable.

The fact that so many of the young people who came out of care were or had been homeless was one element that really shocked a government obsessed with getting homeless people off the streets. Care leavers are one of the most over-represented groups amongst the young homeless, and some 28 per cent of the newly homeless young people who present themselves at Centrepoint projects have been in care. So this is not an occasional, isolated problem. Indeed, before the Children (Leaving Care) Act 2000, one of the main contributory factors for young people's homelessness was a lack of employment opportunities and poor access to what were insufficient benefits. That at least has improved, but supported accommodation, provided or commissioned by social services and housing departments, is still in very short supply, and housing is still reported as one of the biggest issues facing young care leavers.

Centrepoint has been running a support service to help some London boroughs improve their care leaving services and procedures, especially in regard to homelessness, and many children's charities, notably Barnardo's and NCH Action for Children, have done much to help in this area. The Wakefield and Barnardo's project, 'Signpost' is often praised because it helps young people leaving care as well as those who have been or are homeless.* But there are still large numbers of young care leavers who fall through the net, some who do not get the protection afforded by the new legislation, and others who are runaways from care at a

---

* N. Valios, 'Pointing the way to independent living', *Community Care* (27 April–3 May 2000).

younger age, for whom provision is a national disgrace. Young people leaving care who have disabilities, especially learning disabilities, seem to become homeless relatively easily. So despite improvements to legislation in recent years, lack of proper support for young care leavers remains, and this is not an issue that is about to go away.

All in all, people working in the sector believe things are bad for care leavers, for a variety of reasons. The Association of Directors of Social Services (ADSS) has a fact sheet for National Care Leavers' Day entitled 'From Care to Where?', in which it cites four main causes of things being so bad for care leavers. These are: stigma; discrimination, which is particularly acute in the job market; exclusion, since many young care leavers find it hard to be around people who are always talking about getting together with family, holidays, etc.; and disadvantage, for there is no doubt that young care leavers are disadvantaged both socially and educationally. No matter how bright and educationally inclined they are, the system works against their success, with moves from home to home, school to school, and limited space in which to study, plus often having foster families or other peers who are negative about school and education.

Young care leavers often have no one to turn to after the age of 18, though the changes in the law will help that for some, if not all, young care leavers. The Bryn Melyn Group Foundation was set up in 1999 as a charity to provide financial support to care leavers aged 18–26 who have no one else to turn to, precisely because many of them need support longer than the system – even in its new improved state – allows for. It held a seminar in National Care Leavers' Week in 2003 and raised some key issues, including the fact that young care leavers need sup-port long after 21 because the sense of being 'on your own', even if you are a 'successful' young care leaver, never leaves you. Young care leavers may need small amounts of money for tools and books and so on, but they also may need cash awards for access to basic education and training, which the Prince's Trust is providing to an increasing extent; they may also need mentoring for a far longer period than other young people. These concerns should be listened to carefully by government. Now that 16- and 17-year-olds have their money paid to them by the social workers from the local authorities who look after them, there may well be a conflict in the role of the funder and the befriender, and it was clear that 'leaving care workers' were often regarded in a more positive light by the young people than social workers – yet another problem for social workers, who, despite their best efforts, are getting a rough press from pretty well everybody.

But the worst evidence came from young care leavers arguing that the inconsistencies in all sorts of areas made life too complicated and too hard for them to cope. First, there is an inconsistency between what is paid out as a leaving care grant to those going on to further education and those who enter training provision. Second, there is huge variation from local authority to local authority. Third, the experiences of children in foster care were very different from those in residential accommodation, and those at 16 were really too young to take on the responsibilities of independence and had a worse start to care leaving. Fourth, living on your own led to isolation, whilst those in foster care had better networks and fewer negative stereotypes to contend with.

Mental Health

It is little wonder that the statistics on the mental health of young people who leave care are so appalling. In my time at the King's Fund we commissioned Steve Wyler to do a review jointly for the King's Fund and the Oak Foundation on 'The Health of Young People Leaving Care', which showed that many of London's young care leavers experience poor health and that many of them did not know how to use the health services or found NHS services unhelpful. The statistics show that 40 per cent of young care leavers try to take their own lives, 35 per cent harm themselves deliberately, and 17 per cent of them suffer from an enduring mental illness. At the time, Angela Greatley, then King's Fund fellow in mental health, said that 'Care leavers are often very resilient and resourceful young people. But they face an unacceptably high risk of hopelessness, unemployment, isolation and depression.' In the wake of that report, the Fund decided to give a grant to the London Borough of Lewisham to work with the local mental health NHS Trust, the Children's Society, and First Key to improve the mental health of young care leavers. The young people already involved with Lewisham had said that they wanted counselling and personal development programmes alongside existing mental health services. This meant that they needed quite intensive support, something that government is beginning to realize, as the changes in support show, but which is nowhere near as intensive and continuous as young care leavers are saying they need. If young people themselves are identifying the problems and saying what would be helpful, it does seem curious that government, and the voluntary sector, are not acting quickly to put such arrangements in place, given the appalling statistics about what happens to these very same young care leavers.

Steve Wyler's report looked at the 3–5,000 children leaving care in London every year and demonstrated that their physical health is poor, with widespread substance abuse and high levels of mental health problems. In terms of drug use, the Home Office's own data show that former care leavers are at particular risk of developing or having drug problems. Its own study (2001–2) showed that care leavers had higher levels of drug use than the general population, that a third of them said they used cannabis every day, 15 per cent had used Ecstasy in the previous month, and 10 per cent had used cocaine. But lower levels of drug use were reported as the young people began to live independently, except when transitions to independent living were difficult or when other problems occurred. If young care leavers become homeless, their drug use increases again, in common with that of other homeless people, particularly rough sleepers, of whom a surprisingly high proportion are runaways from home or from care. Of the young homeless in general, the majority have been excluded from school, and two-thirds or more have spent time in prison or another young offenders' institution, suggesting that this is a big issue for care leavers, whose presence in the criminal justice system is disproportionately high. For others, it seems that practical responsibilities and parenthood encouraged more responsible behaviours, and former care leavers seemed to grow out of drug use more quickly than the general population, which is a fascinating finding.

The teenage pregnancy rate for care leavers is far higher than the general population – and we already have the highest teenage pregnancy rates in Europe. Yet it is clear that young care leavers do not see the issue of having children as a problem in the way their social workers, key workers, and others do. Many young care leavers just want someone to love, and to love them. Indeed, some young care leavers who were pregnant on leaving care or shortly after report being encouraged to consider having an abortion, rather than inflicting on the child the awful things that had happened to them. But many of them were determined to give their babies a good life, and lots of love. And the truth is that many of them have succeeded, even if poverty remains a problem.

Unhealthy lifestyles, lack of exercise, and poor diets are common amongst young care leavers, yet health advice will often only be accepted in any serious way if it is given within a relationship of trust.* And the young people themselves interviewed for Steve Wyler's work wanted fast-track access to dentistry and opticians and particularly to counselling. Health promotion work is best done by peers, and the Who Cares? Trust has health advice in pamphlets and in its newsletter, in the form of Agony Aunt letters. There are also examples of sports schemes for care leavers and an increasing numbers of specialist drop-in services that offer counselling and support, usually run by voluntary sector organizations and offering a way in to more formal mental health facilities if needed. In Hackney, Off Centre provides one-to-one and group counselling for care leavers or those in care from ages 13–25 and can provide counselling for up to two years, though it believes it is often needed for longer. Care leavers who arrived in Britain as unaccompanied asylum seekers face additional, often serious, health problems, as well.

But the reasons why young people feel that their health may be poor are different

---

* S. Wyler, *The Health of Young People Leaving Care* (2000).

from how adult and official health services might perceive them. Young people identify social and emotional causes for ill health, whilst official health services would point to eating habits, smoking, drinking, and illicit substance use as being critical. Throughout, the way young people themselves talk about these issues gives a strong sense that what those who have left care want is to be treated with respect – just like those who are frequently in touch with the mental health services. They want access to basic health services as of right; finally, and most significantly, they want long-term relation-ships with people they can trust. That would mean General Practitioners who took care to see these young people themselves and not just a member of the team; specialist health workers able to deal with issues relating to mental health and substance misuse who stay the course and do not leave after a few months, and so on.

Yet young people in care often do not trust the mental health services. Nor is it cool to be involved with mental health services; as one care leaver, Heidi Emma Osborne put it, 'the mental health idiots just mess with your head'. She argues* that the services are often provided in poor venues, with young people expected to reveal their most intimate thoughts to strangers, of whom they have often learned to be wary. They have to establish a meaningful relationship with the mental health professional within an established time frame, lest the sessions be stopped. Yet she asks why these sorts of therapeutic relationships need to be formed at such a pace, given that forming any kind of relationship is normally quite time consuming. She continues: 'Yet for some reason, there is an expectation that some of the most damaged people will form a meaningful relationship with a professional in just a few hours over a matter of weeks.' She is right, yet the whole targets and time-allocation culture means that few mental health professionals will be paid for the sort of time that might be needed to really form a relationship with a vulnerable and damaged young person, and certainly are unlikely to find the time to put in the long-term work necessary to establish a truly

---

* Viewpoint, 'In mental health time is the healer', *Community Care* (11–17 December 2003).

therapeutic relationship. Osborne also points interestingly to what she sees as an addiction to the system, where young people in care, despite resenting their every emotion and character trait being opened up to examination, also feel comforted by the concern shown for them by social services and mental health teams. She herself says she is frightened of establishing and building relationships with non-professional people because somehow she has become dependent on the very mental health system that was supposed to be therapeutic. Her words are important and should be heeded.

All these issues concerning care leavers and the care system are all part of a curious attitude to childhood we have in the UK. On the one hand, we want our children to be innocent, and expect them to be so. Yet we allow them to dress up in adult-type clothes, in the height of provocative fashion, from a very young age.* We do not think what childhood should be, we only think of how to protect our children, turning them into a generation

---

* Yvonne Roberts, 'Cheated out of childhood', *The Observer* (21 September 2003).

of lazy, unadventurous computer-loving slobs. On the other, we want our children to feel safe and to be confident when they go out into the world. Then again, we mollycoddle them to such an extent that new evidence suggests that ordinary children carry a daily expectation of being kidnapped by a stranger, being sexually abused by a paedophile, or becoming a victim of terrorism. Meanwhile, urban myths about the Internet and about the prevalence of paedophiles wanting to 'chat up' young people may be stopping children from learning to use the Web properly and to distinguish between truth and false advertising. Parents believe their children are truly at risk, and they believe it especially about the outside world. That fear is transferred to children, who become over-anxious about the outside environment and choose to stay indoors. 'Beliefs about the inherent hostility and danger of public places is commonplace', according to a survey conducted by Demos and the Green Alliance,† which shows that both

† Laura Clark, 'The children who are too frightened to play outside', *Daily Mail* (24 May 2004); Amelia Hill, 'Stranger danger harms kids', *The Observer* (23 May 2004).

parents and children prefer children to remain indoors because of a wholly unrealistic assessment of the risks of the outside world. The result has been that children are too frightened to go outside their own front doors. They will become timid adults, with little chance to develop into independent beings. Carole Easton, Chief Executive of Childline, argues that government and local authorities must take some of the blame for this because there is a lack of safe, easily accessible play space. She argues: 'We have created a very child-unfriendly social environment outside the home. Few communities have accessible play spaces, and even fewer of those spaces are supervised by adults.'

The old fear of infectious diseases carrying off our children has now transmogrified into a fear of strangers and a fear of traffic. Just as children of all social classes travel further afield than they ever did before, their normal everyday movement is further and further curtailed. Planes are a commonplace, but bicycles lead to danger on the road. Travelling to the USA or Spain is no big deal for many children, but an unaccompanied trip on the London underground under the age of 12 or so takes serious negotiation and risk assessment. Traffic is a particular hazard children talk about, but the stranger danger has a particularly fairy tale ring to it. In the words of Gillian Thomas, co-author of the Demos–Green Alliance report, 'on the crime front, my worry is that, because it's turned into a fantasy, they imagine what a stranger looks like and it's always a man with nasty eyes and horrible clothes. It makes them unreal, and they might not be able to recognize real danger.'*

Teachers' unions are increasingly nervous about taking children on school trips, one of the ways for children to gain the adventure experiences that are so important for their growth into mature adults, because they are nervous of being blamed for accidents when they happen. As society becomes increasingly averse to risk, particularly in relation to children, the National Association of Schoolmasters Union of Women Teachers (NASUWT) has advised its members to stop

---

* Julie Wheelwright, 'Streets of fear', *The Guardian* (26 May 2004).

347

supervising children on school trips.* Three union members have been blamed in recent years for the deaths of children on school trips, including Paul Ellis, who ignored warnings and insisted a 10-year-old boy, Max Palmer, jump into a freezing stream in the Lake District. Two others continued with a 'river walking' expedition in the Yorkshire dales after heavy rain and flooding, and two girls died. Court action against teachers has only been taken in recent years where there has been gross negligence, but the NASUWT still claims that accidents are not treated as true accidents and there seems to be a need to blame someone. The National Union of Teachers, Britain's biggest teaching union, does not agree, and has not given its members the same advice.

The former Secretary of State for Education, Charles Clarke, and the Secretary of State for Culture Media and Sport, Tessa Jowell, are trying to prevent an American-style suing culture growing up around school trips and school sports and they believe that teachers, youth leaders, Scout

---

* *Evening Standard* (19 February 2004).

leaders and other volunteers will follow the NASUWT advice and be very careful. For they, too, are averse to risk. Yet unless we can limit the right to sue, particularly suing public bodies, or get a form of legal certificate of risk for parents to sign so that they could not sue unless there was real negligence, the pressure against supervising school trips will continue. Guidance from local authorities asking schools to keep the children out of the midday sun is only the beginning of a worrying trend. Derby City Council has done just that, including guidance about sunscreen, which schools should stock, though teachers 'should not have physical contact with the pupil, and parental consent should be sought for this in case the pupils are allergic to sunscreen'.†

We are at risk of having nervous, obese, and totally un-streetwise children if this continues. We now even make it difficult to volunteer in schools without a major security check. Confidentiality is going out of the window in the name of safety, yet unless a past conviction is child related it seems an

---

† Polly Curtis, 'Schools told to keep pupils out of the midday sun', *The Guardian* (4 June 2004).

odd deterrent to use to try to keep parents out of volunteering in schools, particularly when there is such widespread concern about the lack of male role models for many children.

Where does all this leave us? Overall, it remains a sad story, though with some good and hopeful elements.

Government has tried to improve things for care leavers in a structural way in recent years, with its Children (Leaving Care) Act 2000, with targets for educational achievements (though they are set far too low), with changes to the arrangements for 16- and 17-year-olds, and with ring-fencing money for young care leavers until 2005. All this is undoubtedly positive. The Laming Inquiry and subsequent report, the Kennedy report into child deaths at Bristol, and the Utting report, have all made people more concerned. The changes are good ones.

But there is a real hole in the centre of all this activity. Government is much more concerned about the single tragedies – the Victoria Climbiés, or the Jasmine Beckfords, the Toni-Ann Byfields, or the Kimberley

Carliles – than it is about the underlying sea of grinding misery.

As long as scandals do not blow up concerning children's homes, as happened in North Wales, Islington, and Leicester, there is little public concern about what happens to our most vulnerable children.

As long as we do not hear of a young 15-year-old like Natalie Mills being beaten to death by her boyfriend whilst in care, we relax at the thought of teenagers in violent sexual relationships.

Though our own children do not leave home until, on average, the age of 22, and though parents continue to give children small sums, and sometimes large sums, towards education and training, as well as accommodation, we feel relaxed about young care leavers becoming caught in the benefits maze at the age of 19 when they may be trying desperately to get the GCSEs they missed out on earlier in life.

We can tolerate a huge amount of generalized risk to children and young people, but throw up our hands in horror at the news of one child beaten to death by his or her parents – even though this is commonplace.

We can tolerate widespread and general misery, despite knowing what it might lead to in terms of suicide and breakdown, but find it hard when one individual or agency is blamed.

What we need is a different attitude towards social workers, so that they are held in respect, supported, and properly paid. We need to stop blaming them when things go wrong – for they always will – and instead give them the means to do their jobs. We need to make social work, especially social work with young people in or leaving care, a profession that is popular and hard to get into. And politicians have to stop blaming social workers, unless there is proven gross negligence, and start praising them instead.

Second, we need to ensure that all the leaving care arrangements so recently set in place are maintained and supported, financially and morally, by local authorities up and down the country. Young people need to feel supported and befriended until they are twentytwo at least, and they need to know that it is not only care workers or social workers who will take an interest in them, but that mentors and other young people are available to befriend them. We all need to take a look at what goes on. We all need to be ready to befriend, without the fear of being screened so vigorously that the smallest misdemeanour in our past, such as a minor driving offence, is revealed.

Children's homes need to be opened out to the wider gaze and should once again put on events so that the wider community can come and meet staff and residents. Children with ASBOs must be helped to live a different life, and those children who are troubled must be helped before it is too late and they become desperately damaged adults. We need to show them tough love, and avoid continuously changing the people responsible for their care. If they are prepared to make a relationship with the wider community, then the community should be enthusiastic about its relationship with them.

Lastly, we need to look at the curiously fearful children our society is producing – over protected and frightened of attacks and terrorist outrages – and compare their fears with the exposure to real risk and harm we tolerate when young people leave 'our' care.

FOUR

THE PRISON SYSTEM

On 20 July 1910, Winston Churchill, then Home Secretary and just 36 years old, addressed the House of Commons with these words:

> The mood and temper of the public in regard to the treatment of crime and criminals is one of the most unfailing tests of the civilization of any country. A calm and dispassionate recognition of the rights of the accused against the State, and even of convicted criminals against the State, a constant heartsearching by all charged with the duty of punishment,

a desire and eagerness to rehabilitate in the world of industry all those who have paid their dues in the hard coinage of punishment, tireless efforts towards the discovery of curative and regenerating processes, and an unfaltering faith that there is a treasure, if you can only find it, in the heart of every man – these are the symbols which, in the treatment of crime and criminals, mark and measure the stored-up strength of a nation, and are sign and proof of the living virtue in it.

This chapter tells the story of how we treat people who commit offences, how we punish them and how we do, or don't, rehabilitate them afterwards. It looks at how our present systems have developed from the past and asks whether our modern systems are more enlightened than what went before. It also looks at Britain's love affair with imprisonment, and why we have spectacularly failed to reduce the prison population and develop proper alternatives for the many prisoners who do not need to be there and do not benefit from the experience. It asks whether our desire to avoid risk has contributed to a mechanistic, rule-driven system that has driven out some of the basic humanity needed to bring about a more just society. Though the main area of interest here is how we treat people who have been in contact with the criminal justice system, it is not a subject that can be looked at alone. Alongside it, closely interconnected, are ideas about crime and punishment, about rehabilitation, about acceptable risk to the public or individuals, about how we see the purpose of prison, and how we view alternatives.

The idea of punishment is old as the hills. The Hebrew Bible is full of ideas about crime and punishment, and the Old Testament is viewed as being about a vengeful God, as opposed to the New Testament, which is about a forgiving deity. But an eye for an eye and a tooth for a tooth of the Hebrew Bible means financial compensation for the destruction of an eye or a tooth, not knocking out an eye or in any way damaging the person who has offended by way of retribution. And both the Old Testament and the New Testament warn us of our duty to prisoners. In the Old Testament there is Isaiah's magnificent call to his listeners, God's servants, 'to bring captives out of prison, out of the dungeon where they lie in darkness' (Isaiah 42: 7). In the New Testament we are told 'Remember those in prison as if you were their fellow prisoners and those who are ill treated as if you yourselves were suffering' (Hebrews 13: 3).

Every society, from the Romans and the Greeks to the Anglo-Saxons, and every religion, be it Islam, Judaism, Christianity, Hinduism, Sikhism, or Buddhism, has had its ideas about crime, wrongdoing, punishment, and retribution. So how does our current system work and where do we get our ideas from?

Prisons in London go back to the foundation of Newgate Prison and Fleet Prison in the twelfth and thirteenth centuries respectively. Foul and uncaring, they were plague infested and a scene of spectacle for the masses. But in the eighteenth century, under the influence of Rousseau, amongst others, things changed and people began to think in terms of the perfectibility of human beings. People found guilty of crimes were sent to prisons (where they were not fed unless their families came with food), or fined, transported to the colonies, or executed. A few were branded or had their ears cut off or their tongues bored, one of the punishments that particularly affected the early Quaker settlers in Massachusetts.

The philosopher Jeremy Bentham's view that the only proper measure of right and wrong is the utilitarian principle of the greatest good for the greatest number was beginning to hold sway, and those who offended once were thought to cause harm to the greatest number and therefore imprisoned in ghastly conditions. In most cases, there was no hope for prisoners. They were held in chains and kept in filthy conditions. In France, they were kept in chain gangs, dragging themselves across the country. In England they were pilloried, for all to jeer at. Punishment was a spectacle, and people came to enjoy watching the execution of criminals, or their pillorying, as they also enjoyed going to view the poor inmates of the mental institutions.

By the end of the eighteenth century and beginning of the nineteenth this attitude was beginning to disappear. The first person really to analyse attitudes to crime and punishment was an Italian, Cesare Beccaria, in 1764, whose work was translated into French and English within the first three years or so of publication. It was Beccaria who pointed out that murders described as horrible and violent crimes were then carried out again with horrible violence by the executioners, to the delight of the public. The number of public executions gradually began to fall, whilst the pillory was abolished in France in 1789 and in Britain in 1837.

In many countries, though not England, prisoners had been used to carry out public works of one kind or another, such as sweeping the streets and repairing the roads. In order to stop them retaliating against those who, recognising them by their work and their strange dress and shaved heads, would jeer at them and insult them, they were made to drag heavy chains whilst carrying out their tasks. That, too, was a way of encouraging public humiliation of the prisoners and was abolished in most countries around the beginning of the nineteenth century. The focus started to shift from public humiliation to, as Foucault puts it, 'the trial, and to the sentence'.

John Howard wrote his *State of the Prisons* in 1777, and in 1779 the first Penitentiary Act was passed, authorizing state prisons, as opposed to private ones. In 1780, the Gordon Rioters attacked Newgate Prison, in rage and fury at its conditions, and in 1782 a new Newgate was completed, with public hangings being moved there from Tyburn (in Hyde Park) the following year. Newgate was foul, with cells measuring eight foot by six occupied by two or even three people.

Meanwhile Bentham's influence was increasing. He had designed what he called the Panopticon, a new sort of prison or house of confinement 'applicable to any sort of establishment in which persons of any description are to be kept under inspection', which was backed by the government until it ran out of funds in 1803. Bentham's work was significant for it was designed to make guarding people easy, whether criminals or people with mental illness, and to serve as a place in which they could be confined without too much discomfort. However, the idea of the Panopticon, which Foucault makes clear was a concept rather than a plan or necessarily even a building, was to make it possible for people in the control tower to survey all those who were confined, each in a single cell, unable to see each other, and kept locked up for most of the day and night, just like now. It was a cheap method of surveillance, but it also made it possible to emphasize the difference in power and field of view between the surveyor – either those in charge or those simply coming for entertainment and curiosity – and the contained, whose life was constantly under supervision. This idea fascinated governments, but never quite came to fruition, though some of the new prisons, with their wings easily watched by one or two warders when everyone is locked up, are not far off Bentham's concept of ease of supervision in confinement.

The 1799 Penitentiary Act brought in new prisons with single-occupant cells, enforced silence, and continuous labour. But conditions were still frightful. Elizabeth Fry, the famous Quaker, first visited Newgate's women prisoners in 1813 and was horrified by what she found. Women were hanged with astonishing regularity, and the filth and squalor were unbelievable. Her visits led to her lifelong campaigns for reform. She set up a school for the children of poor prisoners, as well as for some of the children actually imprisoned in Newgate. She also set up a system of 'lady visitors', now only found amongst a few philanthropic organizations. Horrifyingly, some of the conditions she described continue to exist today, for example in Holloway Prison, which is still criticized by every Chief Inspector of Prisons as a place where no civilized society should house vulnerable women.

Part of Fry's success was in the appointing of prisons inspectors from 1835. They tended to favour the separate system of each prisoner having an individual cell. In 1842, Pentonville prison was built as a modern, commodious establishment where prisoners could be kept separate and free from filth and bad influences. Over the next six years fifty-four prisons were built on the same lines, and 11,000 separate cells were now in use. Many of these prisons are still used today. It was a prison building programme the scale of which was not seen again in Britain until recent years.

Conditions in prisons were apparently getting better, or at least less obviously cruel. In 1840, the Insane Prisoners Act had been passed so that prisoners, including those sentenced to death, could be transferred to asylums if they were clearly insane and would not be executed. In 1861 the death penalty was restricted to murder, treason, mutiny and piracy, and was gradually used less. In 1867 the last transportations to Australia took place and 1868 saw the last public hanging in England. Cruelty was out, reform was in. Prisons came under central government control in 1877 but still the purpose of prison was unclear. Was it for punishment, or rehabilitation? And what chance did an ex-convict have of a life after they got out?

Elsewhere, in Italy and to some extent in France, people were beginning to discuss whether crime was shaped by society or whether there were biological reasons for it. The so-called moral statisticians – who would now be social scientists – were arguing for society shaping what human beings do, whilst the great Italian theoretician Cesare Lombroso was telling the world it was all biology, in his *L'uomo Delinquente* (1876), though this was not published in English, and then only partially, until 1911.

In the late 1960s and early 1970s there was a great deal of research in Britain into social deviancy, largely the result of the drug culture at the time. This thinking was particularly concerned with how people's backgrounds led them to criminal behaviours and was often Marxist in its view. Around this time, Michel Foucault published his deeply influential *Discipline and Punish: The birth of the prison* (1976), which took a critical look at confinement in general and prisons, punishment, and torture in particular, as well as the substitution of one form of cruelty – stinking dungeons and instruments of torture – for another: constant surveillance with little or no human interaction.

In the UK, there was a post-war consensus that prison was only to be used in the last resort and that it did not have any effect on crime levels. But with the election of Margaret Thatcher as Conservative Prime Minister in 1979 a tough attitude to crime and sentencing came into play. Much of this attitude remains; so when Tony Blair, the first Labour Prime Minister for eighteen years, came into power in 1997, he promised to be 'tough on crime and tough on the causes of crime'. Prisons filled even faster, new prisons were built, some prisons were privatized, several new ones were built and run by the private sector, and the Probation Service was rebranded. To those who were interested in serious reform of the penal system, it seemed as if little progress had been made. Public attitudes had hardened, and support for increased spending on police and prisons was rising, as the British Social Attitudes Survey showed, from 8 per cent wanting spending on police and prisons to be the first or second government priority for spending in 1983 to 14 per cent in 2002.

Criticism of this attitude mounted – from academics, from the Prison Reform Trust, from the Howard League, from NACRO (the National Association for the Care and Resettlement of Offenders), and from the Chief Inspectors of Prisons in the shape of Sir Stephen Tumim, Sir David Ramsbotham, and Anne Owers. But the public was largely uninterested. Indeed, if anything increasingly authoritarian values held sway, particularly

amongst those with no educational qualifications.* In the light of all this, the Esmée
Fairbairn Foundation set up a project, 'Rethinking Crime and Punishment', in 2001 to
look at these issues over a three-year period.

Despite this increasingly authoritarian
mood, no one can point to a clear relationship between the use of imprisonment as a
punishment (or even as a deterrent) and the
rate of crime. That is true both in the UK and
internationally. In the UK, the Home Office
estimates that a 15 per cent increase in the
prison population only produces a 1 per cent
reduction in recorded crime. Nor is it clear
that more offences are being committed to
account for the rise in prison sentences. It
appears that it is simply the case that offenders are now more likely to go to prison
and to serve longer sentences than used to
be the case. In 2001, magistrates served
prison sentences on 15 per cent of their
cases, compared with half as many ten years
earlier. The Lord Chief Justice, Lord Woolf,
has said: 'There is a continuous upward pres-

---

* A. Park et al., *British Social Attitudes: Twentieth Report* (2003), 139–40.

sure and very rarely any downward pressure on the level of sentences. The upward pressure comes from public opinion and the media, the government of the day and Parliament.' Slogans like 'Prison works' and 'More pensioners sleep safely in their beds because more criminals sleep safely behind bars', became the norm.* So pressure has led to legislation for automatic life sentences for some sex and violent offenders and a mandatory three-year sentence for a third burglary conviction. According to Vivien Stern, policies on juvenile offenders have become much harsher, and the prison population continues to rise. But, she adds, there are signs of doubt within the New Labour government. She quotes David Blunkett, then newly appointed Home Secretary, in the House of Commons after Labour's election victory in 2001: 'we will be judged not by the [number of] people who end up in prison but by the number we prevent from having to be sent to prison. I want to get that on the record. There are now a record 66,500 people in prison – almost

---

* Vivien Stern, *A Sin against the Future* (1998).

50 per cent higher than ten years ago. That is not a record to emulate; it is a record to overcome.'†

Despite such rhetoric, which might have been classed as political leadership if action had really been taken, plans were advanced to build secure institutions for children aged 13 and above. Meanwhile, mandatory sentences for third hard drugs offences, second sex or violence offences, and a third offence of housebreaking came in, even though the judges, not known as the most liberal of British citizens, were strongly opposed.

So what are the facts? Short prison sentences instead of community penalties have almost trebled in ten years from 1991. The number of young people (under 18s) going into custody has almost doubled since 1993, and the number of women going to prison has increased by some 140 per cent between 1993 and 2001, despite the fact that there appears to be no increase in the number of known women offenders, many of them have dependent children, and some one in

---

† Quoted by Vivien Stern, in 'The International Impact of US Policies', in Mauer and Chesney-Lind (eds.), *Invisible Punishment* (2002).

six of them are foreign nationals, mostly convicted on drugs offences. There has also been a huge increase in the number of older people in prison, from 345 over the age of 60 in 1989 to over a thousand in 1999. In 2003, crime remained stable, according to both the British Crime Survey and police recorded crime. So it is not just a matter of more people committing crimes – attitudes towards imprisonment have shifted.

So why the increase in prison populations? At the beginning of 2003, the very year in which the risk of crime and the chance of being a victim of crime was at its lowest level for twenty years or more, the prison population was a staggering 72,000. By the end of January 2004 it was 73,688. The world Prison Population List shows that we are imprisoning people at a rate of 141 per 100,000, compared to France's 93 per 100,000 and Germany's 98 per 100,000. We now jail more people proportionately than Libya, Burma, and Turkey, and it is unclear why. We now have the highest imprisonment rate in the European Union and although our 141 per 100,000 is tiny in comparison with the United States, where one in eight

African-American men between the ages of 25 and 34 is in prison on any given day, and where over two million Americans are in prison at any one time,* it is huge as a proportion of the UK's total population.

The cost is enormous – some £37,500 per head per annum compared with £3,000 for a probation order and £2,000 for a community order. Since 1995, over 15,200 prisoner places have been provided at a cost of more than £2 billion.† It is not just the financial cost that is so worrying, but the social cost of broken families, untreated mental illness, and, of course, the risk of re-offending, since 58 per cent of adult prisoners discharged from jail are back again in two years and nearly three-quarters of young offenders show the same pattern. So if prison provides anything it is as a school for criminals, rather than a deterrent or a place of rehabilitation – ex-prisoners are responsible for about one in five of all recorded crimes. And people who have been in prison and then re-

---

* Mauer and Chesney-Lind, *Invisible Punishment*, op. cit., 1–3.
† Hansard, written parliamentary answers, quoted in Prison Reform Trust Briefing (February 2004).

offend are thought to cost society some £11 billion per year, according to the Social Exclusion Unit.

Overcrowding in our prisons has reached serious levels. At the end of December 2003, 81 of 138 prisons in England and Wales were officially overcrowded, and on 15 July 2003 over 16,000 prisoners were doubling up in cells designed for one person.† The Home Office's own projections show that there is a huge gap between planned usable capacity for prisoners and the forecast prison population. They are forecasting 88,700 prisoners in 2007 but only have 78,700 average usable capacity, which in normal English means serious overcrowding. To add to that, Home Office prison population predictions for the end of this decade are between 91,400 and 109,600 – another huge increase. Yet the Prime Minister's own strategy unit has made it clear that a 22 per cent increase in the prison population since 1997 is only estimated to have reduced crime by around 5 per cent. It states that 'there is no convincing evidence that further increases

---

† Briefing from the Prison Reform Trust (February 2004).

in the use of custody would significantly reduce crime'.‡

There are also large numbers of remand prisoners, some 13,165 at the end of October 2003 – around one in six of the total prison population – of whom 8,093 were people awaiting trial and the rest convicted but not yet sentenced. Eight out of ten people on remand are there for non-violent offences, of whom, in 2002, the largest proportion, some 23 per cent, were there for receiving stolen goods. Of those remand prisoners, half go on to receive a non-custodial sentence, which begs serious questions of the remand system. But, much more worrying, in 2003, 37 people who were in prison awaiting trial took their own lives, more than a third of all prison suicides that year. Given that remand prisoners suffer from a range of mental health problems, one would have expected urgent action to give them help. The Office for National Statistics (ONS) calculates that more than three-quarters of male remand prisoners suffer from a personality disorder,

---

‡ 'Managing Offenders, Reducing Crime' (December 2003), quoted in the Prison Reform Trust briefing, op. cit.

and one in ten have a functional psychosis. Nearly three-quarters of all male remand prisoners and nearly half of female remand prisoners have used at least one illegal drug in the year before going into prison. A third of the men used heroin, and more than 40 per cent of the women. These drug use figures are far higher than for sentenced prisoners. So why not treat them, rather than warehouse them in prison on remand?

The reason for reciting these statistics is that they show we are not locking up the bad and the dangerous – at least not to an extent that makes a significant difference to our crime statistics. We seem to be locking up the inadequate, the miserable, the poor and the sick, sentencing them to an even worse life than they would have had if they had stayed outside prison. The *Daily Mail*, not always the UK's most liberal newspaper, has commented that: 'Too many who end up in jail are inadequate rather than inherently bad, people who are illiterate, mentally ill or addicted to drink and drugs.'* If remand prisoners are five times as likely as sentenced prisoners to have a history of living in unstable or unsuitable accommodation, such as hostels, and if remand prisoners are even more likely than sentenced prisoners not to have had a job before going into prison (and over two-thirds of all prisoners are unemployed), the picture of human misery and deprivation is startling. The prison suicide rate is even more depressing – of the 94 suicides in 2003, 14 were women, of whom five were under 21. It looks as if there is a direct link between overcrowding, which is clearly going to get worse, and suicides: the Prison Service itself has shown that ten of the twenty establishments with the highest incidence of self-inflicted death are also in the top twenty for population turnover. A third of the suicides happen within a week of going into prison, and one in seven within two days, suggesting that the experience of arriving and living in those conditions is literally unbearable for fragile, sad people. Even worse, over fifty prisoners commit sui-

---

* Quoted in Rethinking Crime and Punishment press pack, 'Prison and the Mentally Ill'.

cide shortly after release each year, according to the Social Exclusion Unit.* So these are people who cannot cope. But we seem not to care.

So why are we doing it? The Home Secretary has said it will stop† and that a top limit of 80,000 inmates has been put on the prison population of England and Wales. Yet at the same time, Blunkett was advocating huge 'super-jails' as regional centres, dealing with high-security cases as well as those on short sentences and the less dangerous.

The effect of prison is dislocation and lack of opportunity. The effect of prison shows in mental ill health and in re-offending. The effect of prison is increased numbers of suicides. And there are hidden consequences, too, that are hugely important. In their excellent volume of essays *Invisible Punishment: The collateral consequences of mass imprisonment*, commenting largely on the United States, Marc Mauer and Meda

---

* *Reducing Re-offending by Ex-Prisoners* (SEU, 2002).
† Richard Ford, 'Prevention, not punishment, is best way ahead, says Blunkett', *The Times* (20 July 2004).

Chesney-Lind make it clear that this affects African-Americans disproportionately, with many of their families unable to visit and to maintain contact and with families increasingly growing up with one parent behind bars. There is a disproportionate effect on ethnic minorities in the UK as well. The government claims it wants a criminal justice system that is fair and transparent, but it admits itself that this does not appear to be so. 'We cannot claim to have a Criminal Justice System that is fair, transparent and commands the respect of the public it serves, when we are unsure that people from minority ethnic communities are getting a fair deal.'* NACRO has also looked at this issue (*Barriers to Equality*, 2004) and found disproportionate numbers of black and Asian defendants receiving prison sentences for certain offences compared with white defendants. White defendants were also more likely to receive community sentences in a variety of other situations as well and there was a significantly higher committal rate to the crown court for black and

---

* From the Home Office Criminal Justice Race Unit website.

Asian defendants compared with white defendants. Black defendants charged with theft were more likely to receive custodial sentences than all other groups, and less likely to receive community sentences.

Although the findings show major differences between the experiences of black and minority ethnic groups and white groups as they go through the system, some factors might begin to explain it, such as a lack of fixed abode. Nevertheless, NACRO is convinced these differences are significant and important. At the end of February 2003, there were 17,762 prisoners from a minority ethnic group, one in four of the prison population, compared to the proportion of people from minority ethnic communities in Britain of one in eleven of the general population. More than a third of the prisoners from minority ethnic communities are foreign nationals. Of the British nationals from minority ethnic communities, 12 per cent are black and 3 per cent South Asian. For blacks, this is significantly higher than the 2 per cent of the population they represent. In 2001 there were more African-Caribbean entrants to prison (over 11,500) than there were to UK universities. The imprisonment rate for black people is 1,140 per 100,000, seven and a half times higher than the imprisonment rate for South Asians or whites, at 166 per 100,000 and 170 per 100,000 respectively. If white people were imprisoned at the rate of black people, England and Wales would have around 400,000 people in prison. There is also severe under-representation of staff from minority ethnic groups in the Prison Service, particularly at senior levels.*

The biggest criticism of the system comes from the disproportionate spending on prisons, which takes money away from education and social supports that might improve the lives of communities in such a way as to reduce both crime and the effects of crime. Yet the policy wind is blowing the other way, towards sending more people to prison, and consequently spending more money on keeping them there.

One reason for this is that, in some important way, we seem to need to be able to point to 'evil' and contain it. If we cannot chop evil

---

* Prison Reform Trust Briefing (February 2004).

people up (child molesters are the current favourite, but sometimes it is those who attack and kill old people) or put their heads on spikes outside the city gates after they have been hung, drawn, and quartered (as used to happen to those convicted of treason), we need to be able to point to putting them inside for a significant period. Our evil people are those who kill children – Victoria Climbié's aunt and her boyfriend; Jasmine Beckford's stepfather; Thomas Hamilton, who killed sixteen children and their teacher in Dunblane; Jon Venables and Robert Thompson who killed Jamie Bulger; the child murderer Mary Bell, and so on.

But most prisoners are not evil. If they commit terrible offences, such as offences against children, they are all too often inadequate and pathetic, more than evil. But even these people, whom modern society has particularly chosen to demonize (and with some justification, given the prevalence of child sexual abuse), are a tiny minority of the prison population. Most prisoners are there because they have committed fairly minor offences.

In fact the general public does not think highly of prison as a way of reducing crime. An overwhelming majority of people, however punitive their attitudes are in other respects, think that more use should be made of intensive community punishments, particularly for young offenders. The preferred option for reducing crime is not more prisons but better parenting – as well as more police on the beat, better discipline in schools, and more constructive activities for the young. Despite evidence to the contrary, when respondents to a survey carried out for the Rethinking Crime and Punishment project were asked to rank specified purposes of sentencing, the largest proportion of people ranked rehabilitation highest.*

Prisons are filled with ordinary people, many of them with significant drug and alcohol problems, and even more with significant mental health problems: 72 per cent of male prisoners and 70 per cent of sentenced female prisoners suffer from two or more mental health conditions. Neurotic and personality disorders are particularly preva-

---

* Rethinking Crime and Punishment, *What Does the Public Think about Prison?* (2002).

lent, with 63 per cent of sentenced prisoners having a neurotic disorder, over three times the level in the general population. Bad or mad? Or just sad? Given the numbers, and the fact that so many of the sentenced prisoners are in for relatively minor offences, sad seems to be an accurate description.

This view is reinforced by the proportion of sentenced prisoners who have been treated as in-patient psychiatric patients in the past – some 20 per cent of the men and 15 per cent of the women. Prisoners are also twice as likely to be refused treatment for mental health problems inside prison as outside: of the 39,000 admissions to prison health centres in 2002, only about 30 per cent were for mental health reasons, a far lower proportion than would have been expected given the appalling statistics on the amount of mental distress suffered by prisoners.

It is partly for this reason that the NHS has now taken over prison health services. The prison service has been repeatedly criticized for offering poor health care, and the present prisons minister, Paul Goggins, has recently been forced to apologize to the widow and family of John Tero, who was wrongfully jailed at the age of 72 and died of a cancer that went undiagnosed whilst he was in prison, where he was treated for indigestion for eight months. What made this case worse was that Mr Tero was sentenced to prison in December 2000 but won an appeal against his conviction in 2001, with the case against him being dismissed. However, he was critically ill by the time he came out and died aged 74. A month before his death, the Home Office refused to apologize for his treatment, on the basis that the Prison Service had done nothing wrong. But an independent clinical review of his case suggested that the medical services failed him in both prisons in which he served time, Woodhill and Wymott, and a Prisons and Probation Ombudsman's report criticized Wymott Prison for making him travel home by public transport when he was already seriously ill. In addition to this case, and others like it, a series of reports on doctors working in prisons suggests that recruitment and retention have been a real problem, as well as prison doctors being inadequately trained for what they have to deal with, often working beyond the limits of their ability.*

The decision to move services to the NHS was broadly welcomed, but those who already worked in the system warned of appalling recruitment problems. Paddy Keavney, a Nottingham GP and part-time prison medical officer, said that the services needed more money: 'there are tremendous manpower problems in terms of recruiting and retaining doctors. If recruitment problems in general practice are bad, then they are absolutely diabolical in prisons.'† The first primary care trusts took over responsibility for local prisons in April 2004 (eighteen PCTs to start with). But the statistics they face are terrifying. Indeed, the Prison Reform Trust suggests that around 90 per cent of all prisoners have a mental health disorder, substance abuse problem or

---

* Luke Birmingham, 'Doctors working in prisons', *BMJ* editorial (23 February 2002), and Richard Smith, 'Prisoners: An end to second class health care', *BMJ* (10 April 1999).
† Quoted by Anne Gulland, 'NHS to take over responsibility for prison health services next April', *BMJ* (5 October 2002).

both.† The Prison Officers' Association has also been somewhat critical, whilst welcoming the change in principle. Its general secretary, Brian Caton, was quoted as saying 'You're not dealing with patients, you're dealing with a prisoner who's ill. Prisoners have lots of baggage and are seriously damaged.'‡ These levels of distress and abuse require huge numbers of detoxifications a month; prisoners need to be sectioned under mental health legislation and properly treated in psychiatric care, and the authorities also need to deal with the spread of infectious diseases, such as hepatitis B and C, from needle-sharing and unprotected sex. The challenges for the NHS are enormous, with the NHS expected to have responsibility for all prison healthcare in England by April 2006.

The idea behind the transfer of responsibility for healthcare services from the Prison Service to the NHS was to help reduce re-offending, on the basis that treatment and

---

† Enver Solomon quoted in Roxanne Escobales, 'NHS to take on prison healthcare', *The Guardian* (23 March 2004).
‡ Quoted in *The Guardian* (23 March 2004).

continuing care for people with mental illness was an essential element in the rehabilitation process. In principle, that is absolutely correct. The move is much to be welcomed, and it is clear that prison healthcare should be of an equivalent standard to that experienced outside, and that care should continue, for very damaged people, once they leave prison. But prison itself is unlikely to be an environment conducive to getting well, or even, arguably, remaining stable. Research has shown that 28 per cent of male sentenced prisoners with evidence of psychosis reported spending twenty-three or more hours a day in their cells – over twice as those without mental health problems. Being locked up for so long, with nothing to do, is clearly not therapeutic.

Nor is the way older prisoners are treated. Only two prisons have wings fit for pensioner prisoners, most of whom are physically ten years older than their calendar age and need care and support. Over 80 per cent of those over 65 are chronically ill or disabled, yet the government does not seem to care. Its 'get tough' policy means that older offenders are far more likely to go to prisons that are not designed for them and to face death there.

In his scathing attack on the state of the prisons, Prisongate, the former Chief Inspector of Prisons, David Ramsbotham, argues that, 'Those who need medical treatment benefit when treated as patients first and prisoners second.' He also said: 'Treating prisoners with respect, regarding them as potentially responsible citizens, is one of the key characteristics of a healthy prison.' It can be done, but it requires the necessary skills and an attitude that is less about punishment than about rehabilitation.

David Ramsbotham is not alone. Other prison governors agree with him, against the trend. Amongst them is John Podmore, governor of Brixton Prison, who is outward looking, believes in rehabilitation, and has been turning around a prison that 'sections' one mentally ill prisoner a week so that they can receive proper treatment, an astonishingly high figure out of a total of 800 inmates. He also wants to introduce communal eating in Brixton Prison as a way of encouraging social interaction and common family behaviours amongst his inmates.*

David Ramsbotham's successor as Chief Inspector of Prisons takes a similar view of how prisoners are treated. In her 2002/3 annual report Anne Owers said that 41 per cent of prisoners being held in prison health care centres should have been in secure NHS accommodation. Indeed, the Health in Prisons Project (2001), a World Health Organization initiative, is clear that prisons are not conducive to good health – something of an understatement, one might say – and argues that promoting health issues in prisons is sensible, particularly with reference to drug use and tuberculosis. They suggest that time in prison should be used to try to break the vicious cycle of drug dependency that often leads on to more criminal activity to finance drug habits. They also suggest that those prisoners who are released in a reasonable state of mental health have a better chance of not re-offending if they are free from addiction.

But the issue with remand prisoners, as discussed above, is worse. They are often

---

* Eric Allison, 'I thought Brixton Prison was a dump', *The Guardian* (31 March 2004).

remanded in custody for psychiatric reports. Adults go to local prisons, where conditions can be very poor, and specialist treatment not available. They face prison as people who are often shocked, sick, and unclear what the future holds. Their high suicide rate should not surprise us. What should surprise us is that the system does so little to try to change it. Even the introduction of 'first night' procedures, which happen in some, but by no means all, prisons, would help, where special staff look after prisoners on their first night in a separate part of the prison. It would not be hard to implement this universally.

Home Office officials have acknowledged that thousands of prisoners should be transferred to secure mental health settings immediately. There are problems with the lack of places for people to go to, with a general lack of availability of high-maintenance, high-support care in the community. That translates into worse care in prisons, where prisoners come at the bottom of the pecking order, with the combination of relatively poor care in prison and poor continuity outside making for a disjointed, unsupported environment. A conference in May 2004, held by the Prison Reform Trust and the mental heath charity MIND, and reported in the *British Medical Journal*, called for courts to use alternatives to custody for men with mental health problems who have committed minor offences and for the Prison Service to meet NHS standards, protocols, and targets, especially with regard to staff. Though they did acknowledge that the transfer of responsibility for prison health from the Home Office to the Department of Health had improved things, they also called for an independent agency to monitor mental health provision in prisons.*

Yet there are some signs of very good practice being developed in the new NHS prison partnerships. At Bullwood Hall women's prison, in Essex, the new mental health team, of psychologist, psychiatrist, nursing staff and occupational therapists, is beginning to tackle a prison population where over half the service users have abusive backgrounds and where there is a high inci-

---

* Paul Stephenson, 'Mentally ill offenders are being wrongly held in prison', *British Medical Journal* (8 May 2004).

dence of substance misuse, personality dis-order, and violent behaviour. Wandsworth Prison has a new welfare programme with short-term sessions, because they have such a transient population. The programme is called 'Looking forward: moving on' and combines educational and mental health services so that inmates getter better access to support and training, both inside and outside the prison system. The programme was devised by the Wandsworth primary care trust, the South West London and St George's Mental Health Trust, and Wandsworth Prison itself, and asked the prisoners what they wanted. 'Prisoners aren't often asked what they want ... Education in prison tends to be very focused on literacy and numeracy, but we found people were asking for things like parenting skills. Most interesting was that people said that they wanted things that would improve their employability.'†

The best sign yet is the establishment of a Mental Health Collaborative for prisons, in

---

† Lisa Benzacar, Wandsworth PCT prison lead, quoted in Alice Tarleton, 'Sentence structure', *Health Service Journal* (2 October 2003).

partnership with the National Institute for Mental Health and the NHS Modernization Agency. As long as there are no more substantial reorganizations of the Department of Health that lead to any of the bodies concerned being reorganized or abolished, this should be an important development, empowering staff, as other collaboratives have succeeded in doing, to make improvements in clinical practice because of what they see and do on a daily basis.

This approach is not entirely new. In my time as chairman of Camden and Islington Community Health Services NHS Trust, which then had responsibility for mental health services, the Revolving Doors Agency, commissioned by the District Health Authority and local social services, working with the Community Trust, the housing departments, social services and probation services, carried out a comprehensive survey of all custody records in police stations throughout Camden and Islington for one year (1993–4). It showed that in 576 cases the people detained had some form of documented mental health problems and many others were known to local services. The conclusions were that it might be possible to reduce the demands this group made on the criminal justice system if the local medical and non-medical services were to co-operate more closely in providing better and more flexible support. The result of all this was an experiment with Link Workers in three areas, including Islington, to see if this approach could bring about change. The Link Workers were to be based with police, health, social and housing services to give support and practical help at the time of arrest, to act as advocates and 'go-betweens' to help people re-establish contact with local services, and to play an advisory and support role on a continuing basis for up to two years. The evaluation was funded by the King's Fund and its highlights published in 2003, under the title *Prison Link Workers*. It was found that the Link Workers had helped 76 per cent of clients gain stable housing following release from prison, and a further 24 per cent saw an improvement in their housing compared to before when they went to prison. For all clients, the standard of housing was at least as good as it had been before they went to prison, a complete contrast to the homelessness so often reported by ex-offenders.

Before going to prison, 99 per cent of clients had been unemployed. Despite that, 46 per cent were not receiving any benefits at all when they were referred to the schemes. Link Workers helped 61 per cent of the clients with their benefits applications, arranged benefits agency appointments for a quarter of the clients, and accompanied half of those people to the appointments.

Thirty-four per cent of the clients were not registered with a GP but needed to see one. Link Workers registered 71 per cent of long-term clients with a GP and, by the end of the project, more than 99 per cent of these clients had a GP. Of those clients who could remember, 51 per cent had never had a mental health assessment, nor any contact with mental health services. Link Workers arranged for GP mental health assessments for 36 per cent of clients, and this helped provide evidence to back up claims for Disability Living Allowance and Incapacity Benefit. Finally, Link Workers arranged relevant treatment for 29 per cent of clients (49 per cent had drugs problems and 52 per cent alcohol issues) once they were in the community, and referred 15 per cent of clients in prison to drug services.

The whole project was very successful, and demonstrated that assertive prison inreach and community outreach can make a huge difference to the people with mental problems who come into contact with the criminal justice system. But there were warning signs, both of taking on too many clients – a real British disease, as budgets are constantly squeezed – and being clear about which clients can really be helped.

The American system of mental health courts, a response to the increasingly common arrest and incarceration of people with serious mental health problems, may also help some people to access services they could not otherwise have reached. These special courts bring together the mental health treatment system and the criminal justice system to help defendants with mental health problems through faster case processing time, improved access to public mental health treatment services, and reduced recidivism. In New York City, CASES (the Center for Alternative Sentencing and

Employment Services) works closely with schools and health and housing agencies and arranges for offenders to be placed on its programmes as an alternative to custodial sentencing. Ann-Marie Louison, the Director of Mental Health Programs there, was extremely generous with her time in March 2004, talking me through their system and how they had made, and continue to make, a difference. Where they are different, and have a far stronger can-do mentality than we tend to have in the UK, is in their work with people who have serious and persistent mental illness, what they call co-occurring substance misuse disorders, and we would call 'dual diagnosis', combined with a history of homelessness. These are people our system has found it notoriously hard to treat. But with their Nathaniel Project, they offer an alternative to incarceration and provide intensive case management, on-site psychiatric and nursing services, and monitor compliance with community based referrals. In recent years, the project has become an Assertive Community Treatment (ACT) team licensed by the NY Office of Mental Health. Like our assertive outreach teams, they go out to patients and help people stick to treatment programmes. Unlike our services, they navigate the criminal justice system constantly, and by a mixture of persuasion and insistence – the alternative being prison – get people to cooperate with their treatment programmes and get them established in appropriate housing (100 per cent of their participants are appropriately housed when they leave jail).

It looks, to an outsider, that in a very different, and largely more punitive, system than ours, there is a way of making a difference with a really committed team, working with a mixture of state, city, and charitable funding. But they find it hard to recruit staff and have a client group that often has no experience of being in a stabilizing programme and who has a history of chronic homelessness. They record a history of fighting – politely of course – with both the court system and the mental health system and report that, though the court system is not on the whole reluctant to release offenders to their programmes, sometimes the mental health system can be. The CASES model seems able to deal with the fact that

US communities and judges are as averse to risk as people in the UK. Despite this, they get people released to them, have a low rate of re-offending, and have a formerly risk-averse state system increasingly coming round to working this way with mentally ill offenders.

There are three key ingredients to their success that we might learn from.

First, they maintain manageable caseloads – of one professional to ten people, where our community psychiatric nurses are often carrying caseloads of fifty or more, and our prison mental health services have even fewer staff.

Second, they only hire highly skilled workers, at a Masters Degree level, with a team that has experience in recovery work and expertise in criminal justice, mental health, and substance abuse systems, as well as a commitment to their clients.

Third, they demonstrate to the client an unwillingness to give up. These workers, skilled and experienced, will not abandon clients but will keep them out of prison and in the community, accessing treatment and eventually finding them some kind of daytime activity or even employment. That level of expertise and experience is essential for this kind of work, yet the UK experience is to be understaffed, often to use junior people without adequate experience who simply do not have the toughness and experience to cope.

Many of the people who go into the UK's prisons are young, and many of them have drug and alcohol problems and a history of being in care. On 30 January 2004, there were 10,645 prisoners under 21 in prisons in England and Wales, of whom the majority, over 8,000, were between 18 and 20. By far the majority of young people in prison have been convicted of non-violent offences, a large proportion of which will be burglary and theft. Indeed, those convicted of a social offence between the ages of 18 and 20 have a 72 per cent chance of re-offending. But their experience of prison is not one of training and rehabilitation. Instead, with short sentences, they are more likely to be on the cusp of becoming career criminals than to go straight. Mental health, drug and alcohol abuse problems are all common amongst young people in prison. Of the young adults in prison, nearly three-quarters were excluded from school at some stage, and 63 per cent were unemployed at the time of their arrest. Forty per cent of young men and 27 per cent of young women in prison have been in care during their childhood, compared with only 2 per cent of the general population, whilst 25 per cent of young male prisoners are thought to have been homeless or living in temporary accommodation before going into prison. Young adult prisoners are even more likely to suffer from mental health problems than adult prisoners, and more likely to attempt or succeed in committing suicide than both older and younger prisoners.

The Chief Inspector of Prisons, in her annual report 2002–2003, expressed concern about the lack of a coherent national strategy for 18–21-year-olds in prison, as well a lack of a statement on standards and no new funding. There was commitment in the Labour Party's 1997 manifesto, before it came into government, to improve provision in the prisons for this age group. That is absolutely essential if something is to be done to reduce chances of re-offending and give people the chance of a decent life after they get out of prison.

There is also serious concern about children in prison, for which the UK has been much criticized. On 30 January 2004, there were 2,489 people under 18 in prison in England and Wales, and the number of 15–17 year olds in prison has nearly doubled over the last ten years. The Youth Justice Board, despite having a plan to do so, failed to remove all girls under 17 from Prison Service Accommodation in 2003, even though this was a commitment made by the Home Office in March 1999. Of those in custody of school age, over a quarter have the literacy and numeracy levels of an average 7-year-old or below. Over half of those in custody under the age of 18 have a history of being in care, or have come into contact with social services, and studies show that 45 per cent of them have been permanently excluded from school. They also have particularly high prevalence of behavioural and mental health problems. Amongst prisoners aged 16–20, 85 per cent show signs of a personality disorder and 10 per cent exhibit signs of psychotic illnesses such as schizophrenia. Drugs and alcohol abuse are major problems, and over half the female and two-thirds of the male population of those aged 16–20 had a 'hazardous drinking habit' before going into prison. These people also have a high suicide rate.

For example, Joseph Scholes hanged himself in 2002 from the bars of his cell at Stoke Heath Young Offenders Institution, just a few days after his sixteenth birthday, nine days into a two-year sentence for his involvement in a street robbery, snatching mobile phones. His mother said she had not expected him to survive his sentence, and she also said he had threatened to take his own life, having slashed his face in the run-up to his trial. He had had an unsettled childhood, had been abused by a relative of his father, and showed all the signs of a depressed and difficult young boy, with periodic suicidal thoughts and a history of self-harm. Despite his mother's concern, his warning that he would kill himself was not taken seriously by the judge in his trial, by the Youth Justice Board, who did not give him a place in a secure unit run by the local authority, or by the prison staff. They did not seek to protect him, putting him in an unsafe cell with part-time supervision.

Twenty-five children aged 15 to 17 have taken their own lives in custody since 1990. Between 1998 and 2002 there were 1,111 reports of people under 18 harming themselves in young offenders' institutions, and twelve teenagers killed themselves whilst in custody. Yet these cases rarely make the news and we are not furious, as we would be about the death of someone at the hands of a sex offender.

Society failed Joseph Scholes and his family in not protecting him after a troubled and difficult childhood. Disruptive children in youth prisons are often kept in solitary confinement in bare cells, naked, and are forced to use the floor as a toilet. A report in *The Observer* by Martin Bright in January 2004 revealed that over a hundred children were sent to such punishment cells over the previous year, cells that have no light, ventilation, sanitation, or furniture. Home Office figures showed that such cells had been used systematically, despite official assurances that they were only used in one institution. Huntercombe in Oxfordshire,

Feltham in West London, and Lancaster Farms all used such punishment cells, and Stoke Heath, another young offenders' institution, was found to be using these cells in late 2002. The Prison Service is supposed to have abandoned the use of strip cells for children, and the Home Office insisted that the cells were only used for segregation, not punishment, of children who were extremely difficult and violent.

But the real question that underlies all this is why children as violent and disturbed as this are in young offenders' institutions at all and not in a mental health facility designed for adolescents, where help, treatment, and support are available rather than punishment and sensory deprivation. Even more disturbing, bearing in mind the degree of social exclusion and desperation suffered by many of these young people, is the fact that they are frequently moved from jail to jail to make space for new arrivals. If jail is to do anything for young people, it must be to give them some form of rehabilitation. Moving them around constantly will only serve to disrupt training courses and education and mean that they have no stability in supervision and support.

Support for families visiting young people in prison or young offenders' institutions is weak in the extreme. In 2004, the Visitors' Centre at Feltham Young Offenders Institution closed its doors so that families lost vital support in keeping in touch with their teenagers. The prison cut funding to the centre, a charity, which made it no longer viable. Yet all the evidence suggests that prisoners are six times less likely to re-offend if good family contact is maintained whilst they are in prison, which is extremely difficult for families to do given the rapid moving around of young offenders from place to place. Real investment should be made in visitors' centres and in supporting young people and children in prison. But the public's view, or perhaps more accurately the government's view of the public view, is that people are angry and want these young horrors locked up. They want toughness, not tenderness.

This is complicated by the public's increasing fear of young people – especially young males. Society believes that young people are responsible for far more crime than they actually commit. For example, in 2001, 28 per cent of people believed that young people were responsible for more than half of all offences, whilst a further 55 per cent thought that responsibility for crime is shared equally between adults and young people.* In fact, 76 per cent of detected crime was committed by people over 18 in 1999, and offenders over 21 were responsible for almost 60 per cent of detected offending. Popular perceptions would also suggest that youth crime is on the up and the government's new Anti-Social Behaviour Orders, targeted at uncontrolled young people and their families, seem to confirm that belief. In fact, the numbers of young people cautioned or sentenced for indictable offences has shown a gradual, though not uninterrupted, decline over recent years. Youth crime is at its lowest level since the 1990s.†

There has also been public concern about the numbers of girls and young women who offend, and again there is a belief that the

---

* NACRO, Youth Crime Fact Sheet (July 2001).
† NACRO News (website), 'Children first, offender second?' (16 April 2004).

numbers are rising. But NACRO suggests that the gender breakdown has in fact remained more or less constant for the past ten years or so. Yet, for all that, with evidence of declining detected youth crime, there is a huge extension in the use of custody for children and young people. We have to ask ourselves why. For children are more likely to be victims of crime than the cause of it, and it is adults who commit the vast majority of crime. And prison does not work, since children who are imprisoned are more likely to re-offend.

Concern is so great at the extraordinary way our juvenile prison system is going that several of the largest children's organizations – Barnardo's, NACRO, the Children's Society, the National Children's Bureau, NCH Action for Children, and the NSPCC – have formed an alliance to raise the level of public debate around youth crime by providing clear information and comment on the issues involved. NACRO already made it clear some years ago that the use of punitive sanctions and custody increased throughout the 1990s without being effective deterrents. It cites unstructured psychotherapy, non-directive client-centred counselling, and intervention based on medical models as being demonstrably ineffective in deterring young offenders from re-offending, yet those are precisely what have been offered in many cases. It suggests that cognitive behavioural interventions can be effective, alongside other measures, and that there is a need for skill-based programmes designed to improve problem solving. There is also a need for specific and shorter term programmes for those with drugs and alcohol problems.* If government could see its way to encouraging these sorts of sentences, these interventions might help.

The government, however, seems convinced of the need to use cognitive behaviour programmes, with mixed results. Of those who received a community based sentence and who were given three months of cognitive behaviour counselling, a significant proportion are voting with their feet and refusing to go to the self-help sessions. The Probation Service has been given tough targets to meet on getting offenders into

---

* NACRO, *Effective Practice with Young People who Offend* (1999).

therapy, but nearly two-thirds of the people who start fail to complete. The Canadian and US statistics show a significant fall in re-offending amongst offenders who complete such sessions, but people in Britain tend to get hostile and angry and are ready to drop out after the initial psychometric testing (indeed, a third do). So unwilling are offenders to undertake this kind of group therapy that the Home Office had to cut its target from 30,000 to complete by April 2004 to 20,000 and then to 15,000. Some participants were even telling probation staff they would rather spend three months 'inside' than attend the sessions.*

Despite all the initiatives, including the Home Office's Path-finder projects and the pilot Youth Offender Panels, re-offending has barely gone down. Indeed, Martin Narey, head of the new amalgamated prison and Probation Service, NOMS, the National Offenders Management Service, has promised to quit if the number of repeat offenders does not drop. Yet the evidence is clear. If offenders do not go to jail, they are less

---

* Martin Bright, 'Offenders say no to US-style rehab sessions', *The Observer* (21 September 2003).

likely to re-offend. Government predictions, however, are for the prison population to increase. Judges are being pushed to give longer sentences, including prison sentences for those who would previously have received community punishments. It is likely that Martin Narey will fail in his aim, unless policy changes and unless major political will is put into encouraging alternatives to custody. But despite the fact that many of the young people in prison and young offenders' institutions are there for relatively minor offences, or for repeat offences, there are some who have committed truly horrible offences. It is these who have hit the headlines, and they who have, in some way, coloured the perception of youth and crime.

The most famous example is that of the two children who killed toddler Jamie Bulger. Robert Thompson and Jon Venables were both 10-year olds when they killed the 2-year-old boy. But more recently Terence Lambert and Sergio Pantano, both aged 14 in 1999 when they committed their offence, killed a 26-year-old man, Mohammed Aslan, when they found him sitting on a park bench in Bedford, drunk. The judge told the teenagers that what they did was 'pure unmitigated evil', and described what they did as 'a chilling catalogue of gratuitous violence which gives every indication that it was carried out for the fun of it'. Both adolescents were known by their own gang for their violence, and both were thought to have come from respectable homes, with parents who had done their best to bring up their children well and who were described by the judge as 'God-fearing people'. Neither came from a broken home, both fathers were in work, and they went to a church school. The Revd Nicholas Elder, whose church was attended by the Lambert family, said that 'These were not dysfunctional families. This is a community with close family ties.' Nor does it appear that the murder was racially motivated. The key may lie in the fact that the boys had just moved from their church middle school to a senior school where they had fallen in with a group of boys involved in petty crime. Certainly, there had been some violence before, and there was plenty of bullying and shoplifting. But why these two would have murdered a lone drunk on a park bench is unclear. One of the problems underpinning how we think about children and young people in prison is that we almost need to have a view of them as evil, strange and different. If we thought that what they did had its roots in the rest of society, then we would be to blame. Better let it be the 'evil' within them, the original sin of humanity that was flickering up inside, rather than a reflection of what they watched, what they thought, and how they were brought up

Yet clearly some of it is our fault. David Akinsaya, now a BBC reporter, whose case was discussed in the previous chapter, went straight from 'our' state care system to prison. He suggests that only a few people seemed to really care about him, including one social worker who simply refused to let go and continued to visit him wherever and whatever, including in prison, in her own time. Jenni Randall was the social worker 'who supported me through and after prison, even when I was not officially on her case load', and stopped him going back to prison after he spent nine months in borstal, aged 18. His experience of the care system was that it transferred him from place to place and put him on his own in a house in Basildon, aged 15. He became – unsurprisingly – part of a gang, which led to his sentence for over three hundred offences. He argues that the care system itself is to blame, with 49 per cent of children in care going straight to prison.

There is clearly something desperately wrong with our care system, and with how we think of these young people, if so many end up in our prisons. Yet apparently we want to send more of them there. Despite throwing up our hands at the statistics, public attitudes on youth crime are hardening – even though youth crime is falling. We want, as a society, to get rid of these young people who so annoy and frighten us. Many of them are the ones who came out of 'our' care system. So alternatives to prison are essential, as are ways of supporting young people, however anti-social their behaviour at the time, helping them into jobs and families, and giving them a sense of belonging and self-worth.

Some people are arguing for tagging as an alternative to prison, with community schemes in which young offenders can do something useful and not end up behind bars. The Intensive Control and Change Programme is being piloted in eleven probation service areas and is expected to be rolled out nationally if it works. In this system, 18–20-year-olds will not be put in prison. Instead, they get a combination of training and punishment and, provided they do not breach the conditions of the programme, they do not go to prison. Usually, they get up to six months on a night curfew or electronic tag, up to seven hours a week of community punishments, such as decorating (often old people's homes) and litter collection, and eighteen hours of education and training. Since there are ten thousand or more young men between 18 and 20 imprisoned for a year or less in Britain's prisons, this system, if it works, should reduce prison overcrowding, despite the appalling projections the government has made on expected prison populations for the next few years. But whether the programmes offered will help the young men involved sort out their lives, and whether they will be sufficiently committed to stay with the programme and be helped by their own communities when their punishment is over, is unknown. At least this is a better way of trying to help these young people get a life than automatically putting them behind bars.

Though attempts to deal with drug use by setting up appointments for drug therapy outside whilst still in prison may seem obvious, as has been done in Bradford by the Ripple Project, it has not been the norm. But it is much to be encouraged, in order to stop the endless procession of ex-offenders reoffending because drug dealers get to them quicker than a drug therapy programme or a probation officer. The most significant initiative, though as yet clearly ineffective, is the Drug Treatment and Testing Order, where people who have committed offences to get money for drugs are put on a demanding course of treatment to get them off drugs and are routinely re-tested. Only some 3,400 people a year are on these orders at present, whilst compulsory drug treatment will clearly have to play a far greater role, alongside major social support, in the future. The introduction of these orders was enormously welcomed when it came into force; but, as Helena Kennedy puts it in her book *Just Law*, 'a recent report by probation inspectors found the scheme bedevilled by the failure of Whitehall: too many funding streams, too many targets, central micro-management, of which government is so guilty, and constant reporting back.' So the Probation Service cannot provide for the numbers of orders made, despite the idea being an excellent one.

For drugs are a huge issue. As we have seen, the majority of people in prison have a history of substance misuse, and the rate of the use of heroin, cocaine, or crack cocaine is on the increase. But there are only 1,715 residential drug treatment places available in England, ridiculously few. Drug treatment needs to be an alternative to a custodial sentence for less serious offenders, particularly the young. The relationship between drugs and crime is complex. The Audit Commission reckons that half of drug abusers' annual spend on drugs of £1 billion is raised through crime.* One in six prisoners is there because

---

* Audit Commission 2002, quoted in Rethinking Crime and Punishment, 'Searching for a Fix' (June 2004).

of a drugs offence, very few just for possession. The prison service's own figures show that 11.7 per cent of prisoners failed drugs tests while inside in 2002–3. The Rethinking Crime and Punishment team suggests that this is likely to be an underestimate, as 'a survey of women prisoners found that over a quarter were still using heroin, albeit mainly on an occasional basis compared with daily use outside'.† There is some criticism of the prisons' own detox programmes, with prisoners complaining that the programmes are often not long enough. There is no routine recording of the proportion of prisoners who are given detox and enter one of the prison service's own drug rehabilitation programmes. Yet the link between prison, drug use, and drug crimes is very strong.

There is a further issue. Drug treatment is increasing, but the numbers completing it successfully shows a slight fall (from 59 per cent in 2001–2 to 57 per cent in 2002–3). The government wants to double the numbers in treatment by 2008, to 200,000. The average waiting time to get on a programme is down

---

† Home Office, quoted in Rethinking Crime and Punishment, op. cit.

from 9 weeks in December 2001 to 2.7 weeks in March 2004. The longest waits are for specialist community prescribing and for residential treatment, where the waits are just under four weeks. The problem is that this does not help those who need to get access to treatment in prison, to have their treatment monitored, and to be able to continue it when they get out. This would require no waiting times, along with very good links and partnerships, not a common feature of the prison system. Equally, one might argue that better access to drug treatments and rehabilitation programmes should prevent a large proportion of people entering prison at all. Rethinking Crime and Punishment is saying much of this. What it is not quite saying – though perhaps it should – is that government is to be much criticized for expanding prison populations without dealing first with the drugs issue. If prison is used by some sentencers as the only way to get someone into treatment, and we do not know how many complete treatment in prisons, then the situation is problematic. The way forward should be for treatment to be widely available first, with the offer of a package of compulsory treatment, monitoring and help with other issues as a way of avoiding a custodial sentence second, and only then the need for better treatment of drug abusers within our prisons. All that needs to be combined with proper monitoring and links with outside agencies, to prevent people falling through the net as now occurs on a regular basis.

Equally significant are the numerous Community Rehabilitation Orders, (CROs), which used to be called Probation Orders, and the former Community Service Orders (now called Community Punishment Orders). The widespread changes in the wake of the Carter Review,* largely brought in without consultation, made the Probation Service part of the Prison Service and made its role more mechanistic, more punitive, and less befriending. This should give us pause for thought. The probation service itself resents the change of name from Community Service Orders to Community Punishment Orders. How can those carrying

* Patrick Carter *Managing Offenders, Reducing Crime: A new approach* (Correctional Services Review, December 2003).

them out get a sense of worth from that name? What young person will feel that this work is worth doing if it is purely a punishment, and if it is not seen as much of a deterrent?

Bobby Cummines, Chief Executive of Unlock, a charity specializing in helping ex-offenders, agreed to be interviewed for this book as an ex-offender himself. His story makes for dramatic reading. He started offending when he was very young, in Islington, where he was at grammar school. He started bunking off early. 'There are two types of education: academic and street education, and the street was just more exciting. Older people were grooming you and telling you lies. You believed the myths. At 16 I was into street gangs.' A child of Irish parents, one of eight, 'we never stole off each other. It was a big extended family.' Being 'good with his hands' and a schoolboy boxing champion, he got sent to collect bookies' debts from people not much older than him, and learned that violence 'had a voice'. At 16 he was arrested for possessing a sawn-off shotgun, and his chances of employment were zero. He thinks that if he had been told the truth about what would happen to him if he got involved in crime, he might have listened. 'That's what I do now when I talk to young people. I tell them, I've been there and if it was any good I'd still be in that life.' He then describes how education was liberation, and how he started reading whilst inside. But he also says that many of the teachers in the prisons do not understand the kids inside and are fed up with the overcrowding and the politics and the kids who do not want to learn. 'Then "Unlock" goes in, and when we go in, and talk to kids, there is enthusiasm. We do role plays and work with them', though he admits that the novelty of seeing him fades after only a couple of times. 'But anyway we work with the kids and work out an armed robbery, and we work through a scenario where we work out what they might get and all the hours they'd put in and show it's not worth it. They could be on benefits for more, and not go to jail!' They try to work from where the kids are, so that if they are interested in cars, for instance, they can work on engines, and if necessary learn to read so that they can understand the manuals.

Cummines's own experience was that education and reading were the key for him, and he certainly tries to get the kids he sees to understand that they can get further if they learn something. But, in his view, since the government only funds basic literacy, it fails the kids who are beyond that. His experience was of having people who believed in him – a probation officer who supported him when his mother was dying, and an education officer who showed him compassion – and he argues that the way the system is organized means that staff cannot really talk to prisoners and cannot give the time since it does not count towards their key performance indicators. 'We are dealing with humans, not a jam factory.' And, he adds, that it is 'working against prison staff, too, for if you can talk to a prison officer and get to know them, you don't want to attack them, as you don't feel like attacking someone you have got to know.' His comments on probation are also interesting. For him, the changes to the Probation Service are scandalous, because he does not believe probation officers will be able to give offenders the support and encouragement to get a new life, learn to read, get off drugs, and get a home if they are charged purely with dealing with 'punishment'.

But his most scathing remarks are reserved for the leaving prison period. He points out that you can see your drug dealer the day you get out, but you have to wait for six weeks for the drugs counsellor. With the new National Offender Management Scheme (NOMS), if you have gone through detox, this will be followed up. But, he says, 'It won't. Probation officers are overloaded – they are now like court policemen. How can someone trust the probation officer fully when the next moment he can breach him?' There is a need for better sentence planning, and better discharge planning. The grant at discharge is £46.75 (for prisoners aged 25 and older) if you are of no fixed abode – hardly a good start to a new life – or £37 (for prisoners aged 18 to 24). A higher rate of discharge grant (£94.40) is paid to prisoners on release only if there is a need to seek, obtain, and pay for accommodation. This is only paid to prisoners with no accommodation arranged in advance if this arises through no fault of the prisoner. The current rates were set in 1995, and are under review as part of the National Rehabilitation Plan that the government is drawing up in response to the Social Exclusion Unit's report on reducing reoffending by released prisoners. However, upon leaving prison, people can wait six to twelve weeks for the DSS to release their benefits, so that unless a hostel is prepared to wait for the money they will be made homeless. If they become homeless, all the problems of other homeless people will affect them: their lives will go down and down and they will re-offend, ending up back in prison.

Some people go home to families, but often the families cannot cope as the ex-offender is no longer used to family life. 'In prison, people build up routines to help them cope with being banged up for 23 hours out of 24. They go to sleep at midday. They are not trained for the work ethic.' Cummines argues that what people need when they leave prison is an ID so they can open a bank account, and get a job and a mortgage. And they need an address before they get out, which means proper housing. In other words, they absolutely must not to be left to become homeless. That should not be impossible for us to achieve.

Nor are jobs impossible to find, as the TUC has made clear in arguing that there is a union case for helping ex-offenders get jobs. It would be good to see the TUC itself set up a project, with the unions, to get this under way. For there are some positive signs. Toyota GB has set up a programme of training young mechanics at Aylesbury Young Offenders' Institution. Ford has started a training workshop at Feltham YOI, and National Grid Transco has a very successful scheme operating in Reading YOI. The thinking is obvious. There is a shortage of trained motor mechanics, a skill one can easily learn in prison. But the idea has been slow to catch on. Few other companies are interested, and the figures on those who start the Aylesbury course are not wholly encouraging, with some 50 per cent leaving, for a variety of reasons – 'because they lack the academic ability; others because they get parole or are transferred to an adult prison at 21'. Toyota says the trainees are bright lads but probably have not been to school since their early teens. Geoff Davies, dealer training and development manager for Toyota, is reported as saying: 'In a structured environment, some become star pupils – several of our dealers have taken them on and it's been very successful.'*

Cummines also questions the extent to which we are prepared to ask what prison is for. Just like the Rethinking Crime and Punishment project, he believes we need to ask the question. If it is for retribution, then arguably it might work, though many of those inside just become hardened offenders and will come out and do it all over again. That suggests that a retributive system would be better advised either to punish people in other ways, or to keep them in prison permanently and throw away the key. But as Cummines says, 'if prison is for rehabilitation, and for young offenders it surely must be, then it is not doing a good job'. Prison officers need to be able to spend time with the prisoners, they need to be able to help with personal problems, and they need a manageable workload. But if this is to be achieved, then we need to recruit more

* Stephen Cook, 'Inside Track', *The Guardian* (5 February 2003).

prison officers, and this is hard because it is a thankless task. They are so driven by key performance indicators that they cannot use their professional skills to work with prisoners and help to rehabilitate them, or at least help them suffer less.

Cummines argues that prison should only be for those who really need it, with more rehabilitation and better sentence planning. He also believes in restorative justice, with victims having a voice and with people understanding that most prisoners are not violent. But he also says that 'Prisons are about a lack of love. Prisoners need more contact time with their kids, to let them know the damage they have done to their family, and to let them know what they are losing. Otherwise, it's only other villains who visit them.' His last, and most significant, comment was: 'We need to make ex-offenders feel they have achieved something by going straight. And if they do well in prison they should be rewarded with a lower sentence. There also needs to be a tax incentive for employers to employ ex-offenders.'

Women's Prisons

Some of the worst statistics come from the women's prisons, where suicide rates are high, self-harm is commonplace, and the care of offenders seems to be largely inadequate. From 1,811 women behind bars in 1994, the figure in June 2004 was 4,610. The women are vastly overcrowded, in seventeen prisons with inadequate facilities and staffing. Ten women committed suicide between January and June 2004, compared with fourteen in the whole of 2003, itself a record number. Many young offenders are parents, but only four women's prisons have mother-and-baby units, two taking babies up to nine months and two to eighteen months. A new private women's prison opened in June 2004 with a further mother-and-baby unit for up to twelve women and their babies.

The Prison Service takes babies from their mothers before they are a year old as a matter of course, though most psychologists argue that early separation can lead to long-term psychological problems for the child. In the case of a young woman, Claire Frost, who was jailed for six years in 2002 after being on heroin and attacking and robbing an elderly man, her baby was allowed to stay with her for nine months at New Hall prison in Yorkshire. She then asked to go to Askham Grange open prison, which has a mother-and-baby unit that takes babies up to eighteen months. The prison authorities turned down her request and her baby went to her parents. Ms Frost argued that early separation breached article 8 of the European Convention on Human Rights, respect for a family life, and was backed by the official solicitor. The decision to remove her baby at nine moths was quashed, but the judge said it was up to prison authorities to decide when to move the child. Shortly after her baby went to Ms Frost's parents, she was moved to Askham Grange. One is left completely puzzled at the rationale behind this, when it is clear that it cannot be in the child's best interests to be separated from the mother so early, nor in the interests of good management to refuse a transfer until after the child has been taken away and then send the mother to a place where the child could have gone too.

But this is as nothing compared with the case of Sarah Campbell, from Cheshire. Campbell came from a conservative background and eventually ended up a heroin addict. She was sentenced to three years in Styal, a women's prison, after hassling an elderly man for money for drugs, who, petrified by Sarah and her friends, had a heart attack and died. Sarah had spent six months on remand and had become drug free, to her delight. But she was convicted of manslaughter and was sent to Styal, where she took an overdose within hours of starting her sentence and died three days before her nineteenth birthday. At court, before her sentence, the liaison duty probation officer and a duty psychiatric nurse both warned that she might harm herself. But it made no difference. Her mother Pauline, a civil servant, has become an 'angry vociferous risk-taker'. Her experience of her daughter's death, a child with a known history of depression and drug dependency, has made her furious and has opened her eyes to the fact 'that women are treated with medieval barbarity by our prison system. More and more women are being sent to prison when clearly they should be being treated for mental illness – and conditions once they reach jail are horrific. I have seen women who have used scouring pads and hairgrips to maim themselves'.* Women prisoners are three times as likely as their male counterparts to commit suicide, and despite being only 6 per cent of the prison population, they account for half of all incidences of self-harm. Pauline Campbell argues that women in prison are an invisible issue, that they do not commit violent crimes, and that their offences mostly relate to theft, drugs or unpaid bills. Their separation from their children tells on them very badly. Over half of women prisoners have at least one child under 16, and 8,000 children a year are affected by their mothers going to prison. There has been an astonishing 173 per cent increase in the numbers of women prisoners since 1992, whilst male prisoners have increased by 50 per cent. Even the government has finally got worried. In March 2004, the Prisons' Minister, Paul Goggins, announced the 'Women's Offending Reduction

---

* Quoted in Amelia Hill, 'Mum's Crusade to save women behind bars', The Observer (30 May 2004).

Programme', linking various government departments and units and designed to try to deal with substance misuse, mental health problems and with making community interventions and programmes more suitable and accessible for women. It is clearly needed. But staff are barely available to meet these needs. Nevertheless, it is a step in the right direction. For life inside prison for women is hell. Penny Mellor, a former prisoner, writes movingly in the *British Medical Journal* about life in a women's prison: 'My experience inside three very different prisons was in itself very depressing; listening to the screaming and crying all night leaves you weary, alarms going off at all hours day and night as yet another inmate tries to kill themselves makes you jumpy and renders you physically exhausted, your heart sinking and your mind praying that it won't be someone you've grown fond of that's hurt themselves; prison officers' faces etched in stress related lines as they run to unlock a door not knowing what they will find on the other side, no wonder members of the Prison Service are looking to strike over conditions and pay ...

If you weren't mentally ill when you went in, you certainly are after a very short space of time.'* Some might argue that this is special pleading from a former prison inmate, but it appears not. Suicide and self-harm amongst women prisoners are now at a record high, according to a study by the Prison Reform Trust, funded by the Nuffield Foundation.† The study called on government to invest in mental health provision, drug treatment, and supervision in the community as an alternative to prison for vulnerable women accused of non-violent crimes. It also calls on prisons to provide – via the NHS – better mental health care, which is of a much lower standard than elsewhere. Mental distress is also often exacerbated by prison regimes. One in four of the women in prison have spent time in local authority care as a child, with nearly 40 per cent leaving school before the age of 15 and one in ten at 13 or younger. Over half the women in prison say they have experienced violence at home. The report recommends that community sentences and court diversion schemes that

---

* Penny Mellor, letter, *BMJ* (May 2004).
† *Troubled Inside* (Prison Reform Trust, 2003).

send people who are mentally ill for treatment should be used to divert 'at risk' women from prison whenever possible. That would have saved Sarah Campbell's life. As Juliet Lyon, director of the Prison Reform Trust, said on launching the report; 'Prison is a punishment of last resort. It is cruel to lock up mentally ill women, and it does lasting harm to them and their families.'‡

Helena Kennedy, the redoubtable campaigner for justice and equal rights, agrees. In her passionate book *Just Law* (2004) she argues: 'Women in prison are more likely to be suffering from multiple problems of material deprivation than male prisoners, less likely to be career criminals or dangerous, yet they are at the receiving end of a growing punitiveness. This has partly reflected the growing hostility to single mothers generally, and the judicial inability to understand that equality does not mean sameness, and that they do not have to punish a woman exactly as they would a man if, for

---

‡ Quoted in Owen Dyer, 'Suicide among women prisoners at a record high, report says', *BMJ* (19 July 2003).

example, she has responsibility for dependent children.'

The government's own independent inspectorate of prisons has also been deeply critical of how women are treated in prison. The former Chief Inspector of Prisons, the late Sir Stephen Tumim, annoyed the government of his day with what he said about Holloway and other places, and his successor, Sir David Ramsbotham, did the same when he began his book on the shocking state of Britain's prisons with an account of his first visit – which he refused to complete – to Holloway. In his chapter on women in prison, David Ramsbotham argued that Holloway was the exception to the rule that there had been some improvement in women's prisons around the country in his time. He criticized the fact that women are sent to prisons far away from the places from which they come, which is patently absurd if they are to keep any contact with their children. But Holloway, in Ramsbotham's view, encapsulated the problem not only of how women's prisons were managed, but also of how all prisons are managed. For the Prison Service 'remained stubbornly resistant to making major change until it was forced upon it'.

Everyone agrees that prisons are not the place for vulnerable people, and that women tend to be more vulnerable in prison than men. So why does government not listen? Is it just a desire to be punitive? Do they truly believe that people have a better chance of treatment for drugs and mental illnesses inside prison? Or is it simply that it would not play well in the media to say that women should not be sent to prison unless they have committed violent offences? Just before David Ramsbotham retired from the post of Chief Inspector of Prisons, in July 2001, he gave a lecture to the Prison Reform Trust. As he was about to begin, his wife slapped a piece of paper into his hand on which was written, amongst other things:

If prison worked – less children would be in care and less mothers in prison
If prison worked – we would be shutting prisons, not opening more
If prison worked – there would be work or education for every prisoner

435

THE PRISON SYSTEM

If prison worked – judges would not be seeing in the dock the same people over and over again...*

And so on.

Prison is only a true deterrent for those have something to lose. It is a terrifying and torturing place for people who are mentally ill and vulnerable, and it is undeniably puni- tive. But if you are someone with nothing to lose, the prospect of prison (rather than the reality) is unlikely to deter you – and we know that many ex-prisoners re-offend.

What helps to prevent crime is a feeling that you have a place in society, some de- gree of respect from your fellow citizens, something to lose that would make the loss of liberty frightening and upsetting.

If we cannot work out a way of resettling people who have been offenders so that they do not want to re-offend, then we are not serious about wanting to prevent social ex- clusion. If we cannot get proper drug and alcohol treatment available in the commu- nity, combined with community punish- ments that actually work, then we have no

---

* David Ramsbotham, *Prisongate* (2003), 239–40.

right to argue that we have a welfare state. We need compulsory drug and alcohol treatment for offenders, available instantly on demand, and with the threat of prison if people slip up. We need community punishments to consist of working on things that offenders see as worthwhile. But we also need to understand that if, as a society, we do not give offenders something to strive for, something that is theirs, in the end, we will have done nothing but give them a brief break from a former, unstructured, drug-filled life.

Drugs are a major issue for the prison system, as illustrated by an extraordinary story that came to light in 2004.*

Two offenders, Audie Carr (29) and Benjamin Clarke (23), absconded from Leyhill Open Prison because of their concern that it was rife with drugs. Prison officers discovered the men were missing on the evening of their escape. The following day, having walked for twenty miles, they knocked on the door of Gloucester Prison and asked staff if they could finish their sen-

---

* *The Guardian* (3 June 2004).

tences there. They had been there before, and had both been transferred to Leyhill after beating their drug dependencies, but when they asked to return to a closed jail, because they thought they might succumb to temptation at Leyhill, they were refused. So they walked the twenty miles. There was an attempted prosecution, which was dropped, and they were eventually allowed to stay in Gloucester. However, the Prison Service argued that it was committed to assisting prisoners to stay off drugs at Leyhill, which is clearly not what the two young men found.

Almost all prisoners say that drugs are everywhere in prisons and that beating a drug addiction is not made easy. But there are some wonderful examples of trying to do something about this within, and beyond, the penal system. In New York, there is an extraordinary organization called Family Justice, which attempts family focused justice interventions. It has a system called Family Case Management, which, amongst other things, helps support intensive community based drugs programmes. The work of La Bodega de la Familia, with its family case management model, allows people who are skilled at supporting families and their young with drugs treatment, mental health interventions, housing issues, HIV/AIDS, to work generally with young offenders and those 'at risk'. As well as the usual support, in conjunction with the police department and public housing, police and parole, it offers after-school tutoring, English language proficiency, art and music projects, computer literacy, and job readiness skills. It uses one generation to teach another a useful skill, such as the young teaching the older generation about computer skills, and the older generation teach the youth sewing skills. The idea is that the whole family can use the services, whilst one or more members of the family is under a community supervision order of some kind. That way, the whole family is helped to support the offender, so that they do not lose touch.

There is a pilot project in York, where a small group of known persistent offenders are being targeted by police and probation, visited every day, given help with drug addiction and their housing needs, but made to feel that the two services have their eyes on them. Yet elsewhere families get little support whilst their loved ones are 'inside', and individuals often have great difficulty coming to terms with what family members have done. It is in everyone's interests, not least the State's, to keep the family contacts strong. But we do not do it.

The evidence from Family Justice in the USA demonstrates that such family-based treatment can help to deal with people with dual diagnosis. That particular development should be of enormous interest in the UK, where the incidence of dual diagnosis is sending mental health services into a tailspin, and where there has been real difficulty treating people in the community. Drug treatment is one element of a change programme, and there seems to be no reason why drug and alcohol treatment should not be part of a community punishment or service package. The Social Exclusion Unit's excellent report on *Reducing Re-offending by Ex-Prisoners* makes it clear that the continuity of drugs treatment programmes for remand and short-term prisoners, let alone people who are released, leaves much to be desired. They also describe the issue of alcohol addiction as the poor relation, which it undoubtedly is. Yet if treatment were compulsory, with the alternative to it being the kind of 'breach' that now lands young offenders back inside, then people would try harder to stay out of prison.

Nick Davies tells the story* of Allan Seymour, aged 53, who has been breaking the law for the last thirty-four years. He has been punished with fines, with prison, with community service, and they always say they will rehabilitate him, but they never do. His problem is classic. He is short of £400. He cannot get work (he is a qualified chef) because he has no fixed abode, and he cannot earn enough from part-time work to pay the deposit on a flat, which would be around £400. He gets a bit of casual work in a kitchen some days, around £30, enough for a bed and breakfast for the night and £10 for food. On bad days, he earns nothing, sleeps rough, and eventually has to go and steal something. And, sometimes, he gets caught. Nick Davies comments that, when you look at the people in the courts, they are without

---

* Nick Davies, '£400 short of a life', *The Guardian* (14 April 2004).

exception poor and suffering from mental health problems: 'Through the courtroom go the walking wounded retreating from the battle of life: the mentally ill, the physically disabled, the man who can't leave the cells because he's just had some kind of fit, the endless, bottomless stream of junkies, the alcoholics, the confused, the depressed, the inadequate. Most of these defendants have not got two GCSEs to rub together and a significant number of them admit they cannot read or write.' Davies continues by arguing that the system used to believe that these people should be helped, so that society as a whole would be protected, but that the system has changed. Probation is no longer about befriending, and real assistance is hard to find.

Davies is right, and poverty is part of it. In our so-called welfare state, we have forgotten about the welfare of the damaged and the inadequate. Most wickedly we are truly terrible at providing a programme of real support for people coming out of prison. Allan Seymour cannot even manage to pay a fine, if he is given one, as he has not managed to sign on for his benefits. His old

National Insurance card was not considered enough and he was told he had to have three different kinds of ID. Too hard for him, he drifted off, and now has no benefits. Yet Allan Seymour is neither bad nor mad – he is simply vulnerable, lonely, finds bureaucracy hard, and is not very bright. Yet he is just the kind of person who could be helped, if a home was found for him, with limited support; if he were helped into a job where he could stay because he had a home, and if the home were at least somewhere where there were some others like him so that he could make friends.

It would not be very hard to do. It is just what the Office of the Deputy Prime Minister was recommending in its excellent publication in 2000, *Blocking the Fast Track from Prison to Rough Sleeping*. It means helping single homeless people. It means regarding ex-offenders as vulnerable. It means acting quickly when people come out of prison, or before they leave. The Social Exclusion Unit in its report on reducing re-offending makes exactly the same point. But we do not do it.

We need to look at the hidden effects of our present policies. Banging people up, closing the visitors' centre at Feltham Young Offenders Institution, moving prisoners around – all of this has a serious and deleterious effect on the people concerned and their families and support systems. In a superb chapter in Mauer and Chesney-Lind's collection of essays *Invisible Punishment*, Jeremy Travis, of the Urban Institute in Washington DC, discusses the way the effects on family are an 'instrument of social exclusion'. He discusses the fact that certain rights are removed from offenders and ex-offenders in the US system. Their rights to social welfare, housing support and so on can be denied to them. Though this does not quite apply in the UK, it is clear that the disruption of all social supports, and the lack of an emphasis on resettling people back in the community with the basics of housing, money, and a job, does indeed form a kind of social exclusion.

Ex-offenders are too frequently amongst the homeless in our big cities. Ex-offenders find it very hard to get work. Most ex-offenders, poor when they went into prison, find themselves virtually destitute when they leave because of lack of support and a totally inadequate leaving prison grant. Travis argues: 'these punishments ... create a permanent diminution in social status of convicted offenders, a distancing between "us" and "them".' We do not allow ex-offenders to hold certain offices, usually for a certain number of years; we also require a declaration of a criminal record on job applications; and we put people's names on the sex offenders' register leading to a form of pariah status if the news gets out, as it surely does. These are invisible punishments that need to be thought through if we wish to stop ex-offenders from re-offending.

In his article about Allan Seymour, Nick Davies also looks at the countless junkies, the people, desperate to get drugs, who steal – and worse – to get their fix. He argues that a few years ago the Probation Service would have given some of these people cash to help them get over a bad patch, whilst several decades ago drug addicts would have been given heroin by their GPs to keep them on clean stuff. But our 'war against drugs' has not helped us get people off drugs, has not helped stop a drug culture, and has only made us more punitive towards those who commit offences that are drugs related. A huge percentage of ex-offenders have a drugs problem because, as we have seen, we have been poor at getting people off drugs in prison. One key element of any sensible policy would be compulsory treatment for drugs and alcohol dependency when in prison, with the threat of going back inside if people on community sentences do not comply with a treatment programme. But a punitive and mechanistic approach will not work.

What we need is serious engagement with every person in the prison system by a social worker or probation officer, giving significant time to them, keeping them to their promises, giving them hope of a shorter sentence if they get clean, helping them get access to their children if they stay clean, and so on. And when they leave prison, those same social workers and probation officers – who need to stay with their clients and not see them move from prison to prison, or from one young offenders' institution to another – need to help them get a place to live, a bank account, money, a job, a fresh start. Then they need to stay with them for the next two years, always holding out the hope of better things if they stick with the programme, always threatening a return to prison, and consequently losing their home and access to their children, if they falter.

It will not work for everyone. But that is what is meant by 'tough love', and that is what has been missing for many of these people. In the care system, in the mental health system, in the prison system, they have been unable to make long-term relationships with staff because they keep on being moved around. Prison is the worst, the least planned, the least supportive, of any of these environments, partly because of its punitive purpose; yet those in prison are often the most vulnerable of all, the most needy, the most damaged. A few of them can do us harm, and those must be kept away from the rest of us. But if they are needy, vulnerable, drug- and alcohol-dependent people, we need to help them, rehabilitate them, bring them into our society, and give

447

them a chance. And if we do not do so for the young offender, particularly, then we will have failed a whole generation.

That is the first step. The second is the prevention step, which is a mixture of support for children in care, as discussed earlier, and support for children at risk of serious offending. Mentoring does help: there is a significant reduction in re-offending for young offenders who have been mentored, according to research carried out by De Montfort University. The research found that 77 per cent of young offenders who had been mentored had not re-offended six months later. Other research by the University of Luton found that volunteer mentoring projects with young offenders led to a reduction in offending behaviour, a reduction in problems at school, and an improvement in the young people's self-esteem and self-awareness. We need more of this, to support young people and their families, and indeed to support adult offenders. The question is whether it can become as much something that is expected of most people as paying taxes, getting out of bed, paying bills, and going to the supermarket. For us to repair the huge damage we have done to our prison populations, with the exception of those who have committed violence and pose a serious risk to our safety, we need to make such support for others a normal part of what we do in our daily lives, and not something we shove away, to leave for the professionals.

But this will be impossible for ordinary people, even if they are willing, unless government gives some leadership rather than just pandering to populist opinion that is not always based on fact. Yet all government appears to do in this area is follow public opinion, or even exceed it in some circumstances. For instance, it seems extraordinary that the then Home Secretary, David Blunkett, was not required to resign when Harold Shipman committed suicide in prison in 2003. The fact that we actually tolerate a Home Secretary, responsible for the welfare of prisoners, saying that he felt like celebrating when one of the prisoners in his care killed himself, is deeply disturbing, whatever that prisoner may have done in terms of offending.

We imprison far too many people – even though we know the extent of the harm prison does. It does not reduce crime very much, yet still we do it. We have to ask why, and what we could do to reverse the trend, to make politicians less averse to risk and more concerned with the terrible long-term effects on vulnerable people's lives.

Conclusion

A home, a job, and a chance of not re-offending. That is what we owe offenders. And yet all our policies go the other way. Prisons are overcrowded, and set to become worse. The role of probation officers is changing for the worse. Prison officers are overloaded. Suicides continue to rise. Young lives are wasted.

What we have is a prison system that brutalizes prisoners, and society in general is allowed to ignore what goes on. The isolation of prisoners, and the lack of public knowledge about what a prisoner's life is like, is hugely worrying. Most people would be horrified if they really knew the extent of prisoner isolation and the conditions they have to endure. But we do not know, we do not see, we never go inside – and those who come out of our prison system are usually too damaged to live a normal life with the rest of us and tell us. What kind of society allows this to happen?

It's not rocket science, just common sense.

Get ex-offenders out there working.

Get employers to take them on.

Get prison officers to use their skills in talking to prisoners and supporting them.

Get visits from family made easier.

Don't move young offenders around too much.

Give them a chance of education.

Use the Bobby Cummineses of this world as an example, so that people can see ex-offenders who have gone straight and flourished.

And take the advice of the Social Exclusion Unit and have a 'going straight' contract that will set out what is expected of prisoners in and out of jail, and tell them what they will get if they stick to the deal – in the shape of housing, a job, support, drug treatment or whatever.

Young offenders should be introduced to the victims of their kinds of crime, as has happened very successfully at Exmouth Youth Offending Partnership, where young tearaways were introduced to those who were damaged by their kind of driving, or motorcycle antics, at Exmouth Headway, the centre for people with brain injuries.*

Projects must be set up like the Bridge Project at Doncaster Prison, which links up with Doncaster Action Team for Jobs, gets people into jobs, and pays a rent bond – in lieu of a deposit – for them in advance of release. Brian Anderson, director of resettlement at Doncaster Prison, sees the rent bond as being the key element in the whole strategy: through finding ex-offenders accommodation 'we are reducing the likelihood of re-offending'.†

Once again, the message is that the history of how we treat offenders leaves much to be desired. We are shaped by the past, and conditioned by it. We need to look at offenders differently: get them out of the prisons, un-

---

* Sarah Bartlett, 'Making Headway', *Community Care* (8–14 January 2004).
† Colin Cottell, *The Guardian* (31 August 2002).

less it is vital that they stay there, and try to bring some order to their lives, with tough love and a contract that helps them not to re-offend. This means employment, activity, homes, support, and friendship. And, once again, it means all of us taking an interest and recognizing that our prisons are full of young (and not so young) people who have been through the care system and whom we have failed on many fronts.

FIVE

THE OUTSIDER

In 1937, my mother came to England as a refugee. She was what would now be called an asylum seeker, fleeing from the Nazis in Germany. She had been denied her full civil rights, had a 'J' stamped in her passport as a Jewess, and was given the name Sara, as were all Jewesses, in addition to her other, real, name of Liesel. She had been refused entry to art college as a result of legislation that had stopped all Jews going on to further and higher education. When she came to England she was welcomed warmly by the family she went to live with in Birmingham, the Dobbs family, where she had gone as a domestic, and where she stayed for a few months before they offered to pay for her to go on to further education. An academic family, they took in some twenty young German Jewish women in that time.

Though they were not Jewish themselves, the Dobbs took my mother in because they thought it was the decent and civilized thing to do. One of their daughters, Beatrice Painter, recorded that their home often had a few extra people living there. The family must have brought all these young women in as domestics, because that was the easiest way to get people into the country. But they had every intention of giving them a new start in Britain, in the tradition of British hospitality to those fleeing persecution. Though my mother got her younger brother and parents out of Germany before the war started in 1939, most of the rest of her family perished, the victims of planned cruelty and extermination.

But Britain was not uniformly hospitable to refugees. Long before my mother came, anti-Semitic sentiments were commonly to be heard concerning Jewish refugees and asylum seekers. Sir Alfred Milner, then

British High Commissioner in South Africa, is famous for sending a telegram in 1900 to London warning that a ship called the *Cheshire* was making its way from South Africa to Southampton carrying a boatload of some 350 Jews masquerading as refugees. He continued: 'No help should be given them on their arrival as anyone asking for it would be an impostor.' The *Daily Mail* rallied to Milner's cause, and described what happened when these refugees from the Anglo-Boer war arrived at Southampton: 'Incredible as it may seem, the moment they were in the carriages THEY BEGAN TO GAMBLE ... and when the Relief Committee passed by they hid their gold, fawned and whined, and in broken English asked for money for their train fare.'* As Jeremy Harding puts it in his excellent book, *The Uninvited*: 'How little this has changed can be seen from a headline in the *Mail* in October 1999: "The Good Life on Asylum Alley" over an article revealing "the shocking ease with which refugees play the benefit system".'

---

* *Daily Mail* (3 February 1900), quoted by Kushner and Knox, *Refugees in an Age of Genocide* (1999).

In April 1933, after the boycott by Hitler of Jewish businesses, and as things began to look ominous for German Jews, the British Cabinet approved a reply for the Home Secretary to a parliamentary question as to whether 'the Government will be prepared to consider the granting of asylum to German Jews in this country on a self-supporting financial basis'. The reply ran, and was often repeated: 'the interests of this country must predominate over all other considerations, but subject to this guiding principle each case will be carefully considered on its individual merits ... in accordance with the time honoured tradition of this country, no unnecessary obstacles are placed in the way of foreigners seeking admission.'

But concerns about what was going on in Germany were growing. Questions were asked in Parliament. Eleanor Rathbone MP asked for modification of the regulations (requiring evidence of the ability to be self-supporting) in mid April 1933. Colonel Wedgwood led a debate with a strong plea that the House and the country should 're-alize the value of brains and the duty of hospitality to the oppressed'. Clement Attlee also urged action on the government. Much later, when things became desperate, and after the Austrian Jews began trying to come to Britain after the 1938 Anschluss, Colonel Wedgwood kept up the pressure, asking for the admission of Jewish refugees from Austria for at least six months. He had widespread support, including from the then Archbishop of Canterbury, Cosmo Lang. But the Home Secretary, Sir Samuel Hoare, replied (22 March 1938): 'On the one hand, there is, I am sure, a general desire to maintain the traditional policy of this country of offering asylum to persons who for political, racial or religious reasons have had to leave their own country. On the other hand, there are obvious objections to any policy of indiscriminate admission. Such a policy would not only create difficulties from the police point of view, but would have grave economic results in aggravating the unemployment problem, the housing problem, and other social problems.'

The Home Secretary had general support from the press. *The Times* hoped his line would be interpreted with 'wide liberality', being more generous in its sentiments than the *Daily Mail*. That paper applauded the house's rejection of the Wedgwood motion: 'the floodgates would be opened and we would be inundated by thousands seeking a home'.* The *Express* was even more robust: 'There is a powerful agitation here to admit all Jewish refugees without question or discrimination. It would be unwise to overload the basket like that; it would stir up the elements here that fatten on anti-Semitic propaganda. They would point to the fresh tide of foreigners, almost all belonging to the extreme Left. They would ask: "What if Poland, Hungary, and Rumania also expel their Jewish citizens? Must we admit them too?" Because we DON'T want anti-Jewish uproar, we DO need to show common sense in not admitting all applicants.'†

In the end, some 70,000 or more Jewish refugees came in the 1930s, stayed, and brought good things and prosperity to this country. In most cases they came reluctantly, if gratefully, and never lost their sense of being uprooted. When my mother

---

* *Daily Mail* (23 March 1938).
† *Daily Express* (24 March 1938).

was dying, in 2001, she kept saying that she wanted to go home. And she did not mean to her maker. She meant to Heilbronn, south Germany, to which she had only been back once – with great cajoling from my father – in sixty-four years. 'Home is where the heart is.' For many people, however angry, resentful, depressed, evicted, deprived and oppressed they feel, home is still home.

Britain's record in helping the Jewish refugees in the 1930s was on the whole a moderately good one, at least by comparison with other European countries. The press was generally bigoted and hostile, and politicians were not always as courageous as they might have been. But considerable acts of kindness were shown to many of the refugees, at a time of economic problems and political uncertainty. It is not therefore easy to explain why asylum has now become such a contentious issue and why the term asylum seeker has become a term of abuse. To begin to understand why this has happened, we need to look at the history of refugees and migration into Britain.

This chapter will try to tell that story, and look at some ways through.

Historical Background

After the Romans overran the Celts and the Picts, there was a series of invasions by Germanic tribes, Jutes, Angles, and Saxons, who colonized southern England and became what we now think of as the English. The Vikings arrived some four hundred years later and colonized most of northern England and East Anglia. After the Norman Conquest William I invited the Jews to settle in England in order to be moneylenders. But in 1290 they were expelled, the majority going to France and Italy, from state to state, dukedom to dukedom, in response to toleration or persecution. Indeed, it was Italy that invented the 'ghetto', and thereafter the ghetto, the *Judengasse*, the *Juiverie*, the Jewry, became commonplace in Europe. Some were open – like Old Jewry in London, until the expulsion in 1290. Others were locked at night, and required passes for transit in the day. Restrictions varied in intensity and came and went. But the principle was the same: keep the Jews away from the rest of us – they are alien, different, foreign, dangerous.

In England, after the Jews were deported, animosity was turned towards the Lombards, the moneylenders who replaced the Jews, and other Italians – Venetians, Genoese, and Florentines. There were two anti-Italian mob uprisings, in 1456 and 1457, and in 1517 a London mob started a witch-hunt for aliens. Though the army suppressed the mob, the price of this was a new and even heftier poll tax on foreigners.

Yet the foreigners stayed. Despite the expulsion of the Jews in 1290, there were Jews to be found amongst the court musicians of both Henry VII and Henry VIII. There were Italian court musicians throughout the Tudor period. There was a renowned black trumpeter in Edinburgh in 1505, named, facetiously, John Blanke (*blanc* being white), who played for both Henry VII and Henry VIII. In Elizabeth I's time, Jews started drifting back, Spaniards – despite the wars with Spain – were to be found at court, and towards the end of Elizabeth's reign, black slaves began to appear in England's wealthier households. England also provided a refuge for the Protestants being expelled from France and other European countries.

According to Robert Winder, in his excellent book *Bloody Foreigners*, there were three thousand foreigners in London in the year 1500, 6 per cent of the civilian population: 'Tottenham,' said one alarmed Londoner in Henry VIII's day, 'has turned French.'

Slaves came in increasing numbers in the seventeenth century, and the expansion of the slave trade in the early eighteenth century increased the numbers of black people to be found in England – to approximately 14,000 by 1770. After 1772, thanks to the efforts of the abolitionists, they could not be forcibly deported, but it took until 1807 for Parliament to ban the slave trade – it was too important to Britain's economy, even though it inspired popular revulsion. It was not until 1833 that slavery was abolished throughout the British Empire. As a result of abolition, black people virtually stopped coming to Britain and it was 1892 before the first non-white MP, Dadabhai Naoroji, was elected.

Although Britain has a relatively 'liberal' reputation on immigration and asylum, the law gradually and consistently eroded rights of entry, as soon became apparent with the

Aliens Act of 1905. The 'liberal' approach was only sustained whilst it was still quite difficult for substantial numbers of people to get to British shores. Once mass travel became possible, more and more restrictions were brought in. It is important to stress that all political parties, at whatever stage one examines the history of immigration, have passed legislation that restricts entry. Such legislation is often panic-driven – for instance, in response to actual or potential population movements (e.g. Aliens Act 1905, Commonwealth Immigrants Act 1962 and 1968)

At the same time, immigration from Ireland and from the rest of Europe was increasing. Tens of thousands of Irish arrived between 1830 and 1850, with a huge surge in the 1840s as a result of the potato famine. Then, from 1881, Jews from Eastern Europe started arriving as the pogroms grew in intensity. Bismarck had expelled 'alien Poles', largely but not all Jewish, from Prussia in 1886, and the Russians retaliated by banishing Jews from Moscow in 1890. Meanwhile, Jews were gradually making their way west, many of them thinking they were going to the United States, the so-called golden country, or country of gold. Some were tricked by dishonest shipping agents into thinking that one of the English ports was in the USA, others were unable to afford the fare to the USA, and still others suffered so badly from seasickness on the steamers that brought them that they disembarked in England, unable to bear the thought of continuing on board any longer.

By 1914 over 150,000 Jews had come to Britain from the Pale of Settlement in Russia and Poland. Reactions to them were often hostile. The *Pall Mall Magazine* described the new Jewish immigrants as a 'pest and a menace', and warned of a 'Judenhetz brewing in East London', whilst Major Evans Gordon, the MP for Stepney, said that he felt that the modern Englishman 'lived under the constant danger of being driven from his home, pushed out into the streets, not by the natural increase of our own population but by the off-scum of Europe'.

And so on and so on. The *Evening Standard* was quick to describe the Jewish East End as dangerous and full of foreigners, and politicians gradually wondered aloud about allowing into Britain 'destitute aliens' without restriction. There was a lengthy campaign to get some restrictions, and, after a ten-year campaign, the Conservative government passed the Aliens Act on 10 August 1905, passing all the stages of the Bill in one day. Josiah Wedgwood MP spoke movingly after the applause was over: 'I have never been so ashamed of this House of Commons as I have been today. I have some regard for the traditions of my country. We have never seen such a unanimous spirit of persecution in this house since the time of the Popish plot in 1678.' And Winston Churchill, desperately concerned by the intolerance that was gathering pace, wrote to *The Times* in 1904 saying that there was no good reason to abandon 'the old tolerant and generous practice of free entry and free asylum to which this country has so long adhered and from which it has so greatly gained.' Ford Madox Ford, in *The Spirit of the People: an Analysis of the English Mind*, published in 1904, took a dim view of the government's new view of nationality: 'In the case of a people descended from Romans, from Britons, from Anglo-Saxons, from Danes, from Normans, from Poitevins, from Scotch, from Huguenots, from Irish, from Gaels, from modern Germans and from Jews, a people so mixed there is hardly a man who can point to seven generations of purely English blood, it is almost absurd to use the obsolescent word ''race''. These fellows are ourselves.'* Indeed, it is worth wondering whether the feeling ran so high because this was the first time there had been a significant immigration into Britain of people who were not Christian, unlike the Irish and the Huguenots. Then there was the fact that so many were unskilled and destitute, which may explain some of the feeling that arose later against those coming from the Indian subcontinent.

There was considerable prejudice against the Jews that came in between 1881 and 1905, and an equal, if not greater, prejudice against the Bengali seamen – the so-called lascars – in Scotland and the English ports. The Aliens Act of 1905 was enacted by the Conservatives with considerable support from the trade unions, making clear that im-

---

* Quoted in Winder, *Bloody Foreigners*.

migration, and fear of foreigners, was not a party issue, but a response to deep-seated feeling amongst the population. It targeted 'undesirable aliens' – paupers, lunatics, vagrants, and prostitutes. Many of the young Jewish women who had come to Britain in the 1880s and 1890s had been brought into what was called then the 'white slave trade', and certainly other Jews were the operators of brothels and other houses of ill-repute, so that the Jews were blamed for an increase in degradation and depravity in the country. Diseased people and criminals could be refused entry to Britain as well. Though Britain did not adopt the same stringent health check procedures as the Americans did for immigrants entering the USA through Ellis Island, public health officials did begin to take a tough line about bringing in diseased and degenerate people: it was thought that keeping out the sickest, the most vulnerable, the frailest, the most mentally retarded would prevent British stock from becoming contaminated. The Act, which also targeted those thought to be a charge on public funds, was implemented in response to what was perceived as massive Jewish refugee migration from Eastern Europe, and its introduction was supported by some Jews already in Britain on the basis that they feared what a massive 'unwashed' Jewish presence might do to their fragile place in British society. As synagogues were increasingly anglicizing (the West London Synagogue of British Jews, where I grew up, was so named as the first Reform synagogue in England in 1840), the thought of these Russian and Polish Jews with their chaotic rituals, their Yiddish, their ritual slaughter (for kosher meat) and greasy food repelled many of the Jews already here. They rallied round to help and protect their fellow Jews, of course, but they also tried to persuade them to become truly 'English', to speak English, and to assimilate as fast as possible.

The 1905 Act exempted true 'asylum seekers', suggesting that the view of the Jews was that they were coming for economic reasons, to make a better living, and not that they were genuinely fleeing from persecution – an accusation made frequently, and not always inaccurately, of those claiming asylum now. It is no coincidence that the Act was passed in 1905, for in both 1903 and

1905 there were particularly bloody pogroms in Kishinev, which increased the numbers of Jews trying to get away and seeking entry to Britain. Those that failed to come to Britain after 1905 until the beginning of the First World War continued going to the United States, to Canada, and to South Africa, where immigration continued on a fairly large scale until the 1920s. But when the war began, xenophobia increased and a general fear of foreigners grew in intensity. There were attacks on German butchers and bakers throughout England, and many German-born tradesmen who had lived in Britain for decades fled from their homes in fear of their lives.

More legislation came, in the shape of the Aliens Restriction Act 1914, passed by the Liberal government just as the war broke out. It gave the Crown virtually unlimited powers to control, detain, restrict, and deport aliens in times of war or great emergency, with no procedural safeguards. It also established Home Office control over the internal movement of those defined as aliens, who were required to register with the police, something which continued up to and past the Second World War. The Liberal government also passed the British Nationality and Status of Aliens Act 1914, which affirmed that all inhabitants of the UK, its dominions and its colonies, were British subjects, owing allegiance to the Crown. But it did not allow freedom of movement by all such inhabitants to all parts of the empire. In this legislation, women were denied the ability to transmit their British nationality to their children, and they also lost this nationality on marriage to an alien man (though this was not the case for men who married an alien woman).

After the war, this xenophobia did not subside, as one might have expected. It was a time of high unemployment, with the returning soldiers looking for work, and xenophobia ran high after virtually every family in Britain experienced the huge losses of men on foreign soil. The Liberal government passed more legislation, the Aliens' Restrictions (Amendment) Act 1919, which repealed the 1905 Act but extended the terms of the 1914 Act to peacetime. It introduced new criminal charges for sedition and industrial unrest by aliens, and it removed the rights of former 'enemy aliens' to sit on juries or work for the government, even if naturalized, something which affected members of my originally German Jewish family, though by this time they were fiercely loyal to the British crown and were educating their male children to be English gentlemen.

During the Second World War, former enemy aliens and anyone who had been born in Germany came under general suspicion and many people, including many refugees from Nazi-occupied Europe, were interned on the Isle of Man, or even sent abroad. It was not until after the war that the absurdity of what had been done in the name of national security become apparent. By then there were some 157,000 Poles living in Britain, many of whom had fought with the British and were passionately anti-German and anti-Communist. The Labour government passed new legislation, the Polish Resettlement Act 1947, which allowed them to stay. But concerns about nationality and citizenship still continued.

Under that same Labour government, the British Nationality Act 1948 was passed, which proceeded to define 'citizens of the United Kingdom and Colonies' as a single group. However, as no Commonwealth citizen was an alien, freedom of entry continued as before, which was at least partly in recognition of the great sacrifice made by Commonwealth countries during the war. However, when unprecedented numbers of people began to arrive from the West Indies, India, and Pakistan in the late 1950s onwards, controls were introduced as a so-called temporary measure by the Commonwealth Immigrants Act 1962.

New Legislation

The 1948 Act had enshrined the right of the Commonwealth citizens to enter the UK, work, settle here, and bring their families with them, which is precisely what they proceeded to do. It also established two main categories of citizenship: those who were to be defined as citizens of the United Kingdom and Colonies (CUKCs), and those who were citizens of commonwealth countries. Both groups had the imperial status of British subjects, with an entitlement to settle in

Britain, until too many came for convenience and public tolerance. There was an objection from 11 Labour MPs to the Prime Minister of the time, Clement Attlee, who argued that 'an influx of coloured people domiciled here is likely to impair the harmony, strength and cohesion of our public and social life'. Attlee reassured the MPs that he would modify immigration rules if it resulted in, as he put it, 'a great influx of undesirables'.* There was also, significantly, a third category for citizens of the Irish Republic, probably also in recognition of the large numbers who had fought for Britain in the Second World War (more from the Republic than from Northern Ireland).

At the same time, asylum law began to be formalized in the wake of the 1951 Convention relating to the Status of Refugees (the Refugee Convention) and its subsequent protocol in 1967. (Britain signed the Refugee Convention in 1954 and the protocol in 1968, but it was not until the coming into force of the 1993 Asylum and Immigration Appeals Act that the Convention was directly incor-

---

* Quoted in Suke Wolton, *The History of Immigration Legislation* (1998), 2.

porated into UK law.) A refugee was defined as 'A person who has a well-founded fear of persecution for reasons of race, religion, nationality, membership of a particular social group or political opinion.... Someone who is outside the country of his/her nationality and is unable, or, owing to such fear, is unwilling to avail himself/herself of the protection of that country; or who, not having a nationality and being outside the country of his/her former residence is unable, or owing to such fear, is unwilling to return to it.' The Convention was drafted by member states of the UN in the aftermath of the Second World War, after it became clear that previous refugee agreements had not addressed the needs of the pre-war period or the contemporary realities of large movements of people after the end of the war. The drafters of the Convention thought it would be a temporary measure and would not be needed after the large numbers of refugees in the post-war period had been settled. But it was soon realized that just the same provisions were needed after 1951 for people who became refugees and were not European nationals. So the 1967 protocol removed both the time and geographical limitations that had been written into the original Convention.

Racism Rears Its Head

Nonetheless, this did not apply to the Commonwealth citizens who were beginning to come in ever increasing numbers through the late 1950s and early 1960s to work on the public transport systems, and in the NHS. Feelings began to rise against them, and particularly racist feelings. Race riots in Nottingham and Notting Hill in London dominated the press in the summer of 1958, with the new immigrants, largely from the West Indies, being treated appallingly. MPs did not mention the riots in the election the following year, though the former Fascist leader, Sir Oswald Mosley, used his stance against immigration as a way of trying to get back into Parliament. He failed. It was not uncommon in the early 1960s to see boarding houses displaying a notice saying 'No blacks' in the window, or houses boarded up in streets where black people were settling as the whites moved out. The result of all this, largely a product of racism, was the Commonwealth Immigrants Act 1962, brought in by the then Conservative government, though the Home Secretary of the time, R.A. (Rab) Butler, told the Commons that it was 'only after long and anxious consideration and a considerable reluctance' that the government proposed taking steps to control immigration.

The 1962 Act encapsulated the first major modification to the rights of entry attached to imperial nationality. It was patently racist in that it applied to those UKC subjects not born in the UK and not holding a British passport. It also introduced a three-tiered employment voucher scheme for potential Commonwealth immigrants, which was further modified in 1965. UKC subjects not born in the UK and not holding a UK passport were also allowed to enter for the purpose of study. But things quickly got worse, with race riots in the Birmingham area. Enoch Powell MP began to talk about 'rivers of blood'. As a result, in 1968, with public feeling running high, the Labour government passed the Commonwealth Immigrants Act, which first introduced a distinction between those regarded as Patrials and those who were thought of as non-Patrials. It was passed in response to the 'Africanization' process in Kenya and Uganda (because East African Asians were British passport holders), in the context of a formal right of entry for UKC subjects. Hitherto, anyone who had a British passport was entitled to enter, settle, live, work and bring their families to Britain. The 1968 Act retrospectively denied that automatic right of entry and settlement to East Africans of Asian descent, many of whom were increasingly frightened by the turn of events in Kenya and Uganda. The right of entry of UKC subjects was now only automatically granted if they or a parent or grandparent had been born, adopted, registered, or naturalized in the UK.

As if that were not bad enough, there was a further piece of legislation in 1971, the Immigration Act, this time under the Conservatives, which defined three categories of entry and gave immigration officers powers to detain asylum applicants for the first time other than in wartime. And it created a new immigration status called the 'right of abode in the UK', which still holds force today. The

Immigration Act 1971 gave certain citizens of the United Kingdom and Colonies and other Commonwealth citizens the right of abode in the UK, and stated further that only those with such a right would be free to come and go without being subject to UK immigration controls. This meant that not all people with prime British nationality were equal; some were entitled to enter, reside in, and depart from the UK at will, whilst for others it meant little more than a passport facility, as they were no more able to enter and reside in the UK than other overseas nationals.

But even this did not satisfy an increasingly hostile press, and rising public feeling. So the Conservatives passed the British Nationality Act 1981, which abolished the unified citizenship of the United Kingdom and colonies and replaced it with three new citizenships, British Citizenship, British Dependent Territories Citizenship, and British Overseas Citizenship. This resulted in all those who had been CUKCs with a right of abode becoming British citizens (and in 1983 the 1971 Immigration Act was amended to read that all British citizens had the right of abode). But the remaining CUKCs – those who had become CUKCs by virtue of a connection with a place that continued to be a colony on 1 January 1983 – became British Dependent Territories Citizens (BDTCs), whilst the rest became British Overseas Citizens (BOCs). These could only acquire the right of abode by acquiring British Citizenship itself, no easy matter.

The noose was tightening, with legislation being passed at an ever increasing rate from the 1980s onwards with the aim of keeping out foreigners, particularly black foreigners, or those who were seen as undesirable in other ways, such as the Roma, or even white asylum seekers such as the Kosovans. Though the earliest legislation, such as the 1905 Aliens Act, had specifically excluded asylum seekers, whose definition was unclear at the time, attention was increasingly turning to this category of immigrant. Until 1993, no formal asylum legislation had existed in the UK; very little was written down about the status and rights of refugees, and the status of the UN Convention of 1951 in British law was unclear. However, there had been some significant refugee resettlement programmes before 1993, when the UN Convention finally became enshrined in UK law. In 1956 and shortly thereafter, the UK accepted over 21,000 Hungarians fleeing Communism. During the 1970s and 1980s, numbers of Ugandan Asians were accepted, as well as some Vietnamese, Chilean and other Latin American refugees.

* * *

The pace of developments in the area of asylum and immigration law throughout the 1990s and into the new millennium has been phenomenal. From all that has gone before, one can see that the rate of legislation was increasing. But nothing had happened in the previous century to compare with five major Acts of Parliament in a decade. Visas were introduced for Sri Lankans in May 1985, in advance of the Immigration (Carriers Liability) Act (ICLA), which was passed in 1987. This legislation provided for a charge (currently £2000) to be levied on the owner or agent/operator of a train, ship, or aircraft when a person (who is not a British citizen or European Economic area national) arrives in the UK without a valid passport or other acceptable travel document. This means that carriers are expected to check that documentation is valid, belongs to the person concerned, and has the appropriate visa, if one is needed.

Gradually, other groups were added to the list of who would need visas – for example, Turks needed them from June 1989 after the influx of Kurdish asylum seekers. In May 1997, just after the election of the new Labour government, visas were introduced for Colombians and, in July 1997, for Ecuadorians. In addition, the Dublin Convention of 1990 introduced the concept of a 'safe third country', giving EU countries the option to remove asylum applicants who have travelled via another 'safe' EU country back to that country. In November 1998, new controls were introduced which aimed to deter multiple applications and to filter out fraudulent asylum claims. Some sympathy was demonstrated for people who had genuinely suffered – in 1992, for instance, temporary protection was introduced for Bosnians fleeing from the appalling atrocities in the former Yugoslavia. But in that same year, the Asylum and Immigration Appeals Bill was reintroduced, passed early in 1993.

New Asylum Legislation

The Asylum and Immigration Appeals Act 1993 amended the 1971 Immigration Act. It was the first piece of major legislation to deal explicitly with asylum since the 1905 Aliens Act. Then, in 1995, the Social Security (Persons from Abroad) Miscellaneous Amendment Regulations were first proposed, removing rights to benefits for in-country asylum applicants. In February 1996, new legislative changes came into effect removing all rights to benefits for asylum seekers applying in-country who were appealing against negative decisions on their asylum applications. In June 1996, the Court of Appeal ruled that this was not the proper way to implement these changes, which needed to be done by Act of Parliament. Benefits were temporarily restored to in-country applicants. But, as a result, the government added clauses withdrawing benefits to the Asylum Bill then going through Parliament.

In July 1996, despite considerable objections from a variety of concerned groups, the Asylum and Immigration Act received the Royal Assent, coming into force that August. The 'White List' was introduced of countries that were deemed to be safe and whose nationals were therefore deemed to be at little risk of persecution. The 'safe third country' concept was introduced, to make clear that would-be asylum seekers did not necessarily need to come to the UK. Indeed, had they come through a 'safe third country' they could be required to return there. This legislation also restricted entitlement to housing and other welfare benefits only to those making an application for asylum status at the port of entry, which badly hurt some of those already in the UK who had not realized they had to make an immediate application. Since then, there has been an ongoing tussle between the courts and the government about exactly what asylum seekers are entitled to. The High Court ruled in October 1996 that local authorities were empowered (under the National Assistance Act of 1948) to cater for destitute asylum seekers. But in January 1997, the 1996

Housing Act came into effect, under which asylum seekers lost access to local authority waiting lists. Things were not getting better.

Things Get Worse

Many people concerned with the welfare of asylum seekers expected that the new Labour government that came to power in May 1997 would be less harsh and more inclined to set up a fairer, speedier, more welcoming regime for asylum seekers. It was not to be. In 1997, the Special Immigration Appeals Commission Act 1997 established the Special Immigration Appeals Commission. In 1998, with the Human Rights Act incorporating the European Convention on Human Rights into UK law, many thought that some of the harsher legislation could be tested out against that Act, but little happened. In 1998, the government also published its white paper, entitled *Fairer, Faster and Firmer: A Modern Approach to Immigration and Asylum*. In the following year there was the first reading of the 1999 Asylum and Immigration Act. In horror at what was happening in Kosovo, temporary protection was introduced for Kosovans under the Humanitarian Evacuation Programme (HEP). By the end of the year, however, the Asylum and Immigration Act 1999 received the Royal Assent, and by April 2000 asylum seekers began to be dispersed under NASS (National Asylum Support Service). Some were dispersed to accommodation so awful, to estates so abusive and intolerant, that they had to be taken out, as happened to seven Romanian gipsy families who experienced appalling racist abuse.

Press Views

Indeed, this was at a time that hatred of gypsies, and the depiction of them as 'asylum-seeking gypsy thieves and beggars', was running at an all-time high. The *Sun* newspaper claimed that government research showed that 'begging refugees' was voters' third most important issue after health and education. 'Though the violence of the outcry has been striking, particularly in a boom economy, it isn't very surprising that gypsies are exciting hatred in the press. For hundreds of years they have played a small but lively part in the European imagination, and these days ... Gypsies are perhaps the last group up for grabs,' wrote Isabel Fonseca.* She continued: 'As beggars and as gypsies they are now also emblematic of all asylum seekers: beggars and presumed cheats at the gate of the west.'

Meanwhile, a new refugee integration strategy, *Full and Equal Citizens: A Strategy for the Integration of Refugees into the United Kingdom*, was launched by the then Immigration Minister, Barbara Roche. It aimed to include refugees as equal members of society and to help them develop their potential and contribute to the cultural and economic life of the country. It also set out a clear framework to support the integration process across the United Kingdom, and aimed to facilitate access to the support necessary for the integration of refugees nationally and regionally. It sounded as if the government was truly committed to making life easier for refugees and those with leave to remain in the UK. It was as if two completely separate, apparently mutu-

---

* 'The truth about gypsies', *The Guardian* (24 March 2000).

ally contradictory, policy objectives were being pursued at the same time. For when it came to asylum seekers trying to get into the country, things were getting still harsher, and more unpleasant. In 2001, the Home Secretary announced a substantial package of measures for a fundamental overhaul of the government's immigration and asylum policy. Yet the new Asylum and Immigration Act had only come into force in April 2000, so it had not been given much of a chance to work.

After the events of 11 September 2001 in the United States, attitudes to foreigners hardened – particularly those who might be perceived as Muslim fundamentalists (and who were equated with al-Qaeda sympathizers in the popular mind). In November the UK government introduced the Anti-Terrorism, Crime and Security Bill in response to the increased threat of terrorist activity. Then, in February 2002, it published its White Paper *Secure Borders, Safe Haven: Integration with Diversity in Modern Britain*. This set out the key challenges facing the government on nationality, immigration, and asylum policy and the measures that would be taken to develop a coherent strategy. The Nationality, Immigration and Asylum Bill was introduced into Parliament and passed with Royal Assent by November 2002.

But the government was still not satisfied, as public feelings about asylum seekers, by this time a term of abuse, were continuing to run high. So, in January 2003, it implemented Section 55 of the 2002 Act, which allowed the Home Office to withdraw access to the National Asylum Support Service from those who did not apply for asylum 'as soon as reasonably practicable'. What this means is an effective denial of support to most in-country applicants, who may well simply have misunderstood the system. To add to that, in October 2003, ministers from the Home Office and the Department for Constitutional Affairs published a letter outlining the government's proposals on further asylum reform. This letter provided the background to the 2004 Act and set out a range of proposals. These were intended to unify the immigration and asylum appeals system into a single-tier appeal tribunal with restricted access to the higher courts; to deal with undocumented arrivals; to deal with situations where it is deemed that a country other than the United Kingdom is best placed to consider an asylum or human rights claim; to withdraw family support after appeal from those who are in a position to leave the UK; and to enhance the powers of the Office of the Immigration Services Commissioner (OISC).

In November 2003, the Asylum and Immigration (Treatment of Claimants, etc) Bill was introduced to Parliament in the House of Commons. It was the harshest series of measures yet, containing deeply controversial measures, such as the removal of support for families, which may lead to children being taken into care; the removal of appeal rights; and the introduction of charges for immigration applications. Changes to the legal aid system for asylum and immigration were also proposed. By December 2003, the new Bill had its second reading, with considerable opposition to its harshest measures, including from government backbenchers.

Not satisfied with what it had proposed so far, however, the government tabled a number of amendments to the Asylum and Immigration Bill in June 2004 'as part of a continuing drive to clamp down on abuse of the asylum and immigration system and make clear the rights and responsibilities that come with living in the UK'. According to the Home Office, the measures would accelerate the appeals process relating to the withdrawal of British citizenship and subsequent removal of people from the UK in appropriate cases; it would end back payments of income support for those granted refugee status and require people who are refused permission to live here, but who are unable to leave immediately, to perform compulsory community work – in exchange for the below subsistence-level support given to them.

There is now a time limit of only five days for asylum seekers to appeal to the High Court to be allowed to stay in Britain, despite strong objections from a variety of bishops, cross-benchers, and others in the House of Lords. The right to judicial review of government decisions was reinstated, but the rest was remarkably tough and unbending. The government minister, Lord Filkin, argued that the public was quite clear in wanting the government to ensure 'that the abuse in the system is stamped out, and there is strong support for that position, I believe, not just among the more extreme elements of the popular press, but among those who hold dear the traditions of this society and its responsibilities to consider applicants for asylum'. The language is getting nastier: no one could really believe that those who hold dear the 'traditions of this society' would want to make it impossible for people to have the time to prepare a case for appeal, or deny them a right of appeal, which, arguably, is against the provisions of the Human Rights Act.

To make things worse, the Legal Services Commission has found that more than 120 solicitors' firms have been overcharging millions of pounds from the legal aid budget for handling asylum cases, which has prompted the government to propose a public immigration and asylum legal service, the pilot for which is to be based in Birmingham. Although there have clearly been some abuses of the legal aid system, and the Legal Services Commission has rightly withdrawn contracts from solicitors who overcharge or who do poor quality work, the idea of the public service is part of a different agenda. It is clearly intended to cut costs and, ultimately, to cut the numbers of hours of legal aid an asylum seeker is entitled to. Ministers dropped a proposal to limit the time to nine hours of work,* but they clearly intend to 'choke off' the flow of taxpayer funded legal advice to asylum seekers. One proposal being considered is to withdraw legal aid payments for asylum seekers being interviewed by Home Office staff, though that might be just the time an asylum seeker would need good legal advice and support. The Refugee Legal Centre and the Immigration Advisory Service, both charities and independent bodies, are finding it increasingly difficult to cope, given how hard it is to get proper legal help in an increasingly complex system, which no person arriving on our shores could possibly be expected to understand.

This hardening of official attitudes has been a gradual process but can be seen most clearly if one examines the setting up of the government's own National Asylum Support

---

* Jamie Wilson and Alan Travis, 'Asylum case lawyers milk legal aid', *The Guardian* (16 June 2004).

Service (NASS), which came in under the Immigration and Asylum Act 1999. Such benefit entitlement as remained for asylum seekers – and much had already been removed – was taken away and NASS created to support and disperse destitute asylum seekers. This support was to be provided under a system of vouchers (often called 'asylos'), whilst asylum seekers were to be compulsorily dispersed to designated cluster areas. This was deeply unpopular with asylum seekers, as some of them had come to be near a community of people from their own country or ethnic group. Being dispersed to the poorer parts of Glasgow, and facing racial abuse on a regular basis, was just the sort of thing asylum seekers feared, and just the sort of thing that happened on a regular basis from 2000 onwards.

There is, for instance the story of Zekria Ghulm Salem Mohammed, who committed suicide after a series of horrors in his life as an asylum seeker. He was a young man of 27 who was brought up in a wealthy family in Kabul. His father worked for the United Nations, his brother was a doctor, and his mother was involved in the Red Cross. This was not someone who was going to be a charge upon British society. His moderate political views meant that he fell foul, like so many others, of the Taliban regime, and he fled in fear of his life in 2000, abandoning his dentistry studies at the University of Kabul. He believed Britain would offer him the sanctuary he needed, and he already had family in Southampton. He knew that the Home Office was not deporting people back to Afghanistan because of the political situation there. So he made his way across the border into Uzbekistan, and then on to Hungary. After two months detention there he made his way to the Sangatte refugee camp in Northern France, and then managed to get to Britain and apply for asylum.

The NASS system meant that he was dispersed to Glasgow along with some eight thousand other refugees living there, and he lived in a flat on the twenty-eighth floor of a tower block in Dennistoun. Zekria wanted to continue his dental studies and was sure that the authorities would allow him to repay them for their generosity in granting him entrance to the UK by becoming a dentist, of which there is a desperate shortage

in Scotland. But under the rules, and although he had gone through all the proper
channels, he was not allowed to work or
study and had to rely on benefits, which he
loathed, rather than making his own way. He
also experienced regular anti-asylum seeker
and racist abuse. There has been a huge increase in racist incidents in Glasgow since it
become the asylum capital of Britain, with
two racist murders and five attempted murders in the twelve months before Zekria's
suicide. He tried to carry on, and read vora-
ciously in the local library. He was quiet,
charming, an ambitious and pleasant young
man. But when the government announced
in May 2003 that deportations of refused
asylum seekers from Afghanistan would re-
sume, he lost hope. Fifteen thousand families were allowed to stay on if they had been
seeking asylum for more than three years,
but Zekria was excluded because he was a
single man, despite having been in Britain
for nearly four years. After he had exhausted all the legal attempts to stay in
Britain, he was told he would have to leave
his flat and his £38 a week allowance for
food and essentials was stopped. He was

supposed to get tokens from the NASS for his food, but they failed to arrive. Too proud to scavenge in the bins, and too law abiding to work illegally, he hanged himself. His death is believed to be the third suicide by asylum seekers in a twelve month-period, and it has led to calls for a full inquiry.*

What we are seeing are proud people, who want to be of service and who are terrified of going back to their own countries, being destroyed by the ever more punitive provisions of our legislation. To what end? Even if we want to limit the number of asylum seekers who come to Britain, this has to be done by deterring them from coming in the first place, not by treating those who are already here viciously, bureaucratically, and pointlessly. And when we have such a shortage of dentists, would it not have made sense to allow Zekria, and all the other asylum seekers who come here eager to be of service, to train and work and repay their debt to Britain? Instead, we abuse them, and make life as hard as possible for them.

---

* Paul Kelbie, 'The life and death of an asylum seeker', *The Independent* (29 May 2004).

The Home Office's own experts can talk with equanimity about Britain being 'flooded' by illegal immigrants, as Robert Owen did in a court case about illegal people-trafficking by Chinese Snakehead gangs in Britain.* And Lord Filkin could speak, with apparent equanimity, about those who 'hold dear the traditions of this society'. The traditions of Britain never used to be to pass increasingly punitive legislation concerning asylum at two-year intervals. Nor were the traditions of this society to treat those who came here in fear of their lives and those of their dear ones as if they were idle layabouts. My mother and her relatives worked as domestics, as shop girls, as farm labourers. They were not always treated well, but no one told them they could not work. Indeed, they were expected to do so.

Children

There are serious concerns as to how the government's dispersal policy is affecting

* Alexandra Williams, 'The asylum crisis', *Daily Mirror* (8 June 2004).

children and young people. Technically, children of school age, whether asylum seeking or those with refugee status already granted, are supposed to be treated in the same way as all other children. The education legislation requires local authorities to provide education for all school-age children in their area, and that education is supposed to be appropriate for their age, ability, and aptitudes. High quality, accessible education has been widely acknowledged across all government departments to be vital to the lives of vulnerable children. For asylum-seeking and refugee children and young people, some of whom are extremely vulnerable, there are additional benefits that arise from being placed with peers in an educational setting. In particular, it reintroduces stability into their lives, when events may well have made them feel insecure and lacking in confidence. Local Education Authorities (LEAs) are expected to respond to the needs of asylum-seeking and refugee children living in their area, and are encouraged to develop local policies and procedures to facilitate access to, and support within, local schools. They receive funding for children from asylum-seeking and refugee backgrounds in the same way that they do for all other children on the school roll, and additional funding is available through the Vulnerable Children Grant. There are also measures in place to adjust the presentation of data in primary and secondary school performance tables, so that pupils who have recently arrived from overseas and who have difficulties with English language will not be counted when school performance is calculated.

All these measures ought to remove any barriers to refugee children being offered places in schools. Whether it does is another matter. The Office for Standards in Education (OFSTED) inspects schools for social inclusion and support for specific groups of pupils, including asylum-seeking and refugee children, which ought, once again, to make sure that these children get a decent chance. Once again, it depends how seriously individual schools and local authorities take that responsibility.

For children above the age of 16, placement within a school is at the discretion of the head teacher and the LEA. This can be a real issue for children and young people coming to the UK as lone asylum seekers, and for young refugees. Students who are already attending a school when they reach the age of 16 may continue to do so until they are 18. Different colleges have different policies about fees for asylum-seeking young people, often depending on the funding they receive. Whilst some sixth-form colleges and further education colleges allow 16- to 19-year-old asylum seekers to study free, although they may have to pay a small fee to register, others classify asylum seekers as overseas students, meaning that they have to pay the usually expensive overseas student fees. Some colleges may be reluctant to accept students on to longer courses, such as A-levels or GNVQs, if there is any uncertainty about their asylum application. Yet for any children who want to go on to university and play a useful role in British society, this can be an almost insuperable obstacle. For their hopes are intimately tied up with getting an education and qualifications, and if they are denied educational opportunities there may well be real psychological and social damage.

Those aged 13 to 19 are, however, entitled to use the Connexions Service, the counselling and support service set up by government to give all children and young people in England a better start in life. It provides them with integrated information, advice, and guidance and helps with their personal development. Indeed, Connexions has tried to pull all the issues together, and in a joint initiative with Save the Children, which has taken a strong interest in the welfare of asylum-seeking children and young refugees, has produced *Working Together: Connexions Supporting Young Asylum Seekers and Refugees*, which aims to bring together all the organizations that deliver services to asylum-seeking and refugee children and young people. Save the Children has very properly taken the view that these must be treated as children first and as asylum seekers or refugees second.

When it comes to further education, on the whole young asylum seekers and refugees stand a reasonably good chance of continuing their education. People with refugee status, plus people with Exceptional Leave to Remain (ELR) and asylum seekers who are on income support, job seekers' allowance, or who are supported by social services in exceptional circumstances, are eligible to apply for funding from the Learning and Skills Council. Asylum seekers on NASS support are also eligible and do not need to pay tuition fees. Some others, including those who are beyond compulsory school age and who wish to continue their education, are also entitled to attend further education colleges.

But when it comes to higher education, things become more complicated. Theoretically, eligibility for the home student or overseas student rate of fees is determined by the Education (Fees and Awards) Regulations 1997, which state that people with refugee status or ELR are entitled to pay home fees, as opposed to those for foreigners, which are much more expensive. But this is at the discretion of the relevant educational institution. By no means all institutions have been sympathetic to refugees and asylum seekers. People with refugee status are legally able to study any course at any level, either full-time or part-time, as long as they are able to satisfy the entry requirements and have the financial ability to pay the course fees. Indeed, many training courses are available for free for people with refugee status or ELR and asylum seekers. The most obvious need, however, is for support in learning English, as well as finding ways to recognize and, where necessary, adapt or supplement existing learning, skills and qualifications.

In addition to all this, all LEAs and schools have to comply with the Race Relations Act 1976 and the Race Relations (Amendment) Act 2000 – which means that they must not discriminate on grounds of race. Translation and interpreting services have to be provided, to make it easier for children and young people to enrol in schools and other educational institutions, and also to make it possible to carry out procedures such as special needs assessments. But it is English for Speakers of Other Languages (ESOL) teaching that is vital as a way of delivering education to asylum seekers, refugees, and other ethnic minority groups and individuals, both in terms of language support for school-age children and for those over 16. At present, recognized refugees who need

ESOL tuition can access it under the government's New Deal provision. However, take-up is often low, at least in part because of the particular needs and circumstances of refugees, especially those who are moved time and again and those who need to care for younger brothers and sisters. Everyone, from refugees themselves to teaching providers, agree that there needs to be more ESOL provision: demand has regularly been well in advance of the supply, which begs questions of the government's stated objective of getting refugees integrated quickly, to everyone's advantage.

If one scans the policy territory, therefore, it may seem as if refugees, people with ELR status, and asylum seekers should all be able to access most, if not all, forms of education, provided they have the ability to get onto a course and have the means to pay for it. However, it does not work out like that. Despite the apparent access to education for all children and young people, including refugees and those seeking asylum, the wider context of asylum policy and practice has major implications for their education. Many refugee and asylum-seeking children are not in fact in full-time education. In July 2001, it was estimated that over two thousand refugee children in Greater London were not in school.* A study conducted by Camden LEA in 1999 indicated that at least 50 per cent of 14–19-year-old refugees in that local authority had no contact with any education provider. What causes this is a combination of factors within the broader policy, such as the impacts of dispersal, which is extremely disruptive for children and young people in schools. Although, theoretically, NASS will not disperse a family if the children have been in school for an academic year (three consecutive terms), there is some evidence that dispersal occurs even under these circumstances.

Many refugee children are not in school because they have not been allocated a place. According to Ofsted, this problem is exacerbated by high levels of mobility as a result of dispersal policy and processes.† For example, some families choose to leave the dispersal area (to which they were moved on

---

* Jill Rutter, *Working with Refugee Children* (2003).
† *The Education of Asylum-Seeker Pupils* (Ofsted, October 2003), 5.

a no-choice basis) if they are granted refugee status or some alternative leave to remain. There is also evidence that, whilst some schools and LEAs are excellent in finding spaces for asylum-seeking and refugee children, others appear to be less good at doing so. Schools may be put off by the potential additional needs that refugee children present, such as English language support, adapting to a different curriculum, dealing with depression or trauma, or simply adapting to a new way of learning. There is also some evidence* to suggest that a small minority of LEAs, schools, and professionals are not aware that refugee and asylum-seeking children have exactly the same rights to mainstream education as British children.

Further, many children and young people seeking asylum in the UK are given discretionary leave to remain until they turn 18, after which their future becomes less stable. The practice of awarding discretionary leave to remain 'up to the 18th birthday' acts as a considerable barrier to refugee children,

---

* Rutter, *Working with Refugee Children*, op. cit.

particularly unaccompanied children. Many of them are concerned about their immigration status and – unsurprisingly – find it hard to concentrate on their studies under such circumstances. On the occasion of the first Asylum Seeker of the Year awards for the trust set up in memory of my parents, Walter and Liesel Schwab, held in the London borough of Hillingdon in October 2003, the joy of relatives at seeing their young cousins, children, brothers, and sisters celebrated for their achievements, against all the odds, was tinged with sadness that it did not happen more often, and that the obstacles to success are often unnecessarily great.

There is also the question of accommodation centres. The Nationality, Immigration and Asylum Act 2002 enabled the Government to set up such centres for destitute asylum seekers and their families while their claims are being processed. But the plans to educate children inside these centres rather than in schools is highly contentious and deeply divisive and has been widely criticized by education providers.

Unaccompanied Children

There is a particular issue when it comes to what are called unaccompanied asylum-seeking children. Social services have a duty to provide care and protection to such children from the point at which they arrive in the UK. Yet children's charities have been highly critical of the social services' response to these children. About half come from countries with armed conflict or serious civil disturbance. The other half are a mixture of children who have been victims of direct or indirect persecution, including torture, or who have suffered serious poverty and deprivation, as well as some who have been sent for exploitation – largely, but not wholly, to work in the sex trade. Some are sent out of their countries for their own protection, whilst others have parents who are dead or who have simply gone missing in the upheaval of war. In one study* it was found that a third of the children simply became separated from their

---

* W. Ayotte, *Separated Children coming to Western Europe* (Save the Children, 2000).

509

parents in their country of origin or, in a few cases, in a third country.

Local authorities have a duty of care for these children, and the extent to which they carry it out, and how well, is variable. Young people's experience at the time of arrival – from which point local authorities become responsible for them – is mixed. At best, those arriving at Heathrow airport might be met by the friendly face of James Davies, the young persons' adviser for the Refugee Arrivals Project, whose job it is to provide advice and support to unaccompanied children. But he is the only person in the country with such a role.† It is not uncommon for many others to disappear between their point of arrival and making contact with the local authority. Some argue that that such disappearances happen because some local authorities are reluctant to take on the responsibility for caring for these children. Others suggest that there are doubts about the age of the young people and children who arrive. Whatever the truth, there is a clear concern on the part of some local au-

---

† N. Valios, 'Young Lives in limbo', *Community Care* (2–8 October 2003).

thorities that they have too many asylum-seeking children to care for and too few resources.

Indeed, there has been a dispute as to the extent of local authority responsibility for children of 16 and 17 who are unaccompanied minors. Everyone is agreed that under-16s need foster care or residential care. But some local authorities have argued that the over-16s can be in unsupported accommodation. However, a court ruling in September 2003, in a case brought against Hillingdon local authority, ruled that councils should act as corporate parents to unaccompanied minors until they reach the age of 24. This has huge financial implications; Hillingdon estimated that the ruling would cost it £5 million a year. Objections to the load borne by Hillingdon and other boroughs have been on the increase since the mid 1990s. Indeed, the then chairman of Hillingdon's social services committee, Catherine Dean (Conservative), argued that they needed more funding to look after the 227 unaccompanied children being brought up by the council in 1999, and said: 'As it is, it's taking resources away from local people.'* And indeed it is, unless central government takes on more of the financial responsibility.

It is also increasingly the case that young asylum seekers, where their age is disputed and the immigration authorities think they are over 18, are being processed in the adult units of immigration removal centres. For those who need support and foster care, there is real difficulty for local authorities in finding foster placements that are appropriate to particular ethnic and cultural needs. Local authorities have often been criticized for not taking such issues seriously enough, but in my experience of talking to some of the people responsible, it seems that they try very hard to meet those needs as best they can but experience real difficulty in finding people from similar backgrounds to that of the children.

Many would argue that the main problem is still the in-built view in Britain, Europe, and much of the rest of the developed world that people are trying to enter their coun-

---

* Gaby Hinsliff, 'Councils that spend more on refugees than pensioners', *Daily Mail* (1 September 1999).

tries for reasons other than seeking asylum. So people immediately find themselves having to cope with a culture of suspicion (though, historically, this is nothing new). As Karen Goodman, head of asylum support at Hillingdon, has pointed out, people have already had to cope with serious problems before they even get here, including horrendous journeys as well as the traumas they may have suffered in their own countries. Debt bondage can also be a big problem: 99 per cent of asylum seekers have paid to get to this country – anything from a few hundred to a few thousand pounds.

When people arrive they face all the government restrictions in the asylum and immigration legislation, including Section 55 of the (1999) Nationality Asylum and Immigration Act, which states that if you do not claim asylum immediately you have made yourself ineligible for asylum. Karen Goodman described the many hundreds of unaccompanied children in Hillingdon (the adults are dispersed) and the appalling racism they experience. She also added that a significant number of the children do not know what country they are in when they arrive, as well as often not knowing – or not saying – how old they are. Karen Goodman also argues that the young children who come in as asylum seekers with an adult who is not a parent receive very little attention, probably because they are seen as being in a private fostering arrangement. Such children may well come to suffer abuse and exploitation. This situation may be even worse than for those children who come in as lone asylum seekers.

Health is another issue. Carolyn Bann and Ruth Tennant have argued* that less attention has been paid to the health needs of young asylum seekers than to their needs for education and social care. They are unlikely to have records from their country of origin, they may well not know their own medical history, and may not have had child health surveillance or neo-natal screening for congenital abnormalities. They have probably not had the basic immunizations and, according to the Department of Health, some may be suffering from malnutrition,

---

* *Unaccompanied Asylum-Seeking Children* (King's Fund for National Children's Bureau and Barnardo's, Highlight no. 190, 2002)

HIV/AIDS, tuberculosis, Hepatitis B or C, and malaria, or schistosomiasis. Care for emotional and psychological needs is also patchy: Western psychological and psychiatric models may well not fit these children and, in some cases, may serve to pathologize what they are experiencing.

As mentioned earlier, many young unaccompanied asylum seekers face the prospect of their eighteenth birthday with dread. Instead of birthday cards, they are all too often served with deportation notices by the Home Office. What is at stake is whether children have the right to be treated as young people in need of care, in which case the local authority owes them a duty of care till they are 24, or whether they are only here under temporary arrangements until the age of 18. Many of the children's organizations believe that this emphasis on deporting young people at age 18 is unacceptable in terms of children's human rights.* Indeed, to add to this concern, there are increasing numbers of asylum-seeking children under the age of 18, with a parent,

* Melanie McFadyean, 'Congratulations – now get out', *The Guardian* (12 November 2003).

now being detained. They are removed from school, uprooted from communities, and held in a detention centre or so-called removal centre. But removal may be a long way off. In one well-publicized case, Yurdugal Ay and her four children aged between 7 and 14 were detained for fifteen months before being deported. That is simply unacceptable, but it is increasingly the public face of our immigration system's attitude to asylum seekers and their children.†

One of the bright spots in all this is the work that is being done by befrienders and peer support groups with young refugees and asylum seekers, such as that being carried out by VSU Youth in Action's various teams. It has been working in Kent for forty years or more and has become involved in a variety of projects aiming to integrate young asylum seekers and refugees into local communities and to challenge prejudice. Judith Skinner from VSU in Kent gave an interview for this book and talked about who they were and what they had done. VSU in Kent

---

† Janet Snell, 'Enjoying your stay?' *Community Care* (25 September–3 October 2003).

arose out of a volunteering scheme (working, for instance, in special schools or with old people) originally set up in the 1960s by a teacher at Sevenoaks School. It grew rapidly and now employs thirty full-time staff, with an operating budget of £800,000. Its funding comes mainly from Millennium Volunteers, from the Rank Foundation, and from some local authority funding, though some of the funding sources are coming to an end and cuts may well lie ahead.

VSU in Kent works with some fifteen hundred young volunteers per year across Kent and Medway. The young people concerned are all under 18 and are always supervised by full-time professional staff. Young people are recruited as volunteers via schools, colleges, Connexions, etc., and some have gone on to the Millennium Volunteers scheme. A positive feature is that some people who have come in as 'clients' have gone on to become volunteers themselves. VSU runs several volunteering and befriending schemes, including a club in Medway originally called the Refugee Befriending Club but later renamed the Dosti project (dosti meaning friendship in Dari and Kurdish). However, with dispersal now in place, it has become virtually impossible to run these sorts of clubs. One thing that comes out of Judith Skinner's interview is that these kind of schemes bring huge benefits to everyone, so much so that one might ask if it would be better not to disperse refugee and asylum-seeking families with children so that this kind of welcome can be given, and so that the children and young people can be treated as children and young people first and foremost, and not as so much human flotsam and jetsam, to be moved around at will, to the disruption of education and social links.

Indeed, in two interviews for this book carried out by Ros Levenson with two young asylum seekers who did not want to use their real names (we will refer to them as Daniel and Alice), it was clear that they did not want other young people to know that they were asylum seekers. It was both too dangerous and too dispiriting. Daniel, who is now aged 16 and was 14 when he arrived, was asked how he felt he had been treated as an asylum seeker:

People don't know who I am. But if they knew I was an asylum seeker they'd treat me differently, I know they would. I am used to keeping secrets. I trust myself, and if you don't trust me, I don't care. I don't envy no one. People envy me. I've always got money on me. I don't even tell them about the paper round. I trust myself, not others. Most people are two-faced. Rumour travels quickly. In Africa, I had nothing to hide. I have had to be more wary here. Sometimes, I stop myself saying something. People can be good to you at one point and then a day or two later they can be bad to you. At first I found it hard to speak out. Now I trust [the social worker] and can tell her everything. The boys upstairs [other foster children] – I still don't trust them.

Alice puts it just as strongly. Now 20, she came at 17, with a sister a year younger. She now looks after two brothers as well. To the question of whether anything made it harder for her than it had to be, she said this:

When we were at the airport, then they left us at a hotel for a week but no-one came to help us. We didn't have a number to call. She said someone would come and take us to Croydon. To start with, we only had tea and bread, sometimes chips as I didn't know what to buy. There were not many shops near the hotel. I went to shop like Londis, not like Tesco where you can see what is what and you can see what is a potato. But there was not much round the hotel. You get scared. You don't know what you can say. You can't tell people anything. Anywhere you go, you feel uncomfortable. Or if you have an appointment, you feel you can't ask. It still sometimes happens. I don't talk about where I am from. How can I tell people? People sometimes do understand, and I'll tell them if I can tell they will understand, or if they will listen. I don't socialize. I don't have real friends I can trust. But the people in the hotel were in a similar situation with the same problems. I don't get friends easily here, not like in my own country. Here there are so many different peoples and cultures.

A bleak picture is reflected in both these interviews, and others. Why?

It appears that, as a nation, we are becoming less tolerant. A recent poll for *Prospect* magazine (February 2004) suggests that 40 per cent of white Britons would prefer not to live in multiracial areas. Two-thirds of the population do not count members of another ethnic group as their friends. Concern about immigration is growing, and the government is right to try to respond to that concern. Yet the public tends to exaggerate the numbers of foreignborn UK residents by something like a factor of four,* and 44 per cent of people believe Britain is no better off for its 'multiculturalism'.

The government is picking up on the racist concerns. In June 2004, plans were leaked that showed that the Prime Minister wanted to see restrictions on immigrants from countries such as Nigeria, Sierra Leone, India, Pakistan, and Bangladesh because of fears that schemes allowing young people to come to the UK for working holidays were being abused. Applications from these 'New Com-

---

* Lyndsey Turner, 'Minority Report', *The Guardian* (3 February 2004).

monwealth' countries have risen sharply since the relaxation of the rules in 2003, leading to both the Prime Minister and the then Home Secretary, David Blunkett, wanting to introduce quotas. But there was to be no tightening of the rules for people from the predominantly white countries such as Australia, New Zealand, and Canada. The leaked document said that 'Quotas would require careful handling to avoid accusations or perceptions of discrimination.' But it continued with the words: 'The Prime Minister said that the Home Office should tighten the scheme with a view to ending abuse from new Commonwealth countries.'* Applications have soared from those countries, where people can come for up to two years as long as they do not claim benefits. But surely the only reasons for restriction would be that people were abusing the system to get in as immigrants for the long term. Otherwise why should they not be as welcome as white people on short-term student stays? There have been scams operating with student visas, it is clear, and there

---

* Bob Roberts, 'Migrant race row hits Blair', *Daily Mirror* (6 June 2004).

have now been arrests of people in dawn raids on a group thought to have brought some thousand people to London to bogus colleges.† But scams are scams whoever is operating them, and it is still unclear why black people should be more suspect than white, particularly as, in this particular case, the raids were carried out to coincide with action by the South African police in Durban, showing that a black-led state is just as concerned about fraud as a white-led one.

But there is a fear apparent here, and it appears to be based on the fact that these people are black. Britain is apparently becoming less tolerant of black people coming here, whatever the reason, and by whatever method. But, even if that is the case, should government go along with that view? Many ordinary people feel that asylum seekers and other immigrants are coming in and taking services that should be given to British people, a position often taken by the *Daily Mail*. One particular case was cited by the *Mail* of so-called illegal immigrants coming in from Romania in 1998 and being housed

---

† 'Police smash bogus visa ring', *Daily Mail* (16 June 2004).

in hospital wards, in their view to the detriment of patients who should have been there (even though the facts were that there were no NHS staff available to staff those wards for sick patients because of chronic staff shortages; at the same time, asylum-seeking doctors and nurses are not allowed to work to help staff in tightly stretched NHS facilities).* And the charity Comic Relief was blasted by the media for giving cash aid to asylum seekers, even though they had made it clear that a third of the money raised went to projects in the UK, and a small portion of that went to projects for refugees and asylum seekers: £850,000 over two years, compared with an annual fundraise of over £25 million, was under 2 per cent of the total raised.†

Many Western governments have argued that the original provisions of the 1951 Convention on refugees are out of date. They

---

* B. Davies and T. Judd, 'They couldn't find a bed for my dying granny, but they open the wards for gypsies', *Daily Mail* (8 December 1998).
† (James Clark, 'How Comic relief gives cash aid to asylum seekers', *Daily Mail* (15 March 1999) and A. Cohen, 'Fury at £800,000 Red Nose gift to refugees', *The Sun* (15 March 1999).

argue that it was not designed to manage groups of people fleeing civil war and regional conflict from all over the world but was a specific European measure, after the movements of people after the Second World War, and with reference to the anti-communists in the former Soviet eastern bloc. They argue that the system is being abused by so called 'economic migrants', and they are all trying to deter asylum seekers from reaching their borders. In June 2000 the then Home Secretary, Jack Straw, expressed just such a view, which was echoed by his successor as Home Secretary David Blunkett. The UNHCR has responded to these views and is reexamining the issue. Though the 156 states who are party to the 1951 convention have signed a unanimous declaration to the effect that they still share the underlying principles of the Convention, there is still a desire to push other, closer, countries into bearing the brunt. The UNHCR is advocating the creation of multilateral agreements between countries that will encourage 'responsibility sharing' for the burden asylum seekers place upon them. It also looks as if there may be a serious possibility of some form of EU full harmonization of asylum laws and procedures.

The numbers of those seeking asylum in the UK have now started to go down, which the government sees as a major victory. In the first quarter of 2004, for instance, there were 8,940 applications, 17 per cent lower than the previous quarter, and 44 per cent less than in the first quarter of 2003. In 2003–4, 42,315 asylum applications were received, compared with 80,880 applications in the previous year, a 49 per cent reduction. However, the National Audit Office has challenged the government's figures for the total of asylum seekers receiving welfare and accommodation paid by the taxpayer, and has also criticized the Home Office's own statistics on the numbers of asylum seekers being deported. On the whole, it found the government's figures reliable, but there were several aspects that were 'materially misleading'.* The NAO said that the Home Office's figures on those receiving welfare payments and accommodation from NASS had failed to include up to

---

* *Daily Mail*, news section (25 May 2004).

16,000 asylum seekers supported by local authorities, let alone a further 1,000 supported by the Department for Work and Pensions and around 7,000 unaccompanied children (according to NASS) cared for by local authorities.

So government claims the figures are going down – a clearly important development as public concern rises. But are they? Or are some immigrants not being included in the figures, and others not being added in when they are found here illegally, just so government can say the numbers are going down? In terms of nationality, the largest number of applications in early 2004 were from Somalis, Iranians and Chinese, with Zimbabwean and Iraqi applications not far behind. The only rise in numbers was from Iranians, of 9 per cent.

Of initial decisions, in the same quarter, 4 per cent were granted asylum straight away, with a slight increase in the numbers granted Humanitarian Protection or Discretionary Leave to Remain, of 9 per cent. There were 10,100 appeals received, 11 per cent less than the previous quarter. In the same quarter, 3,320 principal applicants were removed (4,085 people including dependants), 27 per cent more than in the equivalent quarter the previous year. During the year, 17,135 asylum seekers were removed, a sign that procedures are toughening up and that the government is ever more determined to be seen as getting tough on so-called 'bogus' asylum seekers.

Applications for support from NASS were 6 per cent higher in the first quarter of 2004 than the previous quarter, and just over half of these were for accommodation and subsistence support. The applications from Eritrea, where civil war and slaughter are rife, rose dramatically by 54 per cent, putting it in the top ten nationalities of those claiming support. There were 1,330 detainees under the Immigration Act and others were detained under dual immigration and other powers, at Oakington (230), at Immigration Service Removal Centres (980), at short-term holding establishments (30), and at prison establishments (90). Thirty of those held as asylum detainees were under the age of 18, all detained with their families; 90 per cent of asylum detainees were male, and the largest nationalities represented were Jamaican, Turkish, and Chinese.

Political Views

This all shows that the pressure is on. But why do politicians assume that the public is so hostile? It is easy to see why in one way, as one only has to read much of the popular press or to hear people describe 'asylum seeker' as if it is a derogatory term. Yet recently there has been a spate of comments that suggest this is not a universal view. In June 2004 the *Mirror* reported that local politicians had praised asylum seekers renting from private landlords for transforming Broxholme Lane in Doncaster, a former slum.* The area has now moved up market, house prices have nearly doubled in five years, crime has decreased dramatically, and the politicians and the landlords are thrilled. The *Mirror* quotes one of them, Fred Gee, who owns five of the houses in the area, as saying: 'Asylum seekers are very good occupants. In four years I've never had any

---

* Jan Disley, 'Refugees give slum new lease of life', *Daily Mirror* (11 June 2004).

problems with drugs, vandalism or anti-social behaviour.' Indeed, the IPPR (Institute for Public Policy Research) in their *Asylum in the UK* fact file (IPPR, 2003) argues that 'Politicians and policy makers are extremely sensitive to public opinion, yet this opinion is largely ill-informed, wary, defensive and based upon "evidence" presented in crude polls in the tabloid press.'

A Populus poll for *The Times* in February 2003 showed that nine out of ten voters believed that the numbers of asylum seekers in the UK was a serious problem, and 39 per cent thought it was the most serious problem facing the UK. But, at the same time, 78 per cent thought it is right to let in people claiming asylum if their claim is genuine. All this sets politicians a conundrum, and, rather than set a lead in adopting a more humane tone and making it clear that those who have a right to be here will be treated decently, they concentrate on decreasing the numbers seeking asylum. That decrease may be due to increased immigration controls in France, plus the use of immigration officers in the countries of origin, as well as access to welfare benefits being removed from those who do not apply immediately. The notion that asylum seekers may be deported in the future and have their applications dealt with outside the UK may also have depressed the numbers of those who would otherwise have sought asylum in the UK.

The government has tended to argue that all this is to deter 'economic migrants', the so-called 'bogus asylum seekers'. But, as the IPPR stated firmly in their fact file, there is 'limited empirical evidence' that this is the case. It is also clear that most asylum seekers are not fully aware of what is available to them on arrival, nor do they know much about how the determination processes work in different countries, so it is unlikely that all these heavy measures will in fact make a great deal of difference, except to make it harder for people to claim asylum who may be perfectly entitled to do so.

If one looks at the top ten countries from which people have come to claim asylum in the EU over the period 1990–2000, these were places where civil war, extreme oppression of political and ethnic minorities, and human rights abuse were rife – the Former Republic of Yugoslavia; Romania; Turkey; Iraq; Afghanistan; Bosnia-Herzegovina; Sri Lanka; Iran; Somalia; and the Democratic Republic of the Congo (the former Zaire). These are unsurprising as countries of origin. If you look at the same period for applications to the UK alone, those who are particularly likely to come to Britain are Chinese, who often have family connections here already, or Indians and Pakistanis (who also are likely to have relatives in the UK).

Most people fleeing from persecution have very little time to plan their journeys or destinations. They leave at very short notice, so that the pattern of transport networks, visa restrictions and immigration controls tends to make some countries more accessible than others. Desperate asylum seekers often use an agent to help get them out, and the agents' choices of destination may be very different from those of the asylum seekers themselves: as a result, they may well end up somewhere they did not particularly want to be. This is hardly a matter of choice or of conscious planning. It all tends to be fairly desperate and immediate. So why anyone should assume that all or most asylum seekers are really only 'economic migrants' is hard to understand. Indeed, people rarely move permanently unless they are driven by terror or famine. Most people prefer to stay at home, as Saskia Sassen points out. Indeed, she argues if it were easier to get into a country temporarily to work and send money home before returning oneself, then some people would be happy with that option, because it is poverty and famine that is driving them, and a desire to help weaker members of their family, rather than a wish to leave home permanently.*

The image of Britain dishing out benefits to 'dubious aliens' is a parody of the truth. The reasons why particular individuals from specific places move is more complex, and may be less to do with personal repression and oppression than the nature of the society or the circumstances in which people find themselves.

---

* Saskia Sassen, 'Home truths', *The Guardian* (15 April 2000).

Detaining Asylum Seekers

Despite all the argument to the contrary, the vast majority of the world's asylum seekers are not banging on the doors of the UK and the EU. Of the world's estimated 12 million refugees between 1992 and 2001 72 per cent were to be found in the much less rich developing world. At the end of 2000, Pakistan alone had a refugee population – most, but not all, from Afghanistan and India – of two million. And it is not a wealthy country. It is closely followed by Iran, then comes Germany, in third place, with 900,000 refugees. But if you look at it as one should, by the numbers of refugees per 1000 relative to GDP, Armenia comes top of the list, with 79.7 per thousand. The only European country that enters the top ten, at tenth place, is Sweden, with a mere 17.7 per thousand. And though it had more asylum seekers in 2001 and 2002 than any other European country, when the relative size of domestic population is taken into account, the UK ranked eighth in 2002 and tenth in 2001. If it is done according to the wealth of the country, then the UK ranked 7th in Europe in 2002.

Again contrary to what people seem to think, more than one in three asylum seekers in 2002 was found to have been in need of protection or was allowed to stay on humanitarian grounds. In the same year, more than one in five appeals resulted in a grant of refugee status or exceptional leave to remain (22 per cent). Roughly 40 per cent of all who apply or appeal are eventually deemed to be in need of protection from persecution or are entitled to stay for other good, reasons.

Yet the assumption is still made that most of these people are claiming falsely. The government has reacted to that perception by detaining increasing numbers of asylum seekers. It maintains that there is always a need to detain a small number of immigration cases for reasons of security and control. That may well be so. In the past, a person could only be held to prevent their entering the country or to facilitate their removal. But now, after a ruling by the House of Lords, the Home Office can detain asylum seekers for administrative purposes whilst their cases are being decided. Asylum seekers and migrants, including children, can now be detained at any stage of their claim to remain in the UK, for any reason, and with no time limits. The UNHCR suggests that the UK detains more people for longer periods and with less judicial oversight than any comparable country in Europe.

It is not clear why this should be so, unless these are measures purely designed to satisfy public opinion that 'something is being done'. However, one of the unintended consequences is that it seriously compromises the education of the children amongst the detainees. People were already appalled at the idea that children's education might be interrupted by having to go with their families to some kind of accommodation centre specifically for asylum seekers. Education specialists argue that this is clearly against the interests of the children, who should have – indeed, do have – the same rights as any other children. The UK has been roundly criticized by the UN for its attitude to asylum-seeking children, and the Children's Alliance, a coalition of children's charities, has spoken out in the wake of the 2002 UN condemnation, arguing that 'children's human rights are being sacrificed to adult opinion'.

In October 2003 *The Guardian* ran a piece about a Kuwaiti child called Abdullah Shakil. His mother had fled from her abusive husband and they were granted refugee status. But after the authorities discovered that they had wrongly claimed on the asylum application that they had come from Pakistan rather than Kuwait, Abdullah and his two brothers, including one of fourteen months who had been born in Britain, were sent from Bradford to Dungavel detention centre for asylum seekers in Lanarkshire.* The police had come early in the morning and had given them no time to pack. They were taken in a van all the way to Lanarkshire, and did not understand why. His mother was crying, and when they got there they found others crying and shouting too. There were other children there. It was like a prison, indeed it was a prison. 'We had school, but it was too small. There was only one room and there were ten people in and it was too small. There was older boys and girls and younger

---

* 'We were in prison. I did not understand', *The Guardian* (9 October 2003).

than us. In Bradford, I liked school. But I didn't like it in there.' He continued: 'We tried to be good, but sometimes it was hard. Sometimes we were sad and cried.'

According to Save the Children, there are an estimated 82,000 refugee children in the UK. It is impossible to tell how many are being held in detention centres because the government says it would be too expensive to collate the figures, but evidence gleaned from parliamentary answers suggests it is around sixty children at any one time. The government says it would be much worse to split families up when parents are detained. Save the Children and other children's charities, as well as the UN, believe no child should be detained. The answer, therefore, is to find some other way of making sure that people who may not be allowed to remain do not disappear, as well as not detaining people who have children in the first place.

Despite the public being generally sympathetic to the idea that all asylum seekers should be detained while their identities are checked (an ICM poll in February 2003 found 74 per cent of the public in favour of this measure), they almost certainly would not be sympathetic to detaining children for any length of time, nor to detaining people who have lived in the UK for several years and whose children have been born here, and ill treatment of detainees would be universally condemned. And yet evidence has been mounting of systematic physical, verbal, and mental abuse of asylum seekers detention centres.* There is at least one criminal investigation under way, and there are civil claims for damages over a series of alleged assaults, reportedly involving beatings, and, in one case, a death. Detainees at Harmondsworth detention centre have been on hunger strike and employees of the private firm that runs Harmondsworth, UK Detention Services, are being interviewed by the police. Stories of abuse abound: groups who support asylum seekers claim that abuse is commonplace, lawyers report that they are getting claim after claim, and one Labour MP, Neil Gerrard, chairman of the all-party group on refugees, has said publicly: 'What has struck me is the numbers of sim-

---

* James Doward, 'Abuse is systematic at asylum detention centres', *The Observer* (23 May 2004).

ilar stories. They can't all be false. Things are happening that should not be happening.'†

If the allegations are true, it would not be surprising. When government itself talks so negatively of asylum seekers, and puts policies into place that are apparently designed to make life difficult for asylum seekers, it is not in the least surprising that staff are affected by the tone of the public debate and by media hysteria. To add to that, the Chief Inspector of Prisons, Anne Owers, has castigated the government over the filthy and dilapidated state of Lindholme, an immigration removal centre in Doncaster. She had visited it two years earlier, in March 2002, and argued that things had not improved significantly in the intervening period. The communal areas were revolting: 'Paint was peeling, floors had ingrained dirt, and all of the telephone rooms – very important for the detainees' contact with the outside world – were in a disgraceful state. Two lacked chairs, and all were covered in graffiti, among which staff had written up the

---

† *The Observer* (9 October 2003).

Samaritans' number. Inspectors were so concerned that they took photographs of these areas. There had clearly been problems in managing the cleaning contract; but it was noticeable that by contrast the parts of the centre used by staff were in excellent condition.' She also argued that Lindholme still had a prison culture and was quite unsuitable for detainees.

Even more worrying was that troublesome detainees at that same 'filthy and dilapidated' centre had been thrown into punishment cells at a neighbouring prison without proper authorization. This led to the immigration minister, Des Browne, promising the practice would end by October 2004. Yet the whole episode shows the Home Office's uncaring attitude towards the detainees: the first report by Anne Owers should have made it take action. The Refugee Council and the Liberal Democrats have argued, correctly, that immigration detainees are not convicted criminals and should not be treated as such. Essentially, Lindholme is a prison in everything but name, and the Home Office has not moved fast enough to change its culture.* Campaigners have been calling for the setting up of an independent watchdog to monitor conditions and behaviour in the asylum detention centres, as it appears that some people are being held for far too long and others given a very rough time. The conditions have thus far been monitored by so-called independent monitoring boards. But their members are appointed by the Home Office and they are under no obligation to publish their findings. What is needed is objective information and assessment.

Failed Asylum Applicants

As already mentioned, for those whose applications have been rejected there is now a proposal to make those who cannot go back to their countries do compulsory community work. David Blunkett argued that it made 'perfect sense' to give them the opportunity to do community work in exchange for basic subsistence. But what has happened to them is that they sleep in telephone boxes, on

---

* Alan Travis, 'Detainees held in filthy conditions', *The Guardian* (16 June 2004).

542

friends' sofas, or on 24-hour buses. During the day they wander round the streets, too proud to beg, too honest to cheat the system. They are the failed asylum seekers who cannot go home, people like Jabulani, a 24-year-old maths teacher from Zimbabwe, featured in *The Observer* in June 2004.* He was an active member of the Movement for Democratic Change and bore the scars of attacks from Zanu-PF supporters. His application was rejected in September 2003; he was evicted and his food allowance withdrawn, but he could not go home. The Home Office agreed it was too dangerous – so now what? He remains in limbo, dependent on handouts from local charities and soup kitchens. No one knows how many like him there are in the UK.

A Home Office spokeswoman said that making community work an obligation for failed asylum seekers who could not return home would help to solve the problem of destitution. 'It is not a punishment. It is designed to both occupy them purposefully and to enable them to perform useful tasks

---

* Lorna Martin, 'Asylum losers spark city crisis', *The Observer* (13 June 2004).

in return for our providing accommodation at taxpayers' expense.' But Jabulani is a qualified maths teacher, of which we have a chronic shortage. Amongst people like Jabulani are doctors, dentists, nurses and other professionals, because they tend to be the ones who manage to get out. And we do not let them work at what they are qualified to do. Is this sensible? Why couldn't they be granted temporary leave to work? Surely it is better to allow asylum seekers who want to work to do so rather than prevent them working and thereby making them destitute. It cannot be good for us or them to make them feel like criminals, yet that is what we are doing.

At the same time as the community work measures announced by David Blunkett, there was also a measure to restrict the right of successful refugees (and others given leave to remain) to apply for local authority housing other than in those areas to which they had been dispersed by NASS. The system of back payments to successful asylum seekers has been replaced with a loan system to meet the costs of integration. All this goes against the principle of giving a refuge to people who have been abused or oppressed in the countries from which they come.

Health Issues

Many asylum seekers have experienced trauma, war, or violent repression, the destruction of their homes, the death of family members, separation from parents or siblings, and forced displacement. And most of them will have already experienced long periods of uncertainty and mobility. There is also plenty of evidence that children can experience post-traumatic stress disorder (PTSD), which is particularly associated with the violent death of family members. The symptoms can manifest themselves when decisions on asylum applications are awaited. It cannot help those children to be detained in detention centres. The Department of Health is responsible for co-ordinating policy relating to the healthcare of asylum seekers and refugees. But that requires proper co-ordination with NASS, including improving NASS decisions on allocation of asylum seekers, for some will need specialist services not available everywhere, and strengthening communication between NASS and local health service providers. The Department of Health has tried to pilot ways of supporting local health and care agencies in providing good care, including health assessments at the new induction centres for arrivals, and has published an information and resource pack for health workers called *Meeting the Needs of Refugees and Asylum Seekers in the UK*. There have also been some specific moves to ensure that everyone concerned, from health care providers to refugee community groups, knows what the health issues are that confront refugees in general, as well as the specific health issues that may affect particular refugee communities. But there is no special funding from the Home Office or from any other statutory body for the health treatment of asylum seekers, unless one of the new induction centres is situated in the area.

Asylum applicants and those who are granted either refugee status, exceptional leave to remain or enter, or humanitarian protection are entitled to free primary care medical services provided by the National Health Service. However, when a claim to asylum fails, and all appeal processes have been exhausted, asylum seekers become in-eligible for routine NHS primary care treat-ment. GPs and other primary care providers are then supposed to charge them for any treatment. The exception is for emergency treatment, which has to be provided free of charge by the NHS. The result has been that, whilst some Health Authorities undertake some refugee-related work, often in part-nership with other agencies, there are major problems of fragmentation and a lack of co-ordination. There is a real lack of knowledge, for instance, about the needs of refugees in London and other big cities. In May 2002, the NHS London Region (now the Directorate of Health and Social Care for London) spon-sored and supported the production of an information and resource pack for health workers on meeting the health needs of asy-lum seekers and refugees in the UK. Other London bodies, including the Greater London Authority and the London Health Commis-sion, are also showing a keen interest in the health of asylum seekers, and the effect upon them of poor housing and stress.

Although asylum seekers and refugees are legally entitled to access healthcare services from the NHS, in practice they face many difficulties – such as the language barrier and not knowing what they are entitled to. The existing poor health of refugees and asylum seekers is frequently made worse by inequalities in access to health services. Things are even worse where asylum seekers have been dispersed compulsorily by NASS and moved from place to place, which means relationships with health professionals are hard to form. Language difficulties mean that young children often have to act as interpreters, which is obviously fraught with problems.

The children themselves may well have serious health problems, as work for the King's Fund and the Royal College of Paediatrics and Child Health found as far back as 1999. Some will have been malnourished in childhood, others will have suffered trauma and from the effects of poor accommodation – for example, respiratory conditions, asthma, and skin problems.

Though most asylum seekers are relatively healthy on arrival in the UK, the BMA suggests one in six has a physical health problem severe enough to affect their life, whilst two-thirds have experienced significant anxiety or depression. The UK statistical comparison would be 13 per cent of males and 15 per cent of females reporting restrictions on activity due to illness or injury in the two weeks before being interviewed, and a rough figure of 7 per cent of female patients and 3 per cent of male patients being treated for depression by a GP. Even where there are refugee-specific services, there is no clear evidence of their effectiveness because so little research has been done. The signs are that services targeted at specific communities are much appreciated, such as the now well-established Vietnamese Mental Health Project in Lambeth, the Somali Counselling Project in Lambeth, and the Haringey Refugee Development Project. These are quite separate from, though they often work with, the main services for those who have traumatic stress disorder – the Medical Foundation for the Victims of Torture and the Traumatic Stress service, which operates under the auspices of the Camden and Islington Mental Health NHS Trust.

There has been considerable concern amongst the health community about the increasingly tough measures introduced by the government. Where asylum seekers apply for asylum after having arrived in the UK, instead of at the port of entry, they are now denied benefits, support, and accommodation, even though they are still allowed to go on and claim political asylum. They have no money, nowhere to live, and no obvious means of support whilst they apply. One local GP in Dover, which has seen large influxes of asylum seekers, has argued that this poses a public health issue. Dr Peter Le Feuvre gave the example of one of his patients in this situation who had undeniably been a victim of torture: 'the whipping marks were obvious'. He had spent two periods in prison in Angola, 'during which he was branded with a hot iron, and put in a hole with biting ants. He claimed asylum three days after arriving in the UK. The fact that this man is now facing the prospect of sleeping on a park bench in Dover beggars belief. It is grossly inhumane.'*

Dr Le Feuvre argued that he could not even give people a prescription for the medicines they needed because they could not pay the pharmacist, a situation described as ridiculous by the Migrant Helpline at Dover. In a concluding statement to Dr Le Feuvre's article, the British Medical Association expressed deep concern about 'the public health and humanitarian impact of any policy which left a vulnerable group of people both homeless and destitute'. But unless doctors refuse to co-operate with the government on other issues, such as primary care contracts, the BMA's concern will probably make precious little difference, disgraceful though the situation has become.

Work

The fact that asylum seekers are now not allowed to work at all (not even after the first six months as used to be the case) until they have refugee status, or exceptional leave to remain, has had a powerful negative effect

---

* Sally Hargreaves, 'Law against asylum seekers may have public health impact', *BMJ* (24 May 2003).

on them. Depression is common, for many of them are proud people. They are often professionals fleeing oppression and cannot understand why they are not given enough to live on or allowed to work. They would be delighted, in most cases, for their skills to be put to good use for the benefit the UK, and we are foolish not to allow them to do so.

Despite strong and categorical acceptance of the role of employment in ensuring the integration of refugees, the disadvantages faced by asylum seekers continue to have a negative impact on those who are subsequently granted refugee status or leave to remain. It is clear that policy on refugees' and asylum seekers' access to the labour market and to economic activity in general is influenced by the way policy-makers see the wider issue of immigration.

On the one hand, government ministers have begun exploring the idea that immigration could help the UK cope both with current skills shortages in some sectors and with longer-term changes in its demographic structure. On the other, they pick up on the negative feeling towards asylum seekers in large parts of the population. So whilst they develop a plethora of policies to enable 'managed migration' into the country, they have stopped asylum seekers, even those who have the skills of which the UK is desperately short, from working until their case has been resolved. In principle, government policy recognizes the contribution that refugees can make to labour market shortages (including high-skill occupations such as medicine and teaching). Yet refugees often find it very hard to get a job – even when we are crying out for nurses, teachers, and other professionals. The government's own research shows that refugee unemployment is far above the national average for any disadvantaged group in the UK, with women faring worse than men. And those who are in work are not doing what they did in their home countries, with a notable lack of involvement in professional jobs even where pre-migration experience exists. Instead, they tend to end up in low-skill jobs such as catering, cleaning and factory work, and their terms and conditions of employment, as well as rates of pay, are notably worse than those experienced by other people from ethnic minorities.

The Peabody Trust, in a damning report entitled *Refugees: Breaking Down the Barriers to Work*, describes how long it takes for refugees to find work. Over half of refugees who had been in the country for five to eight years are still unemployed, and only 15 per cent hold professional, managerial or employer positions, compared with 43 per cent in their own countries. Of the people interviewed, 11 per cent felt there was definite discrimination against refugees. The government is worried about these figures, but at the same time it has adopted an entirely different policy in relation to asylum seekers, who are not now allowed to enter paid employment until they have received a positive decision on their application. They are no longer able to work or undertake vocational training until they are given a positive decision on their case, regardless of how long they wait for a decision. They can, however, undertake voluntary work, for which they are given travel and lunch expenses.

This relatively new policy preventing access to the labour market by asylum seekers has had a powerful effect. It is supposed to deter people from coming to the UK for work rather than protection. In fact people do largely come for protection. They want and need – for their own self esteem and to prove they are not a burden on the taxpayer – to work and support themselves. But many employers are confused about who can and cannot work, and asylum seekers themselves begin to lose their skills and confidence whilst waiting for a decision to be made about their case. This makes it even more difficult for them to get into work once a decision has been made that they can stay. An employer faces legal action if they employ someone who is not allowed to work; they also find it hard to distinguish between those who are refugees, and allowed to work, and those who are asylum seekers, and are not. Nor are employers immune to the negative press coverage of asylum issues and by the general climate of hostility towards migrant labour. A report published by the Employability Forum* found that employers who do take on refugees are often

---

* *Employing Refugees: Some Organisations' Experience* (2004).

impressed with the calibre of their work. At the same time they are frightened to publicize the fact that they employ them for fear of negative publicity. Its conclusions were reinforced by the fact that five of the ten employers concerned declined to be named. The report warns that fear of negative publicity is a significant barrier to employers considering recruiting refugees.

Returning Failed Asylum Seekers 'Home'

In June 2004 the forced return began of failed Somali asylum seekers to Mogadishu, where the internal conflict had left some two hundred people dead over the previous two months. Both the UNHCR (United Nations High Commissioner for Refugees) and Amnesty International pressed the government, in the shape of the Immigration Service, for urgent clarification over how six men could possibly have been sent back to a war zone as the result of an 'unannounced policy change'. The deportations coincided with a Home Office announcement – slipped out in a Commons written answer – that it was to start forced returns to Iraq 'as soon as the necessary arrangements are in place'.† (There are some 16,000 Iraqis living in Britain who have been refused asylum or exceptional leave to remain.)

An Amnesty International report, published on 14 June 2004, at the beginning of Refugee Week, showed that, according to official statistics, up to 75 per cent of asylum applications in Britain are from people fleeing countries where conflicts are occurring, as defined by the International Institute for Strategic Studies. Both the UNHCR and Amnesty told the Home Office that they were 'extremely concerned' about the unannounced decision to return the six Somali men forcibly, and the UN had already warned against returns south of Galkayo, the area that includes Mogadishu. It was human rights lawyers who spotted a change in the Immigration Service's operational guidance in May 2004. The Home Office stated that the new guidance had been announced in a House of Commons written answer in May 2004, but human rights groups have argued that forced returns had been going

† Alan Travis, 'Deportees sent back to war zone', *The Guardian* (15 June 2004).

on since March. The battle will continue, but the implications are clear.

The UK government, then, is becoming increasingly hostile to asylum seekers. It is returning people when other countries are not (it has been the first country to reach an agreement with the new authorities in Iraq to return asylum seekers there), and its concern is more for public opinion than for the welfare of those who come to Britain seeking asylum from war-torn countries. But we still have a duty to offer a refuge to those suffering persecution, as the journalist Ian Katz put it so well in a 'letter' to the then new Home Secretary, David Blunkett, in June 2001.* He praised the Home Secretary for opening the front door to people with skills Britain was lacking – doctors, nurses, teachers, and so on. But he concluded: 'That does not lessen our duty to treat those who come through the back [door] with fairness and compassion.'

What kind of country are we turning into? Most of us have heard something of the

---

* Ian Katz, 'Leave the back door ajar', *The Guardian* (12 June 2001).

horrors some of these people have been sub-jected to. Rape, torture, watching the rape and torture of others, and being abused reg-ularly are commonplace – we have seen it in Iraq, in Kosovo, in Bosnia, in Sierra Leone. And yet we fail to believe, choosing instead to be hostile.*

In a fascinating piece, written for *The Guardian* back in 2001, Abdulrazak Gurnah, a distinguished novelist from Zanzibar, wrote of his first months in Britain in the late 1960s, having fled a huge violent upris-ing in his home country. 'What a shock it was to discover the loathing in which I was held: by looks, sneers, words and gestures, news reports, comics on TV, teachers, fellow stu-dents. Everybody did their bit, and thought themselves tolerant, or perhaps mildly grumbling, or even amusing. At the receiv-ing end it seemed constant and mean.' He would have left Britain if he had been able, but, having broken the law in his own coun-try, there was nowhere else to go. He con-tinues: 'There is a rational and humane way to conduct this debate, just as there was a

---

* Anabel Unity Sale, 'Haunted by horror', *Community Care* (28 August–3 September 2003).

better way to talk about the arrival of so many non-European people in Britain in the years after 1945. That better way requires knowledge and humanity, not glib and diminishing clichés.'

Rethinking Asylum Policy

What is needed is a complete rethink of asylum policy. In the wake of the discovery in June 2000 of 58 Chinese illegal immigrants found dead in the back of a lorry at Dover, and the ensuing shockwaves, the *Evening Standard* ran a double-page spread by Victor Sebestyen† looking at what was going on and what the alternatives were. Sebestyen, in a broadly sympathetic piece, argued that the refugee problem would not go away, and indeed that it would get worse. He saw that the nub of the problem lay in the fact that public money is used to support people who seem happy to live at the taxpayers' expense but whose claim for 'sympathy and tolerance may appear dubious'. He noted the argument that asylum seekers should be al-

---

† Victor Sebestyen, 'A tidal wave of displaced people', *Evening Standard* (27 June 2000).

lowed to work and not receive benefits; he then considered the various alternative views of the problem, from the ultra-liberal 'let them all in' position to the ultra-right view of wanting to put a No Entry sign at all our points of entry. Or, he argued, we could go for the middle path, and set out to limit and control. This, he argued, is what the government is doing and should continue to do, recognising that the 'the chief burden of the refugee problem is borne by the poorest countries who are least able to cope – a fact the rich First World rarely acknowledges'.

But there are other alternatives that take different factors into account, such as the need for skilled workers and our duty to those who are genuinely seeking asylum. It is also about common humanity and showing political and moral leadership in the face of hysteria and prejudice, as Mary Coussey has done in her work as independent race monitor, appointed by the Home Office to monitor the work of immigration officials. It is her view that the media hype around the whole asylum issue can affect how staff work with asylum seekers and how they view their client group. If the mood 'out there' is negative, and if government does not set a lead, then that mood will affect the people who work closely with asylum seekers. 'It's just not possible for any human being to distance themselves from the relentless coverage that asylum seekers receive. It must affect staff's perceptions, and I think this is an issue that needs to be addressed.'*

Mary Coussey points out that the public generally believes that the UK is a 'soft touch' when it comes to granting asylum but in fact that is not true. We need to look behind and beyond the statistics: 'When you look at the human side, it sheds a whole different light on the issue. I just wish more people would acknowledge that, in the media and beyond.' The media certainly need to ask themselves why they feel it appropriate to peddle hatred about asylum seekers in such a consistent way, as Roy Greenslade has argued cogently:† 'It is a despicable denial of reality for papers to whip up hatred against desperate groups of people who

---

* Mary Coussey, quoted in Janet Snell, 'For fair play', *Community Care* (6–12 November 2003).
† Roy Greenslade, 'Asylum madness? Look who's talking', *The Guardian* (3 February 2003).

have fled from their homes – whether due to political oppression or economic plight – and then wash their hands of the consequences ... With their daily negative stories, the *Mail* (''Asylum on Sea'') and the *Express* (''Surrender to asylum'') and the *Sun* (''Asylum Madness'') are appealing to the basest of human instincts: suspicion of the alien.'

The UK is not alone in its views. Denmark has made it impossible for Danish citizens under 24 to live in Denmark if they marry someone from outside the EU. The Danish government argues that it has to tackle an influx of non-Europeans who rely too heavily on welfare, commit more than their fair share of crime, and do not integrate into Danish society. The result is that these 'love refugees' live in Malmo, in Sweden, and commute the twenty miles across the Baltic Sea back to Copenhagen to work.‡ Ireland has also restricted citizenship, abandoning the long-held right to Irish citizenship for those born in Ireland as a result of reports of heavily pregnant women arriving to give

---

‡ A. Browne, 'Mixed couples cross love bridge to exile', *The Times* (2 October 2004).

birth and then leaving the country again within days.‡

In 2003 the magazine *Community Care* ran a campaign entitled 'Right to refuge', from which a very different picture emerged from the one painted by the government and the media. A poll revealed widespread public support for a change in the law to allow asylum seekers to work, when government has been legislating precisely in the opposite direction. A survey of professionals revealed that 67 per cent of them felt that their asylum-seeking and refugee clients were being treated in a racist way by the authorities, and 87 per cent felt that services were failing this very vulnerable group. In a Christmas sermon in 2000, George Carey, then Archbishop of Canterbury, argued that our ungenerous responses towards asylum seekers are due to fear: 'When people are afraid, generosity is often in short supply. Fear, with its sister insecurity, shuts doors and refuses to allow the stranger in.'* Our

---

‡ David McKittrick, 'Ireland prepares to restrict citizenship', *The Independent* (12 June 2004).

* R Gledhill, 'Carey calls for generosity to asylum seekers', *The Times* (26 December 2000).

fear even extends to potential immigrants from the former eastern bloc countries, as Adam LeBor argued in a fierce piece in *The Times* in April 2004.† We need to stop and think again. As Adam LeBor puts it so gracefully, 'as they say in Germany, the Berlin Wall is gone, but the wall in the head remains'.

Immigration In General

We need to think more positively about immigration or we will not be able to staff many of our services and industries, given our low birth-rate and our increasing numbers of elderly people. Rosemary Righter, in a trenchant piece in *The Times* in June 2000 argued that 'if every political party in the EU were to be scrutinised as critically as Austria's have for hostile comments about immigrants it would be hard to tell the pots from the kettles'. She continued: 'In Britain, politicians are competing to show who is toughest on asylum seekers and illegal immigrants; across Europe, mainstream poli-

---

† Adam LeBor, 'Happy to stay at home', *The Times* (29 April 2004).

tics is becoming, if not frankly xenophobic, at least increasingly anti-immigrant.'

Righter argues that immigration is essential to the welfare of modern industrial and post-industrial economies if we are to pay for pensions and look after our elderly. But, as she also points out, no one dares to say so. And she is right – both that it dangerous to say so and that we need more immigrants, not fewer, whatever the public prejudice. An inadequate skills base is one reason why UK productivity has been poor, not only in the public sector but also in communications and IT, and why a more enlightened and pragmatic immigration policy is necessary.* Back in 2000 the former immigration minister, Barbara Roche, wanted to destigmatize the term 'economic migrant', and her argument still holds good. Unfortunately, it is still a term of abuse as the nation has become more hysterical about immigration, rather than less.

We need to knock down the wall of xenophobia and fear of 'the other'. Asylum seek-

---

* Rosemary Bennett and Christopher Adams, 'Immigrant policy aims to close skills gap', *Financial Times* (11 August 2000).

ers should be allowed to work, even if temporarily. Appeals should he heard more quickly, and detention should not be used unless there are security issues at stake.

Children should never be detained as asylum seekers; and those who arrive unaccompanied should not be deported on their eighteenth birthdays, as sometimes happens. Instead, even if they cannot remain permanently, they should be allowed to complete their education and at least return home with some kind of qualification. Some 26 per cent of local authorities think that there are a 'lot of unidentified unaccompanied children' in their areas, whilst 67 per cent think that young asylum seekers are more at risk of living in sub-standard housing, of neglect, of sexual exploitation, and of exploitation in the workplace.†

Asylum seekers should be treated with respect even if they are not going to be allowed to stay, and their mental and physical health needs should be taken care of. A serious public education campaign needs to take place so that people understand why it

---

† Charlotte Ritchie, 'Children cut adrift', *Community Care* (2–8 October 2003).

is that some asylum seekers have come to the UK. Meanwhile, those who are truly economic migrants should be allowed to come in as and when we need to augment the workforce.

Finally, abuse of asylum seekers and refugees should be seen for what it is: ugly, racist, and a cowardly targeting of the vulnerable. Like any other kind of racism, it should be regarded as unacceptable by society as a whole and should be prosecuted by the authorities where it is sufficiently extreme.

ACKNOWLEDGEMENTS

This book would not have been possible without the help of many people. First, my thanks go to the Rockefeller Foundation for a wonderfully productive four-week residency at its study centre at Bellagio, in Italy. The atmosphere created by Gianna Celli and her team to encourage one to work hard and live sensibly allowed me to write a great deal of the first draft of this book there. Susan Garfield at the Rockefeller Foundation office in New York was patient, supportive, and very kind. My fellow residents at Bellagio were generous with their time and indulgent towards some of the ideas expressed in this book – but they were critical too, and that helped enormously. Second, Ros Levenson, researcher, critic and friend, was quite wonderful in shaping the book. It would not have been possible without her, and I have learned a great deal from her. Thanks also to her daughter, Ellie Levenson, for great help towards the end in editing and shortening two chapters.

My thanks also go to Andy Bell of the Sainsbury Centre for Mental Health, for lots of ideas and support; to Katya Lester for help on the asylum seekers and refugees chapter; to Pam Hibbert of Barnardo's for help with the children and young people leaving care chapter; to Phil Youdan of NCH Action for Children, Judith Skinner of VSU in Kent, Karen Goodman of Hillingdon Council, and to all the young people who agreed to be interviewed – they were wonderful. Thanks to Bobby Cummines of Unlock! and to Heaven Crawley of AMRE Consulting, the team at Rethinking Crime and Punishment, the team at the NSPCC library, and to the library staff at the King's Fund – everyone there was superbly helpful, sometimes spending hours chasing references and half-remembered stories.

Huge thanks too to all the people who helped me so much in the United States. Thanks to Carol Shapiro, of Family Justice; to Ann-Marie Louison of CASES; to Heather Barr of the Urban Justice Center; to Jeremy Travis of the Urban Institute in Washington, DC, who put me in touch with all of them, and was wonderfully helpful in guiding me when my questions were still unfocused; to Tony Hannigan of CUCS; to Patty Inacker of Hall-Mercer Community Mental Health team at Pennsylvania Hospital, Philadelphia; and to Gail Loeb, also at Hall-Mercer, who introduced me to Patty Inacker.

Finally, a huge thank you to Darren Walker of the Rockefeller Foundation, who opened my eyes to looking at the best of what is done in the United States and put me in touch with so many wonderful people and projects, and to my inspirational friend Julie Sandorf, who made me believe anything is possible if you want to do it. All the mistakes are mine, but they all contributed ideas, corrections, inspiration, and new thinking.

ACKNOWLEDGEMENTS

Thanks too to Trevor Dolby at HarperCollins for his wonderful support, his great editing and his tough-minded, no-nonsense approach. It's been great. And to all the team at HarperCollins as well – it has been a huge pleasure. Thanks too to my agent, Clare Alexander, patient friend and excellent listener. This book would not have happened if she had not been so determined to get me to write it. And thanks to Carole Stone, who believed in it from the beginning, introduced the idea to Trevor Dolby, and ... Perhaps some things are just meant to happen. It has certainly been a huge pleasure to work on this project with such extraordinary people, with such commitment to what they do.

Lastly, thanks to my ever-patient friend and assistant Paola Churchill, who has lived though all of this with her usual good humour and forbearance, and my family, Anthony, Harriet, and Matthew. They were all very kind, and I am immensely grateful for all the cups of tea, arguments, corrections, and games of back-gammon they

Acknowledgements

provided when I could not face the computer any longer.

Julia Neuberger
October 2004

BIBLIOGRAPHY

Aitkenhead, D. (2004), 'When home's a prison', *The Guardian* (24 July 2004).

Akinsaya, D. (2002), 'Can children in care avoid prison?' BBC News *http://news.bbc.co.uk/1/hi/talking_point/1979688.stm*

Alibhai-Brown, Y. (1998), 'Age of respect', *Community Care* (10–16 December 1998), 24–5.

Allard, A., Fry, E., Sufian, J. (2004), *Setting the Agenda: What's left to do in leaving care?* : London: Action on Aftercare Consortium.

Allard, A. S. (2002), *A Case Study Investigation into the Implementation of the Children (Leaving Care) Act 2000*, London: NCH.

Allen, M. (2003), *Into the Mainstream: Care leavers entering work, education and training*, York: Joseph Rowntree Foundation.

Allison, E. (2004a), 'Child prisoners "face weakness in system"' *The Guardian* (20 April 2004).

—— (2004b), 'I thought Brixton Prison was a dump', *The Guardian* (31 March 2004).

A National Voice (2002), *Amplify: The Report, 4: The Recommendations* (August 2002): *info@nationalvoice.org*

Appleby, L. (2001), 'Preventing suicides must remain a priority', *British Medical Journal* (6 October 2001).

Ariès, P. (1965), *Centuries of Childhood: A social history of family life*, New York: Random House.

Ashworth, P. (2002), 'Letting go', *The Guardian* (31 July 2002).

Audit Commission (2003), *Actioning the NHS Plan: Assessment of current perfor-*

mance, likely future progress and capacity to improve, London: Audit Commission.

Audit Commission/MORI (2003), *Trust in Public Institutions*, London: MORI.

Ayotte, W. (2000), *Separated Children Coming to Western Europe: Why they travel and how they arrive*, London: Save the Children.

Ayotte, W., and Williamson, L. (2001), *Separated Children in the UK: An overview of the current situation*, London: Save the Children.

Bann, C., and Tennant, R, (2002), *Unaccompanied Asylum-Seeking Children*, London: King's Fund for National Children's Bureau and Barnardo's, Highlight no. 190.

Barnardo's (2002), *Future Citizens*, London: Barnardo's.

—— (2001), *Whose Government is it Anyway?* London: Barnardo's.

Barratt Inquiry (1991), *Regional Fact Finding Committee of Inquiry into the Admission, Care, Treatment and Discharge of Carol Barratt* (chair: Cyril Unwin), Nottingham: Trent Health Authority.

Bartlett, S. (2004), 'Making headway', *Community Care* (8–14 January 2004).

Bean, P., and Melville, J. (1989), *Lost Children of the Empire: The untold story of Britain's child migrants*, London: Unwin Hyman.

Beardshaw, V. (1981), *Conscientious Objectors at Work: Mental hospital nurses – a case study*, London: Social Audit.

Bell, A. (2003), 'Too much in "The Sun"', *British Journal of Health Care Management*, 9: 11, 377.

Bennett, C. (2004), 'The author abused children: should we read his books?', *The Guardian* (27 May 2004).

Bennett, R., and Adams, C. (2000), 'Immigrant policy aims to close skills gap', *Financial Times* (11 August 2000).

Better Regulation Task Force (2004), *Bridging the Gap: Participation in Social Care Regulation*, London: Better Regulation Task Force.

Biehal, N., and Wade, J. (1998), 'Missing links', *Community Care* (12–18 November 1998).

Birkett, D. (2000), 'If it's Daddy, we don't care', *The Guardian* (20 July 2000).

BIBLIOGRAPHY

Birmingham, L. (2002), 'Doctors Working in Prisons', *British Medical Journal* (23 February 2002).

Boseley, S. (2003), 'UK accused of failing child victims', *The Guardian* (9 October 2003).

Boswell, J. (1988), *The Kindness of Strangers: The abandonment of children in Western Europe from late antiquity to the Renaissance*, Harmondsworth: Allen Lane/ The Penguin Press.

Boyd, W. (1996), *Confidential Inquiry into Homicides and Suicides by Mentally Ill People*, London: Royal College of Psychiatrists.

Braid, M, (2000), 'Homing pigeon boy: A modern horror story', *The Independent* (23 August 2000).

Brayfield, C. (1998), 'The death of the family?' *The Times* (12 October 1998).

Bridge Child Care Consultancy Service (1995), *Paul: Death through neglect*, London: BCCCS for Islington Area Child Protection Committee.

Bright, M. (2004a), 'Anger over children locked alone in cells', *The Observer* (11 January 2004).

—— (2004b), 'Most problem "kids" go on to thrive', *The Observer* (13 June 2004).

—— (2003), 'I'd prefer to do time than therapy', *The Observer* (21 September 2003).

Brindle, D. (2004), 'Q. How many care workers does it take to change a light bulb? A. Ask a risk assessor', *The Guardian* (27 March 2004).

—— (2000), 'Staffing crisis hits child protection plan', *The Guardian* (31 January 2000).

Brindle, D., and Carvel, J. (2004), 'Care home rules "stop volunteers helping elderly"', *The Guardian* (8 September 2004).

British Medical Association (2002), *Asylum Seekers: Meeting their healthcare needs*, London: BMA.

British Society of Rehabilitation Medicine (2000), *Vocational Rehabilitation, the Way Forward: Report of a working party*, London: BRSM.

Broad, B. (2003), *After the Act: Implementing the Children (Leaving Care) Act 2000*, Leicester: De Montfort University Children and Families Research Unit Monograph Series No. 3, and the Action on Aftercare Consortium.

Brontë, C. (1847), *Jane Eyre*, Harmondsworth: Penguin Classics edition (2003).

Brown, A. (2000), 'Asylum seekers return to South after "race abuse"', *Evening Standard* (24 July 2000).

Browne, A. (2004), 'Mixed couples cross love bridge to exile', *The Times* (2 October 2004).

Browne, V. (2004), 'Benefits in presidential campaign', *Irish Times* (1 September 2004).

Bunting, M. (2004a), 'The last taboo', *The Guardian* (5 July 2004).

—— (2004b), 'Morality as Polyfilla', *The Guardian* (16 August 2004).

Burleigh, M. (1994), *Death and deliverance: Euthanasia in Germany 1900–1945*, Cambridge: Cambridge University Press.

Campbell, D. (2004), 'At last, the "good dying" guide', *The Guardian* (1 June 2004).

Carey-Wood, J. (1997), *Meeting Refugees' Needs in Britain: The role of refugee specific initiatives*, London: Home Office.

Carter, P. (2004), *Managing Offenders, Reducing Crime: A new approach*, Correctional Services Review/National Probation Service, London: Stationery Office.

Cavendish, C. (2004), 'Public opinion', *The Times* (18 May 2004).

Centrepoint (2002), *Borderline*, Centrepoint Health and Social Exclusion briefing (Summer 2002).

Christophersen, O., Thorpe, K., Upson, A. (2004), *Crime in England and Wales: Quarterly update to December 2003*, London: Home Office Statistical Bulletin, 06/04.

Clark, L. (2004), 'The children who are too frightened to play outside', *Daily Mail* (24 May 2004).

—— (1999), 'How Comic Relief gives cash aid to asylum seekers', *Daily Mail* (15 March 1999).

Clough, S. (2000), 'Teenage sisters guilty of killing widow, 87', *Daily Telegraph* (15 August 2000).

—— (2000), 'Girls who killed widow given long sentences', *Daily Telegraph* (9 September 2000).

Cohen, A. (2002), *A Survey of PCGs*, London: Sainsbury Centre for Mental Health.

Cohen, A. (1999), 'Fury at £800,000 Red Nose gift to refugees', *The Sun* (15 March 1999).

BIBLIOGRAPHY

Cohen, N. (2000), 'Principle witless', *The Observer* (16 April 2000).

Commission for Health Improvement (2003) *What CHI has Found in Mental Health Trusts*, London: CHI.

—— (2003), 'Older people's ward forgotten', *CHI News* (October 2003).

Community Channel (2004), *Walk in our Shoes* (19 August 2004).

Connexions with Save the Children (2003) *Working Together: Connexions Supporting Young Asylum Seekers and Refugees*, http:// www.renewal.net/Documents/ Policy%20Guidance/ Workingtogetherconnexions.pdf

Cook, S. (2003), 'Inside track', *The Guardian* (5 February 2003).

Cottell, C. (2002), 'Finding the key to a life without bars', *The Guardian* (31 August 2002).

Coyle, A. (2002), *Managing Prisons in a Time of Change*, London: International Centre for Prison Studies.

Crewe, C. (2004), 'We can work it out', *The Times Magazine* (1 May 2004).

Crick, B. (2004), 'All this talk of Britain is so ... English', *The Guardian* (12 April 2004).

—— (2000), 'Big Brother belittled', *The Guardian* (19 August 2000).

Curtis, P. (2004), 'Schools told to keep pupils out of midday sun', *The Guardian* (4 June 2004).

Daily Mail (2004), 'Smacking: We plead guilty' (7 July 2004).

Daily Telegraph (2004), 'Politicians take note: the public still trusts GPs', editorial (16 August 2004).

Davies, B., and Judd, T. (1998), 'They couldn't find my dying granny a bed but they open the wards for gypsies', *Daily Mail* (8 December 1998).

Davies, N. (2004) 'Chaos meets order – the result is tragedy', *The Guardian* (13 April 2004).

—— (1998), *Dark Heart: The shocking truth about hidden Britain*, London: Vintage.

Dean, M. (2004), 'Blurred vision of a safer future', *The Guardian* (3 March 2004).

Deer, B. (1985), 'Panic is not a solution', *Sunday Times* (29 September 1985).

Dempsey, A. (2004), 'Too scared to keep children safe?' *Irish Times* (26 July 2004).

Department for Education and Skills (2003a), *Statistics of Education: Care* leavers, 2002–2003, England, DfES Bulletin, 05/03.

—— (2003b) *Statistics of education: Children looked after in England, 2002–2003*, DfES Bulletin, 06/03.

Department of Health (2004), *Prison Health Bi-Annual Report 2001–2003*, London: DoH.

—— (2003a), *Meeting the Needs of Refugees and Asylum Seekers in the UK*, London: DoH.

—— (2003b), *Outcome Indicators for Looked-After Children: Twelve months to 30 September 2002*, London: DoH.

—— (1999a), *Me, Survive, Out There? New arrangements for young people living in and leaving care*, London: DoH.

—— (1999b), *Safer Services: National confidential inquiry into suicide and homicide by people with mental illness*, London: HMSO.

Department of Health, Directorate for Health and Social Care for London (2002), *Information and Resource Pack for Meeting the Needs of Asylum Seekers and Refugees.*

Department of Health, Social Services and Public Safety (2003), *Community Statistics 1 April 2002–31 March 2003*, Belfast: DHSSPS.

Department of Transport, Local Government and the Regions, with the Department of Health, and Centrepoint (2002), *Care Leaving Strategies: A good practice handbook*, London: DTLGR.

Department of Work and Pensions (2002), *Simplicity, Security and Choice: Working and saving for retirement*, London: DWP.

Disley, J. (2004), 'Refugees give slum new lease of life', *Daily Mirror* (11 June 2004).

Doward, J. (2004a), 'Abuse is "systematic" at asylum detention centres', *The Observer* (23 May 2004).

——(2004b), 'I don't want to plan my death', *The Observer* (19 September 2004).

Duffy, B. (2004), 'Free rider phobia', *Prospect* (February 2004).

Durrant, J. (2000), *A Generation Without Smacking: The impact of Sweden's ban on physical punishment*, London: Save the Children.

BIBLIOGRAPHY

Duval Smith, A. (2004), 'J'Accuse', *The Observer* (23 May 2004).

Dyer, O. (2003), 'Suicide among women prisoners at a record high, report says', *British Medical Journal* (19 July 2003).

Ellen, B. (2000), 'What would we do without evil?' *The Observer* (5 March 2000).

Employability Forum and Institute for Employment Studies (2004), *Employing Refugees: Some organisations' experience*, London: Employability Forum.

Ennals, P. (2003), 'We are not criminals', *Community Care* (9–15 October 2003).

Escobales, R (2004a), 'Women offenders and reducing reoffending', *The Guardian* (12 March 2004).

—— (2004b), 'NHS to take on prison healthcare', *The Guardian* (24 March 2004).

Family Justice (2003a), *Families are Part of the Solution*, New York: Family Justice.

——(2003b) *Families: A natural resource for drug courts. Looking at practitioner perspectives on the role of families in therapeutic jurisprudence*, New York: Family Justice, issue brief.

Federation of Irish Societies (2004), *Consulting the Irish Community on Inside*

Outside: Improving mental health services for black and ethnic minority communities in England – The community response and its evaluation, London: FIS.

Fenton, S., and Azra, S. (1993), *The Sorrow in my Heart: Sixteen Asian women talk about depression*, London: CRE.

Fernando, S. (1991), *Mental Health, Race and Culture* London: Macmillan Press in association with Mind Publications.

Fernando, S., Ndegwa, D., and Wilson, W. (1998), *Forensic Psychiatry, Race and Culture*, London: Routledge.

Fonseca, I. (2000), 'The truth about gypsies', *The Guardian* (24 March 2000).

Ford, R. (2004a), 'One-stop prisons will cost £500 million', *The Times* (4 August 2004).

—— (2004b), 'Prevention, not punishment, is best way ahead, says Blunkett', *The Times* (20 July 2004).

Fostering Network, The (2004), 'News on the amendment to the Children Bill' (website news item, 27 May 2004).

Foucault, M. (2001), *Madness and Civilisation: A history of insanity in an age of reason*, tr. Richard Howard, London: Routledge.

—— (1977), *Discipline and Punish: The birth of the prison*, Harmondsworth: Penguin.

Frean, A. (2000), 'Parents are pariahs of modern Britain', *The Times* (20 October 2000).

Frith, M. (2004), 'The difficult child, his mentor and a new life free from crime', *The Independent* (7 June 2004).

General Medical Council (1992), 'Nigel Cox', *GMC News Review Supplement* (December 1992).

George, S. (2003), 'How collective insanity has taken a grip on the world', *New Academy Review*, 2: 3 (Autumn 2003).

Gidley, S. (2004), 'Call ourselves civilised? Just see how we treat older prisoners', *The Guardian* (12 May 2004).

Gill, L. (2004), 'Abuse is a wicked secret', *The Times* (1 January 2004).

Gillies, N., and MacErlean, N. (2000), 'Tell me the old, old story', *The Observer* (23 July 2000).

Gledhill, R. (2000), 'Carey calls for generosity towards asylum seekers', *The Times* (26 December 2000).

Glouberman, S. (1990), *Keepers: Inside stories from total institutions*, London: King Edward's Hospital Fund for London.

Goater, N., King, M., Cole, E., et al. (1999), 'Ethnicity and the outcome of psychosis', *British Journal of Psychiatry*, 175: 1 (July 1999).

Goldie, N. (2003), *Money for Mental Health*, interim report, London: Sainsbury Centre for Mental Health.

Goodhart, D. (2004), 'Too diverse?' *Prospect* (February 2004).

Gorin, S. (2004), *Understanding What Children Say*, York: Joseph Rowntree Foundation.

Gosling, P. (2000), 'The truth they didn't want to hear', *Community Care* (4–10 May 2000).

Gould, M. (2004), 'Social exclusion reports "milestone" in ending stigma', *Health Service Journal* (17 June 2004).

Grand, S. (2004), 'Let's be risk averse out there', *The Guardian* (10 June 2004).

Greenslade, R. (2003), 'Asylum madness? Look who's talking', *The Guardian* (3 February 2003).

BIBLIOGRAPHY

Grewal, H. K. (2004), 'When Irish eyes aren't smiling', *The Guardian* (11 March 2004).

Grimley Evans, J. (1997), 'The Rationing Debate. Rationing Health Care by Age: The case against', *British Medical Journal* (15 March 1997).

Grove, V. (2004), 'No redemption for the rude girls', *The Times* (1 September 2004).

Guardian, The (2003) 'The asylum seeker: "We were in prison. I did not understand"', *Guardian* Child Protection Special (9 October 2003).

Gulland, A. (2002), 'NHS to take over responsibility for prison health next April', *British Medical Journal, London* (5 October 2002).

Hansard (2004), Lords Hansard (30 March 2004).

HARCA [Poplar Housing and Regeneration Community Association] (2004), 'Security gates and grilles', *HARCA Life* (April 2004).

Harding, J. (2000), *The Uninvited: Refugees at the rich man's gate*, London: Profile Books.

Hargreaves, S. (2003), 'Law against asylum seekers may have public health impact', *British Medical Journal*, (24 May 2003).

Harris, A. (2003), 'Whatever happened to trust? *Patient Centred Care* (October 2003).

Harris, P., and Bright, M. (2003), 'The whistleblower's story', *The Observer* (6 July 2003).

Health Advisory Service (2000) *'Not because they are old': An independent inquiry into the care of older people on acute wards in general hospitals*, London: HMSO.

—— (1995), *A Place in Mind: Commissioning and providing mental health services for people who are homeless*, London: HMSO.

Health in Prisons Project (2001), *Why promote health in prisons?* (www. hipp-europe.org/background).

Healy, A. (2004), 'Researchers find Irish schizophrenia gene link', *Irish Times Health Supplement* (30 March 2004).

Heffernan, I. (2003), 'Diatribe', *Mental Health Today* (October 2003).

Helm, S. (2000), 'Kids' stuff', *Independent on Sunday* (3 September 2000).

BIBLIOGRAPHY

Hencke, D. (2004), 'Plan to end Whitehall sleaze rule', *The Guardian* (16 August 2004).

HM Inspector of Prisons (2003), *Annual Report 2002/3*, London: HMSO.

Her Majesty's Inspectorate of Probation (2002), *Annual Report 2001/ 2002*, London: Home Office.

Herbst, K. (2001), 'Drug offenders stay clean', *Changemakers Review* (December 2001).

Hill, A. (2004a), 'Mum's crusade to save women behind bars', *The Observer* (30 May 2004).

—— (2004b) '"Stranger danger" drive harms kids', *The Observer* (23 May 2004).

Hinsliff, G. (1999), 'Councils that spend more on refugees than pensioners', *Daily Mail* (1 September 1999).

Home Office (2004), *Asylum Statistics: 1st Quarter 2004 United Kingdom*, London: Home Office, National Statistics.

—— (2004), *Race and the Criminal Justice System*, London: Home Office (http://www.homeoffice.gov.uk/justice/race.html).

Hopkins, G. (2003a), 'Small steps, giant leaps', *Community Care* (13–19 November 2003).

—— (2003b), 'It all clicks into place', *Community Care* (6–12 November 2003).

—— (2003c), 'This is my life', *Community Care* (9–15 October 2003).

Houston, M. (2004), 'Falling staff hits psychiatric care', *Irish Times Health Supplement* (30 March 2004).

Huber, N. (2000), 'Guidance says treat child prostitutes as victims', *Community Care* (25–31 May 2000).

Hughes, R. (1987), *The Fatal Shore: The transportation of convicts to Australia 1787–1868*, London: Harvill Press.

Humphrey, D. (2004) *The Good Euthanasia Guide 2004: Where, What and Who in Choices in Dying*, Eugene, Oregon: Norris Lane Press.

Hutton, W. (1995), *The State We're In*, London: Jonathan Cape.

Ignatieff, M. (1999), 'Ascent of Man', *Prospect* (October 1999).

Institute for Public Policy Research (2003), *Asylum in the UK: An IPPR fact file*, London: IPPR.

Ironside, V. (2003), 'Dilemmas', *The Independent* (17 November 2003).

James, E. (2004), 'People don't like to get involved when there's a fracas on the train. But sometimes there's no choice', *The Guardian* (20 May 2004).

Jenkins, G., Asif, Z., Bennett, G. (2000), *Listening is Not Enough*, London: Action on Elder Abuse.

Jenkins, J. H. (1998), 'Diagnostic criteria for schizophrenia and related psychotic disorders: Integration and suppression of cultural evidence in DSM-IV', *Transcultural Psychiatry*, 35: 3 (September 1998).

Jenkins, S. (2004), 'Who will protect us from the health and safety set?' *The Times* (12 August 2004).

—— (2001) 'Have we all lost the nerve to think?' *The Times* (3 January 2001).

Judge David L. Bazelon Centre (2003), *Criminalisation of People with Mental Illnesses: The role of mental health courts in system reform*, Washington, DC: Judge David L. Bazelon Centre.

Katz, I. (2001), 'Leave the back door ajar', *The Guardian* (12 June 2001).

Keizer, B. (1997), *Dancing with Mister D: Notes on life and death*, London: Black Swan.

Kelbie, P. (2004), 'The life and death of an asylum seeker', *The Independent* (29 May 2004).

Kennedy, H. (2004), *Just Law: The changing face of justice – and why it matters to us all*, London: Chatto & Windus.

King, A. (2004), 'Analysis: NHS patients still want their own doctor', *Daily Telegraph* (16 August 2004).

King, M., Smith, G., Bartlett, A. (2004), 'Treatments of homosexuality in Britain since the 1950s – an oral history: the experience of professionals', *British Medical Journal* (21 February 2004).

King's Fund (2003), *Prison Link Workers*, London: King's Fund.

—— (2003), *Mental Health Inquiry: London's State of Mind*, London: King's Fund.

—— (1987), *The Need for Asylum in Society for the Mentally Ill or Infirm: The third King's Fund Forum consensus statement*, London: King's Fund.

BIBLIOGRAPHY

Kushner, T., and Knox, K. (1999), *Refugees in an Age of Genocide*, London: Frank Cass.

Laurance, J. (2004), 'Is there a doctor on the plane? No, they're too worried about being sued', *The Independent* (31 May 2004).

—— (2003), *Pure Madness: How fear drives the mental health system*, London: Routledge.

Layard, R. (2005), *Happiness: Lessons from a new science*, London and New York: Penguin.

LeBor, A. (2004), 'Happy to stay at home', *The Times* (29 April 2004).

Leason, K. (2003), 'Concerns over abuse are cue for MPs to investigate measures to tackle it', *Community Care* (6–12 November 2003).

Lenzer, J. (2003), 'Whistleblower charges drug company with deceptive practices', *British Medical Journal* (22 March 2003).

Levenson, E. (2004), 'After Nimbyism – Jimbyism', *The Guardian* (24 March 2004).

Levenson, R., with Greatley, A. and Robinson, J. (2003), *London's State of Mind*, London: King's Fund.

Levenson, R., and Sharma, A. (1999), *The Health of Refugee Children*, London: King's

Fund and the Royal College of Paediatrics and Child Health.

Lewin, T. (2004), 'Want to volunteer in schools? Be ready for a security check', *New York Times* (11 March 2004).

Lewis, G., Croft-Jeffreys, C. and David, A. (1990), 'Are British Psychiatristsracist?' *British Journal of Psychiatry*, 157: 3 (September 1990).

Local Government Data Unit, Wales (2003), *Children Looked After by Local Authorities* (21 March 2002).

London Research Centre, *Refugees: Breaking down the barriers to work*, London: London Research Centre and Peabody Trust.

Love, M. (2004), 'This much I know', *The Observer* (4 April 2004).

Lydall, R. (2004), 'Early dip swimmers face ban in safety row over open air pool', *Evening Standard* (19 July 2004).

McGavin, H. (2004), 'Feltham guards "laid bets on fights in cells"', *The Independent* (29 May 2004).

McIlvenna, M. (2003), 'Foreign aid', *The Guardian* (18 June 2003).

BIBLIOGRAPHY

McKee, M. (1999), 'Sex and drugs and rock and roll', *British Medical Journal* (15 May 1999).

McKittrick, D. (2004), 'Ireland prepares to restrict citizenship', *The Independent* (12 June 2004).

McLeod, A., and Hudson, J. (2003), 'Invisible politics', *Children's Express* (November/ December 2003).

Madge, N. (2003), *Is England Child-friendly Enough?* London: National Children's Bureau.

Maier, E. (2003), 'Reforming Character', *Third Sector* (1 October 2003).

Manzoor, S. (2004), 'Work in a gap year? Give me a break', *The Guardian* (11 August 2004).

Marks, A. (2003), 'A new weapon in the war on drugs: family', *Christian Science Monitor* (30 April 2003).

Martin, I. (2004), 'Asylum losers spark city crisis', *The Observer* (13 June 2004).

Martin, N. (2002), 'Woman, 102, takes home plea to Blair', *Daily Telegraph* (19 March 2002).

Mauer, M., and Chesney-Lind, M. (eds.) (2002), *Invisible Punishment*, New York: The New Press.

Mawer, C. (1999), 'Preventing teenage pregnancies, supporting teenage mothers', *British Medical Journal* (26 June 1999).

Mellor, P. (2004), 'Suicide rates', *British Medical Journal*, rapid responses (7 May 2004).

—— (2003), 'And another female prisoner is dead', *British Medical Journal*, letters (15 January 2003).

Mills, J. (2004), 'Danger: Jam sponge. Cakes the ladies of the WI bake for patients are banned by hospital as a potential health hazard', *Daily Mail* (29 July 2004).

Minnis, H., McMillan, A., Gillies, G., et al. (2001), 'Racial stereotyping by psychiatrists in the United Kingdom', *British Medical Journal* (20 October 2001).

Mitchell, F. (2003), 'The Social Services response to unaccompanied children in England', in *Child and Family Social Work* 8 (2003).

Morris, N. (2004), 'Female prisoner suicides soar in overcrowded jails', *The Independent* (9 June 2004).

Mulholland, H. (2000), 'Fifty reasons to be cheerful', *The Guardian* (3 April 2000).

Mullan, P. (2002), *The Imaginary Time Bomb: Why an ageing population is not a social problem*, London: I. B. Tauris.

Murphy, E. (1991), *After the Asylums: Community Care for people with mental illness*, London: Faber.

National Association for the Care and Resettlement of Offenders (2004), *Barriers to Equality*, London: NACRO.

—— (2004), *Children First, Offender Second?* Press release (16 April 2004).

—— (2001), *Youth Crime Fact Sheet: Some facts about young people who offend*, London: NACRO Youth Crime.

—— (1999), *Effective Practice with Young People who Offend*, NACRO briefing.

Neate, P. (1995), 'Catalogue of disaster', *Community Care* (13–19 July 1995).

Nestlé Family Monitor (2000), 'Mapping Britain's Moral Values', *Nestlé Family Monitor*, consultant Professor Helen Haste (March 2000).

NG Inquiry (1996), *Report of the Independent Inquiry Team into the Care and Treatment of NG* (chair: J. R. Main, QC), London:

Ealing, Hammersmith, and Hounslow Health Authority and the London Borough of Hounslow.

NHS Confederation (2003), *The Draft Mental Health Bill: An assessment of the implications for mental health service organisations*, London: NHS Confederation.

Office of the Deputy Prime Minister (2000), *Blocking the Fast Track from Prison to Rough Sleeping*, London: ODPM.

Ofsted (2003), *The Education of Asylum-Seeker Pupils*, HMI 453 (October 2003).

O'Neill, O. (2002), *A Question of Trust: The BBC Reith lectures 2002*, Cambridge: Cambridge University Press.

Orr, D. (2000), 'Adoption is not always the answer', *The Independent, Review Supplement* (25 February 2000).

Osborne, H. E. (2003), 'Viewpoint. In mental health time is the healer', *Community Care* (11–17 December 2003).

Park, A., Curtice, J., Thomson, K., Jarvis, L., Bromley, C. (2003), *British Social Attitudes: The twentieth report. Continuity and change over two decades*, London: National Centre for Social Research and Sage Publications.

BIBLIOGRAPHY

Parry, V. (2004), 'Risk taking is good for you', *The Guardian* (15 July 2004).

Pettinger, N. (1998), 'Age-old myths', *Health Service Journal* (27 August 1998).

Phillips, L. (2004), 'Does nobody care?' *Daily Mail* (7 July 2004).

Phillips, M. (2004), 'The real agenda? Labour's power over parents', *Daily Mail* (7 July 2004).

Phillips, T. (2004), 'Multiculturalism's legacy is "have a nice day" racism', *The Guardian* (28 May 2004).

Philpot, T. (2003), 'Bad company?' *Community Care* (6–12 November 2003).

Porter, R. (2002), *Madness: A brief history*, Oxford: Oxford University Press.

—— (1987), *A Social History of Madness: The world through the eyes of the insane*, London: Weidenfeld & Nicolson.

Potter, J. (2004), *Responding to Elder Abuse*, London: Community and District Nurses Association.

Prasad, R. (2001), 'Care leavers give social workers a vital lesson', *The Guardian* (14 February 2001).

Prison Reform Trust (2004), Briefing (February 2004).

—— (2003), *Troubled Inside: Responding to the mental health needs of women in prison*, London: Prison Reform Trust.

Quindlen, A. (1993), *Thinking Out Loud: On the personal, the political, the public and the private*, New York: Fawcett Columbine.

Rabiee, P. (2000), 'Mind the gap', *Community Care* (8–14 June 2000).

Ramsbotham, D. (2003), *Prisongate: The shocking state of Britain's prisons and the need for visionary change*, London: Free Press.

Rees, G., and Smeaton, E. (2001), *Child Runaways: Under 11s running away in the UK*, London: The Children's Society.

Reith, M. (1998), *Community Care Tragedies: A practice guide to mental health inquiries*, Birmingham: Venture Press.

Repper, J., and Brooker, C. (1996), *A Review of Public Attitudes Towards Mental Health Facilities in the Community*, Sheffield: SCHARR (Sheffield Centre for Health and Related Research), occasional paper 96/1.

Rethinking Crime and Punishment (2004), *Searching for a Fix: Drug misuse, crime and the criminal justice system*, London: Rethinking Crime and Punishment.

—— (2004), *The Art of Rehabilitation: Attitudes to offenders' involvement in the arts*, London: Rethinking Crime and Punishment.

—— (2004), *Restorative Justice – An idea whose time has come?* London: Rethinking Crime and Punishment.

—— (2003), *Media and the Shaping of Public Knowledge and Attitudes Towards Crime and Punishment*, by Marie Gillespie and Eugene McLoughlin, London: Rethinking Crime and Punishment.

—— (2002), *What Does the Public Think about Prison?* London: Rethinking Crime and Punishment.

Revolving Doors Agency (1998), *People with Mental Health Problems in Contact with the Criminal Justice System: A service mapping project in Camden and Islington*, London: Revolving Doors Agency.

Richardson, B. (2004), 'At work, age does matter', BBC News Online (16 June 2004).

Riddell, M. (2004), 'In thrall to scaremongers', *The Observer* (11 January 2004).

—— (2003), 'Childhood betrayed', *The Observer* (16 November 2003).

—— (2002), 'The subliminal fear that stalks us all', *The Observer* (8 September 2002).

Riddell, P. (2004), 'Getting the grey vote', *Parliamentary Monitor* (November 2004).

Ritchie, C. (2003), 'Children cut adrift', *Community Care* (2–8 October, 2003).

Ritchie, Jean H., QC (chair) (1994), *The Report of the Inquiry into the Care and Treatment of Christopher Clunis*, London: HMSO.

Roberts, A. (2001–), *Crimtim: A criminology and deviancy theory history timeline*, Middlesex University (http://www.mdx.ac.uk/www/study/crimtim.htm).

—— (3.1999) *Society and Science History Timeline*, Middlesex University (http://www/mdx.ac.uk/study/sshtim.tim).

—— (1981–), *Mental Health History Timeline*, Middlesex University (http://www.mdx.ac.uk/www/study/sshtim.htm).

Roberts, B. (2004), 'Migrant race row hits Blair', *Daily Mirror* (6 June 2004).

Roberts, Y. (2003), 'Cheated out of childhood', *The Observer* (21 September 2003).

Robinson, T. (2004), 'This shameful neglect', *Daily Mail* (13 January 2004).

Rogers, N. (2003), 'Children refugees –first and foremost children', *Child and Family Law Quarterly*, 15: 4 (December 2003).

Rose, D. (2001), *Users' Voices: The perspectives of mental health service users on community and hospital care*, London: The Sainsbury Centre for Mental Health.

Roth, M., and Kroll, J. (1986), *The Reality of Mental Illness*, Cambridge: Cambridge University Press.

Royal Commission on Long-Term Care (1999), chair: Sir Stewart Sutherland, London: Stationery Office.

RSGB [Research Surveys of Great Britain] Omnibus (2003), *Attitudes to Mental Illness*, survey commissioned by the Department of Health and carried out by RSGB Omnibus, a division of Taylor Nelson Sofres (May 2003).

Rubino, F. (2004), 'Doing family time', *Hope Magazine*, New York (March–April 2004).

Rutter, J. (2003), *Working with Refugee Children*, York: Joseph Rowntree Foundation.

Ryan, M., and Orchard, S. (2003), 'Love thy neighbours?' *Community Care* 18 December 2003–7 January 2004).

Sainsbury Centre for Mental Health (2003), *The Economic and Social Costs of Mental Illness*, London: SCMH.

—— (2003), *Money for Mental Health: A review of public spending on mental health care*, London: SCMH.

—— (2002), Breaking the Circles of Fear: *A review of the relationship between mental health services and African and Caribbean communities*, London: SCMH.

Salari, N. (2003), 'Are health and care services ready for a surge in Alzheimer's cases?' *Community Care* (28 August–3 September 2003).

Sale, A. U. (2003), 'Haunted by horror', *Community Care* (28 August–3 September 2003).

Sassen, S. (2000), 'Home truths', *The Guardian* (15 April 2000).

Save the Children (1995), *You're On Your Own*, London: Save the Children.

Save the Children and Greater Glasgow Council (2002), *Starting Again: Young asylum seekers' views on life in Glasgow*, Save the Children, Scotland.

BIBLIOGRAPHY

Scottish Executive (2003), *Children's Social Work Statistics 2002–03*, Statistics Publications Notice: Health Care Series.

Scottish Executive (2002), *Child Protection Statistics for the Year Ended 31 March 2002*, Edinburgh: Scottish Executive.

Sebestyen, V. (2000), 'A tidal wave of displaced people', *Evening Standard* (20 June 2000).

Selten, J. P., Veen, N., et al. (2001), 'Incidence of psychotic disorders in immigrant groups to the Netherlands', *British Journal of Psychiatry*, 178: 4 (April 2001).

Seshamani, M. and Gray, A. (2004), 'A longitudinal study of the effects of age and time to death on hospital costs', *Journal of Health Economics*, 23: 2 (March 2004).

Shapiro, C., and Schwartz, M. (2001), 'Coming home: Building on family connections', *Corrections Management Quarterly*, 5: 3 (2001).

Sharpley, M., Hutchinson, G., McKenzie, K., et al. (2001), 'Understanding the excess of psychosis among the African-Caribbean population in England. Review of current hypotheses', *British Journal of Psychiatry*, 178 (April 2001).

Sheff, D. (2004), 'The good jailer', *New York Times Magazine* (14 March 2004).

Sherman, A. (1994), *Island Refuge: Britain and refugees from the Third Reich 1933–1939*, second edition, London: Frank Cass.

Shorter, E. (1997), *A History of Psychiatry. From the era of asylum to the age of Prozac*, New York: John Wiley.

Skinner, J. (2002), 'Befriending young refugees and asylum seekers', *Youth Action* (Autumn 2002).

Smith, G., Bartlett, A., King, M. (2004), 'Treatments of Homosexuality in Britain since the 1950s – an oral history: the experience of patients', *British Medical Journal* (21 February 2004).

Smith, R. (1999), 'Prisoners: an end to second class health care', *British Medical Journal* (10 April 1999).

Snell, J. (2003), 'Enjoying Your Stay?' *Community Care* (25 September–1 October 2003).

Social Exclusion Unit (2004), *Mental Health and Social Exclusion*, London: SEU/Office of the Deputy Prime Minister.

—— (2002), *Young Runaways*, London: SEU/ Office of the Deputy Prime Minister.

Spector, R. (2001), 'Is there a racial bias in clinicians' perceptions of the dangerousness of psychiatric patients? A review of the literature', *Journal of Mental Health*, 10: 1 (2001).

Steele, L. (1998), 'Good enough for your own kids', *Community Care* (12–18 November 1998).

Stein, M. and Wade, J. (2000), *Helping Care Leavers: Problems and strategic response*, Social Work Research and Development Unit, University of York, Department of Health, London.

Stephenson, P. (2004), 'Mentally ill offenders are being wrongly held in prisons', *British Medical Journal* (8 May 2004).

Stern, V. (2002), 'The International Impact of US Policies', in Mauer, M., and Chesney-Lind, M. (eds.), *Invisible Punishment*, New York: The New Press.

—— (1998), *A Sin Against the Future*, Harmondsworth: Penguin.

Street-Porter, J. (2004), 'I'll do anything except go into a care home', *The Independent* (6 February 2004).

Sugarman, P., and Duggan, L. (2004), 'Vulnerable prisoners', *British Medical Journal*, rapid responses (7 May 2004).

Szasz, T. (1974), *The Myth of Mental Illness: Foundations of a theory of personal conduct*, rev. edn, New York: Harper & Row.

—— (1972), *The Manufacture of Madness*, London: Paladin.

—— (1963), *Law, Liberty and Psychiatry*, London: Macmillan.

Tarleton, A. (2003), 'Sentence structure', *Health Service Journal* (2 October 2003).

Taylor Nelson Sofres plc (2000), *Attitudes to Mental Illness: Summary report*, London: Taylor Nelson Sofres.

Teather, D. (2004), 'Pfizer pays $430m to settle "off label" drug pushing case', *The Guardian* (16 May 2004).

Thompson, A. (2000), 'Why are they being failed?' *Community Care* (4–10 May 2000).

Thornicroft, G., Davies, S., and Leese, M. (1999), 'Health Service research and forensic psychiatry: A black and white case', *International Review of Psychiatry*, 11: 2/3 (May 1999).

Times, The (2004), 'Children in care are failed', Public Agenda (3 August 2004).

—— (2004) 'Big Blunkett is watching you', Public Agenda (3 August 2004). Toynbee, P. (2004a), 'Nanny Blair would win it', *The Guardian* (2 July 2004).

—— (2004b), 'Voting's too good for 'em, *The Guardian* (4 June 2004).

—— (2003) 'Burn her!', *The Guardian* (17 November 2003).

Trades Union Congress (2002), *Employment and Ex-Offenders*, London, TUC briefing.

Travis, A. (2004), 'Detainees held in "filthy" conditions', *The Guardian* (16 June 2004).

—— (2004), 'Deportees sent back to war zone', *The Guardian* (15 June 2004).

—— (2004), 'Private women's prison brings in the interior designers', *The Guardian* (9 June 2004).

—— (2004), 'Nuisance neighbours face compulsory life skills classes', *The Guardian* (1 June 2004).

Travis, J. (2002), 'Invisible Punishment: An instrument of social exclusion', in Mauer and Chesney-Lind (eds.), *Invisible Punishment*, New York: New Press.

Turner, L. (2004), 'Minority report', *The Guardian* (3 February 2004).

Utting, W. (1997), *People Like Us*, London and Cardiff: Department of Health/Welsh Office.

Valios, N (2003a), 'Running on empty', *Community Care* (30 October– 5 November 2003).

—— (2003b), 'Young lives in limbo', *Community Care* (2–8 October 2003).

—— (2000), 'Pointing the way to independent living', *Community Care* (27 April– 3 May 2000).

Vandereycken, W., and Van Deth, R. (1994), *From Fainting Saints to Anorexic Girls: The history of self-starvation*, London: Athlone Press.

Verkaik, R. (2004), 'Compensation culture harms British way of life, says judge', *The Independent* (21 June 2004).

Wade, J., Biehal, N., Clayden, J., Stein, M. (1998), *Going Missing: Young people absent from care*, London: Wiley.

Walker, D. (2003), 'Taxed by inconsistency', *The Guardian* (11 December 2003).

Wallcraft, J., and Bryant, M. (2003), *The Service User Movement in England*, London: Sainsbury Centre for Mental Health.

BIBLIOGRAPHY

Ward, J., Henderson, Z., Pearson, G. (2003), *Findings: One problem among many: Drug use among care leavers in transition to independent living*, London: Home Office.

Ward, K. (2003), *ICAR [Information Centre about Asylum and Refugees in the UK] Navigation Guide – UK asylum law and process*, London: ICAR.

Wayne, P. (1998), 'Very bad boys', *Prospect* (January 1998).

Weaver, C. (2004), '"40 deaths a year caused by mentally ill"', *Evening Standard* (3 September 2004).

Wellard, S. (2003), 'Thanks for having us', *zero2nineteen*, 12 (December 2003).

Williams, Prof. A. (1997), 'The Rationing Debate. Rationing Health Care by Age: The case for', *British Medical Journal* (15 March 1997).

Williams, A. (2004), 'The asylum crisis', *Daily Mirror* (8 June 2004).

Williams, S. (1999), 'Don't cast aside Britain's reputation for humanity', *Independent on Sunday* (8 August 1999).

Willmore, I. (2003), 'Passing the buck', *The Guardian* (4 February 2003).

Wilson, J., and Travis, A. (2004), 'Asylum case lawyers milk legal aid', *The Guardian* (16 June 2004).

Wilson, M. (1993), *Mental Health and Britain's Black Communities*, London: King's Fund Centre.

Winder, R. (2004), *Bloody Foreigners: The Story of immigration to Britain*, London: Little, Brown.

Wolton, S. (1998), *The History of Immigration Legislation, or: Why immigration controls are racist*, Students against Campsfield (http:// www/ closecampsfield.org.uk/background/ Immigration–history.html).

Woolf, L. (1939), *Barbarians at the Gate*, London: Victor Gollancz.

Wyler, S. (2000), *The Health of Young People Leaving Care: A review for the King's Fund/Oak Foundation*, London: King's Fund.

Lightning Source UK Ltd.
Milton Keynes UK
02 December 2010

163778UK00001B/5/A